R. Barri Flowers, MS

Kids Who Commit Adult Crimes
Serious Criminality by Juvenile Offenders

Pre-publication
REVIEWS,
COMMENTARIES,
EVALUATIONS . . .

*"**K**ids Who Commit Adult Crimes* provides a broad overview of adolescent deviance. It provides an excellent multidisciplinary theoretical base for explaining this most pervasive phenomenon. The text also provides an excellent historical chronology of adolescent offending and means used to rehabilitate this population. The statistical analysis is most useful in understanding the pervasiveness of the problem. This text would be very useful to anyone interested in studying juvenile delinquency."

Cassandra J. Bowers, PhD
BSW Coordinator,
Wayne State University,
School of Social Work,
Detroit, MI

*"**K**ids Who Commit Adult Crimes* serves as a current and essential handbook for criminology students. The data provided is easy to digest. The structure of the book follows the format of most criminology courses, with a strong section on intrafamilial causes of delinquency. This is an area of explanation that is much neglected. The section on dating violence will be especially useful in the college classroom. The chapter on school crime does a service by placing the issue of gang violence next to the more media-driven issues of mass shootings. I found the discussion of juvenile courts to be very clear, when the subject can often be confusing because of the incredible variations in court procedures. 'Juvenile delinquency' used to mean running away from home and shoplifting. Now that youth are more likely to be involved in serious offenses, Flowers' book is essential."

Randy Blazak, PhD
Assistant Professor,
Portland State University,
Oregon

Kids Who Commit Adult Crimes

Serious Criminality by Juvenile Offenders

HAWORTH Criminal Justice, Forensic Behavioral Sciences, & Offender Rehabilitation
Nathanial J. Pallone, PhD
Senior Editor

New, Recent, and Forthcoming Titles:

Treating Sex Offenders in Correctional Institutions and Outpatient Clinics: A Guide to Clinical Practice by William E. Prendergast

The Merry-Go-Round of Sexual Abuse: Identifying and Treating Survivors by William E. Prendergast

Chaplains to the Imprisoned: Sharing Life with the Incarcerated by Richard Denis Shaw

Forensic Neuropsychology: Conceptual Foundations and Clinical Practice by José A. Valciukas

Inaccuracies in Children's Testimony: Memory, Suggestibility, or Obedience to Authority? by Jon'a F. Meyer

Kids Who Commit Adult Crimes: Serious Criminality by Juvenile Offenders by R. Barri Flowers

Family Empowerment Intervention: An Innovative Service for High-Risk Youths and Their Families by Richard Dembo and James Schmeidler

Kids Who Commit Adult Crimes
Serious Criminality by Juvenile Offenders

R. Barri Flowers, MS

The Haworth Press®
New York • London • Oxford

The Haworth Press, Inc., 10 Alice Street, Binghamton, NY 13904-1580.

Cover design by Marylouise E. Doyle.

Library of Congress Cataloging-in-Publication Data

Flowers, Ronald B.
    Kids who commit adult crimes : serious criminality by juvenile offenders / R. Barri Flowers.
        p. cm.
    Includes bibliographical references and index.
    ISBN 0-7890-1129-8 (alk. paper)—ISBN 0-7890-1130-1 (alk. paper)
    1. Juvenile delinquency—United States. 2. Juvenile justice, Administration of—United States.
3. Juvenile delinquents—United States—Psychology. I. Title.

HV9104 .F635 2002
364.36'0973—dc21
                                                                            2001039709

To the best thing to ever happen to me.
Here's another one for you, H. Loraine!
Love forever and a day!

ABOUT THE AUTHOR

R. Barri Flowers is currently a research criminologist and crime writer with 29 published books to his credit, many in the fields of juvenile delinquency and criminology. A frequent winner of the Choice Award for writing and academic excellence, Mr. Flowers has a BA and an MS from Michigan State University's School of Criminal Justice. His area of expertise includes youth crime, violence, and victimization. His books on this topic include *Children and Criminality; Minorities and Criminality; The Adolescent Criminal; The Victimization and Exploitation of Women and Children; Female Crime, Criminals, and Cellmates; The Prostitution of Women and Girls;* and *Runaway Kids and Teenage Prostitution.*

Mr. Flowers is a member of the American Crime Writers League, American Society of Criminology, Child Abuse Prevention Network, MSU Alumni Association, Mystery Writers of America, Police Writers Club, and Sisters in Crime. His other nonfiction, academic criminology, and crime books include *Murders in the United States: Crimes, Killers, and Victims of the Twentieth Century; Sex Crimes, Predators, Prostitutes, Perpetrators, and Victims; Domestic Crimes, Family Violence, and Child Abuse; Drugs, Alcohol, and Criminality in American Society; Women and Criminality; Demographics and Criminality;* and *Criminal Jurisdiction in Indian Country.*

CONTENTS

PART IV: RESPONDING TO JUVENILE DELINQUENCY AND CRIMINALITY

Preface

Serious juvenile crime and violence are occurring in alarming numbers across the United States. The proliferation of school shootings and other school violence, possession and deadly use of firearms by juveniles, gang involvement, and substance abuse are all indicative of the greater problem of out-of-control youth in our society.

While juvenile violent and chronic crime has declined in recent years, the reality is that too many kids are still involved in serious delinquent conduct and criminally aggressive behavior. Studies show that youth violence and deviance are interrelated with child abuse, family violence, peer violence, drug and alcohol abuse, the availability of guns, and the limitations of the juvenile justice system in dealing with serious juvenile offending.

In response to the problem of juvenile crime, more and more states are getting tough on juvenile offenders—making it easier to try and convict them as adults, no longer viewing underaged serious and violent offenders as unaccountable for their actions. This and other measures of juvenile crime control and deterrence notwithstanding, the dynamics of youthful antisocial behavior remain in place in our society and continue to influence and affect juvenile delinquency and criminality.

Kids Who Commit Adult Crimes: Serious Criminality by Juvenile Offenders examines the relationship between youth and serious and violent antisocial behavior in our society. It explores the precursors, onset, situational, and motivating factors of juvenile violence and crime, as well as examining explanations and responses to the growing problem of juveniles committing serious crimes.

This book is recommended as an appropriate primary or supplementary text for coursework in juvenile deviance in undergraduate and graduate studies in disciplines including criminal justice, juvenile delinquency, criminology, sociology, psychology, child abuse, racial and ethnic studies, law, substance abuse, and related fields. It is also suitable reading material for professionals in child welfare, law enforcement, psychology, sociology, and medicine, as well as policy-makers, and general readers concerned about troubled youth and the implications on society.

I would be remiss if I did not give my sincerest gratitude to my research assistant and other half, H. Loraine, without whom this book would never have been completed.

The pages that follow should add to the body of literature on juvenile criminality, while presenting a fresh perspective on the subject of serious and violent offending by youths.

Introduction

The increasingly serious nature of juvenile criminal behavior has been felt across the country as youth violence, violent youth gangs, drug-related offenses, and other delinquent and criminal conduct has changed the way we regard minors and delinquent behavior. Recent times have seen an explosion in school tragedies, juvenile homicides, teen battering, date rape, youth family violence, teenage alcohol and drug abuse, and related youthful offenses. This has led to greater efforts to understand the roots, causes, and correlates of juvenile violence and chronic delinquency, as well as develop more effective means of identifying at-risk youth and treating serious and violent juvenile offenders. The juvenile and criminal justice systems have done this.

In response to the greater numbers of youth entering the justice system for violent crimes, including murder, rape, aggravated assault, drug offenses, and domestic crimes, more and more juvenile offenders are being transferred to adult courts where the punishment can better fit the crime. While many support this hard stance, others believe that young offenders do not belong in the criminal justice system, pointing out associated factors such as child abuse and family violence that predispose young people to extreme behavior and ramifications that they may not fully comprehend.

Kids Who Commit Adult Crimes examines the realities and dynamics of serious and violent youth offending and its implications. The book is divided into four parts. Part I explores serious juvenile crime including its magnitude; youth violence; kids, drugs, and crime; school crime and violence; youth gangs and criminality; dating violence; and family violence.

Part II examines explanations of juvenile delinquency and criminal behavior, including biological, psychological, and sociological perspectives; and intrafamilial causes and correlates of delinquency.

Part III addresses juvenile crime and the justice system, including the police and juvenile offenders, youths and the juvenile and adult courts, and juvenile offenders in custody and confinement.

Part IV examines responses to the problem of serious and violent juvenile offending and its precursors, including federal laws and prevention, intervention, and control strategies.

PART I:
EXPLORING JUVENILE CRIME

Chapter 1

The Magnitude of Juvenile Crime

At the dawn of the twenty-first century, one of our nation's most pressing problems concerns serious crime and violence perpetrated by juvenile offenders. Researchers studying the dynamics and scope of chronic delinquent and youth violent criminality have recognized its magnitude as a social problem (Blumstein, 1996; Flowers, 1989; Snyder and Sickmund, 1996; U.S. Department of Justice, 1999). According to experts, the cost of juvenile criminality to the individual and to society is staggering (Cohen, 1998; Flowers, 1989).

Although recent trends indicate a decline in overall serious violent juvenile crimes (Elliot, 1994; Federal Bureau of Investigation, 2000; Snyder, 1997), an increase has occurred in school violence and family violence committed by youths (Flowers, 2000; Flowers and Flowers, 2001; National Center for Education Statistics, 1998). Moreover, drug use has risen among youth, often a precursor to crimes of violence and other delinquent behavior (Federal Bureau of Investigation, 2000; Flowers, 1999; Inciardi and Pottieger, 1991; Riley, 1997).

Persons under the age of eighteen account for approximately 25 percent of personal crimes including rape, assaultive offenses, robbery, and theft (Snyder and Sickmund, 1996; U.S. Department of Justice, 2000b). Arrest figures indicate that while juveniles represent nearly 18 percent of all persons arrested for total crimes, they account for approximately 28 percent of those arrested for serious and violent crimes (Federal Bureau of Investigation, 2000).

The proliferation of guns and their use by juveniles along with their increasing involvement in delinquent juvenile gangs further reflect the sobering reality and serious implications of youth violence in America today (Bjerregaard and Lizotte, 1995; Curry and Decker, 1998; Hutson, Anglin, and Pratts, 1994; Zimring, 1996).

DEFINING JUVENILE CRIME AND DELINQUENCY

Crimes committed by juveniles are typically defined by legal and nonlegal definitions. Legal definitions tend to reflect state and federal statutes on juvenile offenses and offenders. Nonlegal definitions are derived from interpretations of the law, community norms, social trends, and delinquency authorities. Most legal or nonlegal definitions differentiate serious and violent juvenile offenders from juveniles who perpetrate status offenses such as running away or truancy which are applicable only to minors.

Legal Definitions

Legally, a juvenile delinquent is anyone who has broken a criminal law of any state or federal jurisdiction. The California statute provides a typical example of laws governing juveniles and criminality. Under the Welfare and Institution Code, Section 602 summarizes the state's legal definitions of juveniles and delinquents.

> Any person who is under the age of 18 years when he or she violates any law of this state or of the United States or any ordinance of any city or county of this state defining crime other than an ordinance establishing a curfew based soley on age, is within the jurisdiction of the juvenile court, which may adjudge such person to be a ward of the court. (Welfare and Institution Code, Section 602, 2002)

All juveniles who commit criminal offense are charged under Section 602, whether the offense is murder, motor vehicle theft, or drug abuse violations. Although the wording may vary from state to state, the basic premise of the California statues on juvenile crime and delinquency applies in every state.

Juvenile court jurisdiction over juvenile offenders is not uniform across all states; it varies based on the age of the juvenile and the state in which the offense occurs. Currently only six states have established a minimum age for a juvenile referral to the juvenile court. In four of these states, the minimum age is ten years old (Task Force on Juvenile Justice and Delinquency Prevention, 1977). Under common law, it is presumed that criminal liability cannot be applied to a person under the age of seven; however, there are no state statutes that reflect this.

In thirty-eight states, the District of Columbia, and federal codes, the maximum age for which the juvenile court has original jurisdiction over a juvenile offender is seventeen. In eight other states, the age is sixteen, while in four states, the highest age of juvenile court jurisdiction is fifteen (Flowers, 1990; Office of Juvenile Justice and Delinquency Prevention, 1999a). Therefore a person seventeen or under who commits a crime may be referred to the juvenile or adult court, depending on the offender's age and/or jurisdiction of the state.

In some instances, juvenile offenders may be tried as adults in criminal court even if their age and the state place them under the original jurisdiction of the juvenile court. Under some exclusion statutes, statutory juvenile codes specify that when a juvenile is charged with a serious crime such as murder, or is a chronic offender, the juvenile court has no jurisdiction regardless of the age of the accused. Juvenile offenders may also be subject to adult criminal court jurisdiction in cases of "concurrent jurisdiction," which allows the prosecutor the option of filing charges in criminal or juvenile court. Typically juvenile cases come before criminal courts through judicial waiver or transfer from the original jurisdiction of the juvenile court. In ten states there is no minimum age limit for which juvenile cases may be waived to criminal courts. For states that have such a limit, the age generally ranges from fourteen to sixteen (Torbet and Szymanski, 1998; U.S. Department of Justice, 1999).

In a number of states, a person over seventeen years of age can be placed under the jurisdiction of the juvenile court usually up to the age of twenty-one (U.S. Department of Justice, 1999). However, by and large, the "legal age" of any given state determines if an offender will fall under juvenile or criminal court jurisdiction (Flowers, 1986).

As more states crack down on serious juvenile criminality, new laws have been passed to make it easier to remove violent youths from the juvenile justice system and into the criminal justice system. From 1992 to 1997, forty-five states enacted laws allowing the transfer of such juvenile offenders to criminal court jurisdiction (Office of Juvenile Justice and Delinquency Prevention, 1999a).

Nonlegal Definitions

Nonlegal definitions of delinquency are often interpretative, a reflection of norms, cultures, biases, and subjectivity. Such definitions can vary considerably even from profession to profession:

> Sociologists define the juvenile delinquent as a person who not only commits a delinquent act, but who is also labeled by the way society reacts to it. Psychiatrists' definitions emphasize the emotional tones and attitudes involved in any mental pathology. Psychologists view the delinquent not only by the act of delinquency, but by the way the juvenile thinks about it. (Flowers, 1986, p. 118)

Defining the delinquent can be as much individualistic, subjective, or societal, as based on legal definitions. Some conduct deemed delinquent in the United States may be acceptable behavior elsewhere in the world. Even in this country, labeling a delinquent may reflect prejudices and discrimination. For example, racial and ethnic minority juveniles are often disproportionately represented as delinquents in arrest and juvenile custody figures (Bilchik, 1999; Flowers, 1988; LaFree, 1995). Whereas similar conduct among white juveniles may be interpreted differently or seen as merely "sowing their oats." This speaks to the variance in nonlegal definitions and the problems it can create in defining juvenile misconduct.

THE NATURE OF JUVENILE OFFENSES

The range of juvenile antisocial behavior falling within legal definitions of juvenile crime and delinquency varies from the least serious offenses—such as status offenses—to the most serious violations of criminal laws. Juvenile status offenders—including runaways, truants, and incorrigible youths—represent the most frequent type of juvenile offender arrested.

Petty offenses such as alcohol- and drug-related crimes, shoplifting, and vandalism are most often committed by juveniles. Most of these crimes go undetected. Those that are detected rarely result in the arrest of the offender. It is estimated that petty crimes represent as much as 90 percent of all juvenile delinquent acts (Flowers, 1990; Sanders, 1981).

Serious crimes or felonies—including murder, rape, aggravated assault, and robbery—are the least common, yet most publicized types of juvenile delinquency and criminality. Violent crimes account for roughly 5 to 10 percent of all juvenile arrests. Approximately 15 to 20 percent of all serious delinquent acts fall into this category (Federal Bureau of Investigation, 2000; Flowers, 1986; Strasberg, 1978). The most common types of juvenile felonies are property crimes such as burglary, grand larceny, and motor vehicle theft, in which no violence is used.

MEASURING THE EXTENT OF JUVENILE CRIME

Assessing the magnitude of juvenile crime and delinquency is the most important means of understanding the nature of the offenses and seeking the means to detect, control, and prevent the behavior. The three primary sources for measuring juvenile criminality are: (1) official statistics, (2) victimization surveys, and (3) self-report surveys.

The most prominent of these sources is the Federal Bureau of Investigation's annual *Crime in the United States: Uniform Crime Reports*. Since 1930, the FBI's Uniform Crime Reporting (UCR) Program has collected crime and arrest statistics from law enforcement agencies measuring the scope, type, frequency, and fluctuation of crime in the United States. Offenses are divided into two categories: Type I (Crime Index) and Type II (nonindex). The Crime Index consists of eight offenses that gauge fluctuations in the total volume and rate of crime. These offenses represent the most serious crimes reported to law enforcement including, *violent crimes*: murder and nonnegligent manslaughter, forcible rape, robbery, and aggravated assault; and *property crimes*: burglary, larceny, motor vehicle theft, and arson. Nonindex offenses, considered less serious, include forgery and counterfeiting, fraud, embezzlement, vandalism, prostitution and commercialized vice, offenses against family and children, and vagrancy (Federal Bureau of Investigation, 2000).

Slated to replace the aging UCR Program is a redesigned, more advanced crime measurement system known as the National Incident-Based Reporting System (NIBRS). Currently being used in nineteen states, the NIBRS collects information on every single incident and arrest that falls within twenty-two categories (Federal Bureau of Investigation, 2000). This modernization of crime and delinquency information and collection methodology will make data on the characteristics and incidence of juvenile delinquency and criminality more complete as a supplement to other crime measurement systems.

Victimization surveys on crime offer another important means of learning about juvenile crime. These surveys use random victim samples to describe the nature of the criminal victimization and estimate the age and other characteristics of the offender.

Self-report surveys are the third major source of obtaining information on the frequency and distribution of delinquency and criminal offenses. Such surveys rely on asking juveniles what types of delinquent acts they were involved in and which ones led to arrest or detention.

Although these measurements of juvenile crime are significant, they also have drawbacks that limit their overall effectiveness. They will be examined later in the chapter.

OFFICIAL ARREST STATISTICS

Law enforcement agencies gather two types of arrest statistics pertaining to juvenile offenders. One of these focuses on Crime Index offenses cleared or solved "when at least one person is arrested, charged with the commission of an offense, and turned over to the court for prosecution" (Federal Bureau of Investigation, 2000, p. 201). For most clearances involving only offenders under the age of eighteen, the clearance is recorded when the juvenile suspect is cited to make an appearance in juvenile court or before other authorities in the juvenile justice system.

As shown in Table 1.1, in 1999, 19.3 percent of the Crime Index offenses cleared involved persons less than eighteen years of age. Juveniles accounted for 12.4 percent of the violent crime clearances and 21.8 percent of the property crimes cleared nationwide. Murder and nonnegligent manslaughter reflected the lowest percentage of involvement of persons under eighteen at 6.3 percent, while arson represented the highest. Almost half of the arson cases cleared involved juveniles.

Regionally, the Midwestern states had the highest percentage of Crime Index offense clearances involving persons under eighteen at

TABLE 1.1. Offenses Cleared by Arrest of Persons Under 18 Years of Age, 1999[a]

	Total All Agencies: 11,243 Agencies; Population 203,514,000[f]	
	Total clearances	Percent under 18
Crime Index total	1,773,115	19.3
Modified Crime Index total[b]	1,784,246	19.5
Violent crime[c]	479,569	12.4
Property crime[d]	1,293,546	21.8
Murder and nonnegligent manslaughter	7,1981	6.3
Forcible rape[e]	30,781	11.8
Robbery	75,925	15.3
Aggravated assault	365,665	12.0
Burglary	203,172	19.1
Larceny-theft	968,773	22.7
Motor vehicle theft	121,601	19.3
Arson[b]	11,131	49.0

Source: Derived from Federal Bureau of Investigation, *Crime in the United States: Uniform Crime Reports 1999* (Washington, DC: Government Printing Office, 2000), p. 209.

[a] Includes offenses cleared by exceptional means.
[b] It is not necessary to report clearances by detailed property classification to be included in this table. The Modified Crime Index total is the sum of the Crime Index offenses, including arson.
[c] Violent crimes include murder, forcible rape, robbery, and aggravated assault.
[d] Property crimes include burglary, larceny-theft, and motor vehicle theft.
[e] Forcible rape figures furnished by the state-level Uniform Crime Reporting (UCR) Program administered by the Delaware State Bureau of Investigation and the Illinois State Police were not in accordance with national UCR guidelines and were excluded from the forcible rape, violent crime, Crime Index total, and the Modified Crime Index total categories.
[f] Population figures are rounded to the nearest thousand.

24 percent, followed by Western states at 22 percent. Juveniles constituted offenders in 17 percent of the clearances in Northeastern states, and 16 percent of the Index crimes cleared in Southern states (Federal Bureau of Investigation, 2000).

The second means of measuring juvenile offenses by police agencies is by recording the number of persons arrested for a particular crime. These data track the number of individuals taken into custody, as a person may be arrested multiple times during a given year for the same or different offenses.

Table 1.2 reflects total arrests in the United States by age in 1999. Persons under the age of eighteen accounted for 17.4 percent of all arrests, while those under fifteen constituted 5.5 percent of total arrest figures. More than 80 percent of all persons arrested were age eighteen and over.

For Crime Index offenses, juvenile arrestees under age eighteen accounted for 27.8 percent of total arrests, or more than one out of every four persons arrested. The figures are even higher for property crime where persons under eighteen represented 32.3 percent of arrests, or nearly one-third of total arrestees. More than 16 percent of the arrests for violent crimes involved persons younger than eighteen.

The top ten most frequent arrests of juveniles in 1999 can be seen in Table 1.3. "All other offenses (except traffic)" was the offense for which most arrests of persons under eighteen occurred, followed by larceny-theft. Burglary was the tenth most frequent offense of juvenile arrestees. There were only two Crime Index offenses in the top ten most frequent arrests of juveniles. Other serious offenses on the list include other assaults (ranked third), drug abuse violations (ranked fourth), and vandalism (ranked ninth). More than 25 percent of arrests of persons younger than eighteen was for Crime Index offenses in 1999 (Federal Bureau of Investigation, 2000).

Characteristics of Juvenile Arrestees

Arrest statistics reveal that most juveniles arrested for crimes are white male older teenagers (Flowers, 1990; Snyder, 1999; U.S. Department of Justice, 1999). According to the UCR, in 1999 there were 1,157,142 arrests of males under eighteen years of age, compared to 431,697 arrests of females under eighteen in the United States (see Figure 1.1). Male juveniles were nearly three times as likely to be arrested as female juveniles for all offenses. For violent crimes, the difference was even greater. There were almost five arrests of males for every one arrest of females under the age of eighteen for violent crimes. However, the arrest ratio was smaller for property

TABLE 1.2. Total Arrests, Distribution by Age, 1999

Offense charged	Total all ages	Ages under 15	Ages under 18	Ages 18 and over
Total[a]	9,141,201	506,817	1,588,839	7,522,362
Percent distribution[b]	100.0	5.5	17.4	82.6
Murder and nonnegligent manslaughter	9,727	114	919	8,808
Forcible rape	18,759	1,221	3,182	15,577
Robbery	73,619	4,888	18,735	54,884
Aggravated assault	318,051	16,139	45,080	272,971
Burglary	192,570	24,561	64,481	128,089
Larceny-theft	794,201	100,635	249,100	545,101
Motor vehicle theft	94,335	8,508	33,255	61,080
Arson	10,811	3,874	5,791	5,020
Violent crime[c]	420,156	22,362	67,916	352,240
Percent distribution[b]	100.0	5.3	16.2	83.8
Property crime[d]	1,091,917	137,578	352,627	739,290
Percent distribution[b]	100.0	12.6	32.3	67.7
Crime Index total[e]	1,512,073	159,940	420,543	1,091,530
Percent distribution[b]	100.0	10.6	27.8	72.2
Other assaults	844,728	64,980	151,645	693,083
Forgery and counterfeiting	69,853	565	4,481	65,372
Fraud	225,934	1,730	7,940	217,994
Embezzlement	11,208	68	1,101	10,107
Stolen property; buying, receiving, possessing	802,426	5,044	18,865	61,561
Vandalism	182,043	33,736	76,319	105,724
Weapons; carrying, possessing, etc.	113,880	8,945	27,596	86,284
Prostitution and commercialized vice	63,927	126	877	63,050
Sex offenses (except forcible rape and prostitution)	60,120	5,384	10,641	49,479
Drug abuse violations	1,007,002	20,428	128,286	878,716
Gambling	7,023	95	835	6,188

TABLE 1.2 *(continued)*

Offenses against family and children	92,849	2,137	6,093	86,756
Driving under the influence	931,235	391	13,803	917,435
Liquor laws	427,873	10,748	103,734	324,139
Drunkenness	437,153	1,861	14,082	423,071
Disorderly conduct	421,662	42,467	113,303	308,359
Vagrancy	20,213	326	1,597	18,616
All other offenses (except traffic)	2,416,544	78,007	275,397	2,141,147
Suspicion	4,907	330	1,153	3,754
Curfew and loitering law violations	114,220	31,513	114,220	—
Runaways	96,328	37,996	96,328	—

Source: Adapted from Federal Bureau of Investigation, *Crime in the United States: Uniform Crime Reports 1999* (Washington, DC: Government Printing Office, 2000), p. 222.

a Based on 8,546 agencies; estimated population 171,831,000.
b Because of rounding, the percentages may not add to total.
c Violent crimes include murder, forcible rape, robbery, and aggravated assault.
d Property crimes include burglary, larceny-theft, motor vehicle theft, and arson.
e Includes arson.

crimes. Approximately two and a half male juveniles to every one female juvenile were arrested for property crimes.

The majority of juveniles arrested fall between the ages of fifteen and seventeen, in descending order, as shown in Figure 1.2. In 1999, seventeen-year-olds accounted for the most total arrests of persons under eighteen, followed by sixteen-year-olds. For Crime Index offenses, arrestees fifteen to seventeen years of age constituted more than 60 percent of those arrested. Research on serious juvenile offenders has consistently supported official data on serious delinquency and criminality and the peak age group of juvenile offenders at fifteen to seventeen (Flowers, 1990; Office of Justice Programs, 1999; Tatem-Kelley et al., 1997).

TABLE 1.3. Most Frequent Arrests of Juveniles, 1999

Rank	Offense
1.	All other offenses (except traffic)
2.	Larceny-theft
3.	Other assaults
4.	Drug abuse violations
5.	Curfew and loitering law violations
6.	Disorderly conduct
7.	Liquor laws
8.	Runaways
9.	Vandalism
10.	Burglary

Source: Compiled from Federal Bureau of Investigation, *Crime in the United States: Uniform Crime Reports 1999* (Washington, DC: Government Printing Office, 2000), p. 222.

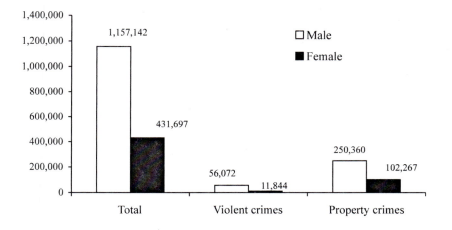

FIGURE 1.1. Juvenile Arrests, by Gender, 1999. (*Source:* Derived from Federal Bureau of Investigation, *Crime in the United States: Uniform Crime Reports 1999,* Washington, DC: Government Printing Office, 2000, pp. 224, 226.)

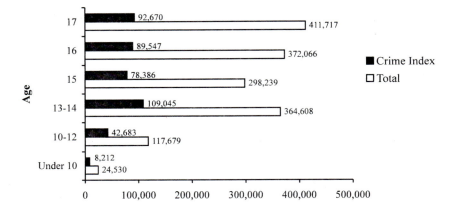

FIGURE 1.2. Juvenile Arrests, by Age, 1999. (*Source:* Derived from Federal Bureau of Investigation, *Crime in the United States: Uniform Crime Reports 1999,* Washington, DC: Government Printing Office, 2000, p. 222.)

White juveniles are much more likely to be arrested for total crimes and serious or violent crimes than juveniles in minority groups (Flowers, 1986; Hindelang, 1978; Sampson and Lauritsen, 1997). As shown in Table 1.4, whites under the age of eighteen accounted for nearly 72 percent of all juvenile arrests and more than 67 percent of the Crime Index arrests in 1999.

Black youths made up more than 25 percent of the persons arrested under age eighteen for all crimes, but represented over 29 percent of the persons arrested for Crime Index offenses and nearly 41 percent of the violent crime arrestees. The overrepresentation of black juveniles in serious and violent crime arrest figures has been documented in a number of studies on differential arrest rates and race (Bilchik, 1999; Flowers, 1988; LaFree, 1995; Snyder, 1999; Wolfgang, Figlio, and Sellin, 1972).

Among other racial minority groups, juveniles of Native American and Asian origin combined represented 3 percent of overall arrests of persons under eighteen, and 3.5 percent of Crime Index arrests.

Although UCR data do not measure ethnic minority crime, studies show that Hispanic youths are disproportionately arrested for violent,

TABLE 1.4. Juvenile Arrests for Crime Index Offenses, by Race, 1999

Offense charged	Arrests under 18					Percent distribution[a]				
	Total	White	Black	American Indian or Alaskan Native	Asian or Pacific Islander	Total	White	Black	American Indian or Alaskan Native	Asian or Pacific Islander
Total	1,584,718	1,140,123	398,010	20,295	26,290	100.0	71.9	25.1	1.3	1.7
Murder and nonnegligent manslaughter	923	434	452	16	21	100.0	47.0	49.0	1.7	2.3
Forcible rape	3,176	2,001	1,096	35	44	100.0	63.0	34.5	1.1	1.4
Robbery	18,709	8,101	10,184	133	291	100.0	43.3	54.4	0.7	1.6
Aggravated assault	45,003	27,993	15,819	486	705	100.0	62.2	35.2	1.1	1.6
Burglary	64,360	46,736	15,749	773	1,102	100.0	72.6	24.5	1.2	1.7
Larceny-theft	248,523	173,430	65,645	3,787	5,661	100.0	69.8	26.4	1.5	2.3
Motor vehicle theft	33,202	18,998	12,901	441	862	100.0	57.2	38.9	1.3	2.6
Arson	5,759	4,595	1,049	56	59	100.0	79.8	18.2	1.0	1.0
Violent crime[b]	67,811	38,529	27,551	670	1,061	100.0	56.8	40.6	1.0	1.6
Property crime[c]	351,844	243,759	95,344	5,057	7,684	100.0	69.3	27.1	1.4	2.2
Crime Index total[d]	419,655	282,288	122,895	5,727	8,745	100.0	67.3	29.3	1.4	2.1

Source: Adapted from Federal Bureau of Investigation, *Crime in the United States: Uniform Crime Reports 1999* (Washington, DC: Government Printing Office, 2000), p. 231.

[a] Because of rounding, the percentages may not add to total.
[b] Violent crimes include murder, forcible rape, robbery, and aggravated assault.
[c] Property crimes include burglary, larceny-theft, motor vehicle theft, and arson.
[d] Includes arson.

17

property, and drug-related offenses (Bilchik, 1999; Flowers, 1988; Hawkins et al., 2000; Pope and Feyerherm, 1993).

Juvenile Arrest Trends

Long-term arrest trends indicate that although overall juvenile arrests have risen, arrests for serious and violent crimes by juveniles have been on the decline. According to official figures, as shown in Table 1.5, between 1990 and 1999 juvenile arrests for all crimes increased 11 percent. However, for Crime Index offenses, arrests decreased by more than 20 percent. Arrests of persons under eighteen for violent crimes dropped nearly 5 percent over the span. The biggest decline—down 55 percent—was for murder and nonnegligent manslaughter. Arrests for aggravated assaults rose almost 4 percent

TABLE 1.5. Juvenile Arrest Trends for Serious and Violent Offenses, 1990-1999

Offense charged	Number of persons arrested under 18 years of age		
	1990	1999	Percent change
Total	1,166,660	1,294,513	+11.0
Murder and nonnegligent manslaughter	1,478	665	−55.0
Forcible rape	2,871	2,498	−13.0
Robbery	18,096	15,138	−16.3
Aggravated assault	34,735	36,095	+3.9
Burglary	79,068	53,847	−31.9
Larceny-theft	250,129	211,621	−15.4
Motor vehicle theft	49,193	25,142	−48.9
Arson	4,476	4,896	+9.4
Violent crime[a]	57,180	54,396	−4.9
Property crime[b]	382,866	295,506	−22.8
Crime Index total[c]	440,046	349,902	−20.5

Source: Adapted from Federal Bureau of Investigation, *Crime in the United States: Uniform Crime Reports 1999* (Washington, DC: Government Printing Office, 2000), p. 216.

[a] Violent crimes include murder, forcible rape, robbery, and aggravated assault.
[b] Property crimes include burglary, larceny-theft, motor vehicle theft, and arson.
[c] Includes arson.

during the ten years. Although juvenile property crime arrests decreased nearly 23 percent, arrests for arson grew by more than 9 percent. These data are consistent with studies on recent juvenile arrest patterns and a general decline in arrests for the most serious and violent offenses (Office of Justice Programs, 1999; Snyder, 1997; U.S. Department of Justice, 1999).

Limitations of Arrest Statistics

In spite of the importance of arrest data in the overall measurement of juvenile crime, there are serious shortcomings to this approach. Perhaps the most glaring weakness of official data is that it is subject to uncontrolled factors. A number of researchers, such as Wolfgang (1963) and Sellin (1961), have pointed this out in criticizing arrest statistics. Criminologists Edwin Sutherland and Donald Cressey describe the unreliability of crime data:

> The statistics about crime and delinquency are probably the most unreliable and most difficult of all statistics. It is impossible to determine with accuracy the amount of crime in any given jurisdiction or any particular time. Some behavior is labeled "delinquent" or "crime" by one observer, but not by another. Obviously a large proportion of all law violations go undetected. Other crimes are detected but not officially recorded. (Sutherland and Cressey, 1978, p. 29)

Other criticisms of official statistics include:

- Official data reflect only offenses law enforcement agencies are aware of.
- Statistics are not gathered for all offenses.
- What constitutes a crime is inconsistent (i.e., arrest, charge, conviction).
- There is reliance on percent changes in the total volume of Crime Index offenses.
- The index of the gravity of crime is inadequate.
- The basis of crime rates is flawed.
- Uniform Crime Reports data vary in criminal statistics.
- There is differential enforcement of criminal statistics.
- The voluntary means by which criminal statistics are gathered limits its overall effectiveness. (Flowers, 1990)

VICTIMIZATION SURVEYS

Crime victimization surveys are an important complement to arrest statistics in measuring juvenile crime and delinquency. Victimization surveys contact randomly selected households and ask respondents about criminal victimization details from the perspective of the victim. This information includes estimating the age of the perpetrator(s) of such crimes.

The most extensive victimization survey has been conducted by the U.S. Justice Department's National Crime Victimization Survey (NCVS) Program. Started in 1972, its annual survey *Criminal Victimization in the United States: A National Crime Victimization Survey Report* focuses on crimes with specific victims (i.e., sexual assault and robbery) who "understand what happened to them and how it happened and who are willing to report what they know" (Flowers, 1990, p. 13). Data are collected annually from a sample of an estimated 45,000 households with more than 94,000 individuals age twelve or older. The NCVS defines a victim as one who has been victimized through personal or property crimes, including forcible rape, assault, and household burglary (U.S. Department of Justice, 2000b).

According to the NCVS, one in three single-offender victimizations in the United States are perpetrated by offenders under the age of twenty. As shown in Table 1.6, in 1995 there were over 7.2 million single-offender victimizations in this country. Of these, nearly 24 percent were crimes of violence where the offender was perceived to be age seventeen or younger. Violent juvenile offenders were most likely perceived to be between fifteen to seventeen years of age.

Multiple-offender victimization data indicate that most violent crimes committed by more than one offender involved youth offenders. Nearly half the crimes of violence with multiple offenders in 1995 were perpetrated by offenders age twenty and younger (see Table 1.7). For rape and sexual assaults, almost 56 percent were believed by victims to have been committed by multiple offenders younger than twenty.

Victimization data show that young violent offenders tend to most often victimize young people. In 1995, in nearly 60 percent of single-offender victimizations—when the offender was perceived as age seventeen or under—the victim was between twelve and nineteen years of age (U.S. Department of Justice, 2000b). Similarly, in almost 70 percent of multiple-offender victimizations of crimes of vio-

TABLE 1.6. Percent Distribution of Juvenile Single-Offender Victimizations, by Type of Crime and Perceived Age of Offender, 1995

Type of crime	Number of single-offender victimizations	Total[a] %	Perceived age of offender (%)		
			Under 12	12 to 14	15 to 17
Crimes of violence	7,287,430	100	1.3	10.6	12.0
Completed violence	2,023,180	100	1.1[b]	9.1	12.3
Attempted/threatened violence	5,264,250	100	1.4	11.2	11.9
Rape/sexual assault[c]	303,240	100	0.0[b]	3.2[b]	6.0[b]
Robbery	623,710	100	1.2[b]	7.4	9.3
Completed/property taken	381,850	100	0.0[b]	7.8	10.1
With injury	90,660	100	0.0[b]	0.0[b]	6.3[b]
Without injury	291,190	100	0.0[b]	10.2	11.3
Attempted to take property	241,850	100	3.2[b]	6.9[b]	8.1[b]
With injury	51,130	100	0.0[b]	13.1[b]	5.5[b]
Without injury	190,720	100	4.0[b]	5.3[b]	8.8[b]
Assault	6,360,470	100	1.4	11.3	12.6
Aggravated	1,346,930	100	1.6[b]	6.6	11.5
Simple	5,013,530	100	1.3	12.6	12.9

Source: U.S. Department of Justice, *Criminal Victimization in the United States, 1995: A National Crime Victimization Survey Report* (Washingtion, DC: Government Printing Office, 2000b), p. 192.

a Total of all single-offender victimizations. Detail may not add to total because of rounding.
b Estimate is based on about ten or fewer sample cases.
c Includes verbal threats of rape and threats of sexual assault.

lence—when the offender was believed to be age twenty and under—the victim was age twelve to nineteen.

For violent young multiple offenders, the persons targeted for certain crimes tend to be elderly. For example, more than 40 percent of assault and robbery victims of multiple offenders perceived to be twenty or younger, were age sixty-five and over (U.S. Department of Justice, 2000b).

TABLE 1.7. Percent Distribution of Youthful Multiple-Offender Victimizations, by Type of Crime and Perceived Age of Offenders, 1995

Type of crime	Number of multiple-offender victimizations	Total[a] (%)	All under 12 (%)	All 12-20 (%)
Crimes of violence	2,147,890	100	0.9	46.9
Completed violence	720,030	100	0.3[b]	41.9
Attempted threatened violence	1,427,860	100	1.1[b]	49.5
Rape/Sexual assault[c]	32,480	100	0.0[b]	55.9[b]
Robbery	496,710	100	0.0[b]	44.6
Completed/property taken	346,500	100	0.0[b]	43.3
With injury	127,110	100	0.0[b]	42.9
Without injury	219,380	100	0.0[b]	43.6
Attempted to take property	150,200	100	0.0[b]	47.5
With injury	43,420	100	0.0[b]	50.4[b]
Without injury	106,770	100	0.0[b]	46.3
Assault	1,618,700	100	1.2[b]	47.5
Aggravated	497,580	100	0.9[b]	37.6
Simple	1,121,110	100	1.3[b]	51.9

Source: U.S. Department of Justice, *Criminal Victimization in the United States, 1995: A National Crime Victimization Survey Report* (Washington, DC: Government Printing Office, 2000b), p. 52.

a Total of all single-offender victimizations. Detail may not add to total because of rounding.
b Estimate is based on about ten or fewer sample cases.
c Includes verbal threats of rape and threats of sexual assault.

NCVS trends support official data in revealing that juvenile perpetrated serious and violent victimizations in the United States are on the decline (see Figure 1.3). From 1993 to 1997, the number of crimes of violent victimizations in which at least one offender was a juvenile decreased by approximately 33 percent.

Limitations of Victimization Surveys

Victimization surveys have been criticized for their methodology and reliability. Most notably, victims must be willing to discuss their

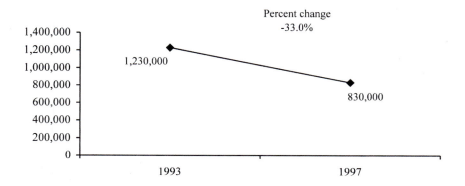

FIGURE 1.3. Trends in Juvenile Violent Crime Victimizations, 1993-1997. (*Source:* Constructed from U. S. Department of Justice, *Juvenile Offenders and Victims: 1999 National Report,* Washington, DC: Office of Justice Programs, 1999, pp. 62-63.)

victimization. Most are not willing to do so. Studies show that more than 60 percent of personal crimes are never reported (Flowers, 1994; U.S. Department of Justice, 2000b).

Victim perception can also be questioned. Victimization surveys require victims to estimate the age of an offender. This is subject to interpretation and can easily be flawed due to the stress of the moment, limited lighting at the time of the victimization, the height or size of the offender, and other factors.

Another major shortcoming of victimization data in recording delinquency or youth criminality is that the survey's primary focus is on the victim, not the offender. Furthermore, most victimization surveys measure personal victimization of individuals age twelve or over, leaving a gap in the total picture of victimization by ignoring the perception of victims under age twelve.

Other weaknesses of victimization research relate to communication barriers, the truthfulness of victims, and selective recording of victimization. For instance, certain crimes—such as kidnapping or drug abuse—are not measured. Since dead victims cannot be questioned, the crime of murder is also excluded from victimization research.

SELF-REPORT SURVEYS

Self-report surveys offer a third important means for gauging the magnitude and nature of juvenile crime and delinquency. Unlike victimization surveys that rely on a victim's interpretation of offender characteristics, self-report studies ask juveniles themselves whether they have ever committed delinquent or criminal acts. This allows researchers to gain more insight into the dynamics of juvenile delinquency to supplement official and victimization data.

Self-report data have revealed that juvenile involvement in crime and delinquency is far more widespread than arrest statistics alone would indicate (Cernkovich, Giordano, and Pugh, 1985; Chaiken, 2000; Elliot, Huizinga, and Morse, 1986; U.S. Department of Justice, 1999). In a self-reported survey of 2,000 Canadian youths ages twelve to eighteen, 93 percent admitted committing at least one offense during the previous year that could have resulted in referral to juvenile authorities. Eighty-two percent had committed criminal acts such as theft and drug use. Nearly 10 percent of youths admitted to serious or violent crimes such as aggravated assault (LeBlanc, 1980).

In one of the most comprehensive surveys of self-reported delinquent behavior, the Institute for Justice Research interviewed 2,122 Illinois youths between the ages of fourteen and eighteen (Kratcoski and Kratcoski, 1980). The survey revealed that:

- Forty-seven percent had been in fistfights.
- Fifty-one percent had committed petty theft.
- Forty-six percent had shoplifted.
- Twenty percent had possessed firearms.
- Sixteen percent had participated in gang fights.
- Fifty-nine percent had consumed alcohol without parental permission.

Other self-report surveys have examined gender differences in delinquency. The National Institute of Mental Health's study of national self-report findings in different years concluded that male juveniles were far more likely to commit every type of delinquent act than their female counterparts (U.S. Department of Justice, 1980). However, in a study conducted by Cernkovich and Giordano (1979) of 822 Midwestern teenagers—though males were more likely to have engaged in serious delinquent activities than females—the gap between boys and girls was smaller than indicated in official data. Gold and Reimer's (1975) study of self-reported delinquency revealed an increase in delinquent behavior among girls, but primarily for non-serious crimes such as drug and alcohol use.

Self-report studies have also focused on racial and ethnic differences in delinquency with mixed results. Some studies have found that black youths were disproportionately involved in serious and violent offending (Elliot, 1994; Elliot and Ageton, 1980; Office of Justice Programs, 1999). Other research, such as the National Youth Survey, has been inconclusive in its findings on racial variations in delinquent behavior (Hawkins et al., 2000), or found no significant variations in reporting rates of violent crime by race (Elliot, Huizinga, and Morse, 1986).

In the 1997 National Longitudinal Survey of Youth, which sampled 9,000 youths aged twelve to sixteen, black and Hispanic males were more likely than white males to have ever been arrested or arrested more than once. However, relatively equal proportions of white, black, and Hispanic females had ever been arrested or arrested more than once (Bilchik, 1999).

Limitations of Self-Report Surveys

Self-report studies on delinquent behavior have a number of drawbacks that limit their reliability (Cernkovich, Giordano, and Pugh, 1985; Hawkins et al., 2000). They depend mostly on the honesty and accuracy of the respondents. For instance, it is practically impossible to determine the extent of under- or overreporting on the prevalence and nature of juvenile delinquency and criminality. Another shortcoming can be seen in attempts to verify self-report findings through juvenile court records or other data. Verification would compromise the anonymity of the respondents, thereby affecting their ability to be truthful without fear of punitive actions.

In addition, biases in self-report surveys reduce their reliability. These include variables of sampling, communication barriers, and problems with measurement techniques. The majority of self-report research on juveniles and crime is done locally rather than nationally and must rely on both official permission (such as gaining entry to an institution) and individual cooperation.

Chapter 2

Youth and Violence

Kids who commit violent crimes have dominated the news in recent times, fueled by mass slayings at schools, gang related drive-by shootings, and a rise in assault crimes (Flowers and Flowers, 2001; Howell, 1998; Office of Justice Programs, 1999). The increased use of firearms in juvenile violence and their frequently random nature are of particular concern to law enforcement authorities and criminologists (Cornell, 1990; Chaiken, 2000; Flowers, 1990; National Youth Gang Center, 1999; Office of Juvenile Justice and Delinquency Prevention, 1998).

Minority youths tend to be disproportionately involved in violent criminality in terms of arrest and detention (Bilchik, 1999; Flowers, 1988; Hawkins et al., 2000). However, white youths account for more than half of juvenile arrests for crimes of violence each year (Federal Bureau of Investigation, 2000). Substance abuse is commonly associated with juvenile violence, along with family troubles, school problems, mental illness, environment, and other correlates (Flowers, 1999, 2000; Hawkins et al., 1998; Rojek and Jensen, 1996).

Youth violence is often directed toward young victims, creating a vicious cycle in which both the offender's and victim's lives are forever damaged (Finkelhor and Ormrod, 2000; Flowers, 1994; National Youth Gang Center, 1999; U.S. Departments of Education and Justice, 2000). The seriousness of the problem of juvenile violence has caused many states to change laws to make it easier to try violent youthful offenders as adults (Office of Juvenile Justice and Delinquency Prevention, 1999a; U.S. Department of Justice, 1999). Many believe this shift in policy toward serious and violent youth is long overdue, with increasingly stringent measures expected in the future.

27

TRENDS IN JUVENILE ARRESTS
FOR CRIMES OF VIOLENCE

According to official figures, overall arrests of juveniles for violent crimes continue to be on the decline. In 1999, more than 54,000 arrests of juveniles for violent crimes in the United States occurred. As seen in Figure 2.1, between 1990 and 1999, arrests of persons under the age of eighteen for violent crimes dropped nearly 5 percent. The biggest decline came for murder and nonnegligent manslaughter at more than 55 percent, while arrests for forcible rape went down almost 13 percent, and robbery 16.9 percent. However, juvenile arrests for aggravated assault grew almost 4 percent during the period.

Table 2.1 shows ten-year violent crime arrest trends for males and females under the age of eighteen. From 1990 to 1999, decreases in male arrests for every violent crime occurred, with a 55.9 percent drop in arrests for murder and nonnegligent manslaughter, followed by a 16.9 percent drop in arrests for robbery, 12.9 percent for forcible rape, and 5.1 percent for aggravated assault. Total male juvenile arrests for violent crimes declined by almost 11 percent.

Overall, arrests of female juveniles for violent crimes rose nearly 40 percent over the ten-year span. Aggravated assault arrests in-

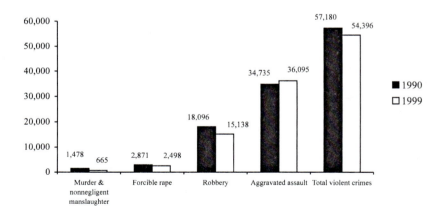

FIGURE 2.1. Ten-Year Arrest Trends for Violent Juveniles, 1990-1999. (*Source:* Derived from Federal Bureau of Investigation, *Crime in the United States: Uniform Crime Reports 1999,* Washington, DC: Government Printing Office, 2000, p. 216.)

TABLE 2.1. Ten-Year Arrest Trends for Violent Juveniles by Sex, 1990-1999

	Male			Female		
Offense	1990	1999	Per-cent change	1990	1999	Per-cent change
Murder and nonnegligent manslaughter	1,397	616	−55.9	81	49	−39.5
Forcible rape	2,814	2,450	−12.9	57	48	−15.8
Robbery	16,580	13,784	−16.9	1,516	1,354	−10.7
Aggravated assault	29,667	28,147	−5.1	5,068	7,948	+56.8
Total violations	50,458	44,997	−10.8	6,722	9,399	+39.8

Source: Derived from Federal Bureau of Investigation, *Crime in the United States: Uniform Crime Reports 1999* (Washington, DC: Government Printing Office, 2000), p. 216.

creased 56.8 percent. However, arrests for other violent crimes decreased. Murder and nonnegligent manslaughter arrests dropped more than 39 percent, forcible rape arrests by 15.8 percent, and arrests for robbery dropped 10.7 percent.

Arrest data have consistently shown that over 50 percent of youths under the age of eighteen arrested for violent crimes are white, more than 40 percent are black, and approximately 3 percent are other racial minorities (Federal Bureau of Investigation, 2000).

FIREARMS AND YOUTH VIOLENCE

Studies have found a strong relationship between the accessibility, possession, and use of firearms by youth and juvenile violence (Block and Block, 1993; Ewing, 1990; Howell, 1998; Kennedy, 1998; Mercy and Rosenberg, 1998). This is particularly true for juvenile homicides (Bailey, 1996; Cornell, 1993; Flowers and Flowers, 2001; Goetting, 1989; Lasseter, 1998; Office of Justice Programs, 1999) and youth gang violence (Bjerregaard and Lizotte, 1995; Hutson, Anglin, and Eckstein, 1996; Sheley and Wright, 1995).

According to findings in juvenile violence studies funded by the Office of Juvenile Justice and Delinquency Prevention (Office of Justice Programs, 1999), firearms were used in juvenile-related homicides as follows:

- Ninety-one percent of murders involving a juvenile in a Los Angeles study
- Eighty-three percent of juvenile-perpetrated homicides in a Milwaukee study
- Eighty-five percent of the juvenile homicide victims in a Washington, DC, study

Studies have shown that firearms were fairly easy to obtain for youths, especially those living in high-risk neighborhoods (Mercy and Rosenberg, 1998; Newton and Zimring, 1969; Office of Juvenile Delinquency and Prevention, 1998). In the Los Angeles study, 40 percent of the youths had possessed or knew of others who owned a firearm. Among those who reported having a gun, 70 percent said they had acquired it from a friend. Twenty-five percent of youths indicated they knew on average four places where they could obtain a firearm (Office of Justice Programs, 1999).

In 1999, nearly 26,000 youths under the age of eighteen were arrested on weapons charges, including carrying and possessing weapons in the United States (Federal Bureau of Investigation, 2000). Many more violent youths are believed to possess or have access to firearms. In self-report data, 20 percent of juvenile arrestees reported carrying a firearm most or all of the time. Juveniles arrested were almost twice as likely as nonjuveniles arrested to report having stolen a gun. Gang members and drug dealers tended to be more likely than other individuals arrested to have stolen a firearm (U.S. Department of Justice, 1999).

THE DYNAMICS OF VIOLENT JUVENILE OFFENDING

Various individual and contextual factors and correlates of juvenile violence have been established by researchers (Flowers, 1986; Hawkins et al., 1998; Loeber and Farrington, 1998). These include the following:

- Early introduction to violence
- Hyperactivity
- Aggressive behavior

- Risk taking
- Family dysfunction
- School troubles
- Additional antisocial behavior
- Community circumstances

Neighborhood circumstances have been shown in a number of studies to be related to the onset and continuation of juvenile violence (Flowers, 1989; Office of Justice Programs, 1999). These include neighborhoods characterized by the following:

- Poverty
- Family disruption
- High crime rate
- High rate of racial and ethnic minorities
- High stress levels
- Single-parent families
- Family violence
- Weak economic opportunities
- Other disadvantaged neighborhood or household factors

Prevalence of violence studies have consistently found that in most cities or neighborhoods, a small percentage of youthful offenders tend to perpetrate a large proportion of the crime (Chaiken, 2000; Flowers, 1990). In the Washington, DC, youth violence study, 7 percent of the male youths interviewed had committed 36 percent of the reported delinquency, including 20 percent of the juvenile assaultive offenses, and nearly 50 percent of the property crimes and drug dealing offenses (Office of Justice Programs, 1999).

CHARACTERISTICS OF VIOLENT JUVENILES

Gender and Youth Violence

Demographic predictive studies of violent youthful offenders indicate late adolescent boys and young male adults are considerably more likely than girls or older males to be serious or violent offenders (Chaiken, 2000). Overall, males commit the vast majority of violent crimes (Flowers, 1990; Tatem-Kelley et al., 1997; U.S. Department of Justice, 1999). In the Washington, DC, study of juvenile violent offenses, males were responsible for more than 80 percent of the 2,686 seriously violent crimes juveniles were charged with, including murder, rape, robbery, and aggravated assault. Similarly, in a South Carolina homicide study, between 1992 and 1994 nearly 90 percent of juvenile homicide offenders were male (Office of Justice Programs, 1999). In addition, male youths were twice as likely as female youths to bully peers in physical assaults, often a precursor to other antisocial behavior.

Some research has found that although violence is far more prevalent among male youths, violence by female youths appears to be gaining ground (Adler, 1975; Flowers, 1995). For example, in one study, at the age of thirteen, 18 percent of the female sample group reported perpetrating violent offenses, compared to 16 percent of the male sample (Office of Justice Programs, 1999).

Age and Youth Violence

Research shows that violent juvenile offending typically begins around fourteen to fifteen years of age (Flowers, 1989; Stouthamer-Loeber et al., 1997). In the Washington, DC, study, almost 40 percent of the youths charged with serious violent offenses were age fifteen or younger. In the South Carolina study, the mean age of the juvenile homicide offenders was 15.8, with the assault and battery offenders at 15.6 years, and other serious juvenile offenders at 15.1 years (Office of Justice Programs, 1999).

Other studies have found the rate of male violence to peak between fifteen and seventeen years of age before declining (Tatem-Kelley et al., 1997). Research on the onset of serious male delinquency indicates that most offenders committed their first serious nonviolent criminal act by the age of fourteen (Stouthamer-Loeber et al., 1997).

Race and Youth Violence

Although youth violence occurs among all racial and ethnic groups, black youths are overrepresented in violent crime arrest figures relative to their numbers in the juvenile population (Elliot, 1994; Federal Bureau of Investigation, 2000; Flowers, 1998; Snyder, 1999). For instance, in the Washington, DC, study of juvenile violence of 2,686 juveniles arrested and charged with homicide, rape, robbery, or aggravated assault, 98 percent were African American (Office of Justice Programs, 1999). Some studies suggest that police biases or other factors may affect differential rates of arrest and estimates on violent youthful offending with respect to race and ethnicity (Flowers, 1988; Hagan and Peterson, 1995; Mann, 1993).

In general, self-report surveys of juvenile violence tend to support official data on higher prevalence and incidence rates of violent offending among racial and ethnic minority groups such as African Americans and Hispanics (Elliot and Ageton, 1980; Farrington et al., 1996; Office of Justice Programs, 1999). However, some studies have found little statistical variation in rates of self-reported violent criminality by racial groups (Elliot, Huizinga, and Morse, 1986) or otherwise questioned prevailing views on the self-reported disparity of juvenile violent offending among racial and ethnic populations (Flowers, 1988; Hindelang, 1981; Huizinga and Elliot, 1986).

VICTIMS OF JUVENILE VIOLENCE

Violent juvenile offenders victimize people of all ages, racial groups and ethnicities, classes, and income levels (Flowers, 1990; Office of Justice Programs, 1999). However, in general, violent juveniles tend to perpetrate violent offenses against victims of similar age, race, ethnicity, and socioeconomic background (Flowers, 1988, 1994; U.S. Department of Justice, 2000).

According to the National Crime Victimization Survey (NCVS), nearly three in ten serious violent victimizations in 1997 involved offenders under the age of eighteen (U.S. Department of Justice, 1999). These included:

- Twenty-seven percent of aggravated assaults
- Fourteen percent of sexual assaults
- Thirty percent of robberies

Juveniles were twice as likely as adults to commit serious crimes of violence in groups. Multiple offenders were involved in 50 percent of violent victimizations by persons younger than eighteen in 1997.

Juveniles typically commit violent offenses against other juveniles. The National Incident-Based Reporting System reported that juvenile offenders are responsible for approximately 45 percent of juvenile victimizations known to law enforcement, while representing 53 percent of the total identified perpetrators of juvenile victims (Finkelhor and Ormrod, 2000).

Much juvenile serious and violent crime offending is never reported to law enforcement authorities, and therefore not included in official juvenile crime data (Flowers, 1994; U.S. Department of Justice, 2000). The NCVS found that in 1997, 58 percent of the serious violent offenses perpetrated by offenders under the age of eighteen were never reported (U.S. Department of Justice, 1999). Juvenile violent crimes unreported to law enforcement departments included:

- Forty-nine percent of sexual assaults
- Fifty-eight percent of aggravated assaults
- Sixty percent of robberies

Homicide Victims of Juvenile Offenders

Juvenile murderers tend to kill primarily males and acquaintances—most often with a firearm (Ewing, 1990; Flowers and Flowers, 2001; Lasseter, 1998). Approximately 70 percent of victims of juvenile killers were killed with a gun (U.S. Department of Justice, 1999). Approximately 25 percent of victims of juvenile homicides are youths under the age of eighteen (Office of Justice Programs, 1999).

According to the Office of Juvenile Justice and Delinquency Prevention, between 1980 and 1997, the following trends were established for characteristics of homicide victims of juveniles (U.S. Department of Justice, 1999):

- Eighty-three percent were male.
- Forty-two percent were white.
- Forty-seven percent were black.
- Twenty-seven percent were juveniles.
- Fifty-five percent were acquaintances.
- Fourteen percent were family members.
- Thirty-one percent were strangers.
- Seventy percent were killed with a firearm.
- Twenty-seven percent of victims of female juvenile homicide were killed by non-firearm means.
- Young children were proportionately far more likely to be killed by female juveniles than male juveniles.

THEORIES ON VIOLENT JUVENILE OFFENDING

Various delinquency theories and perspectives have been applied to the study of youth violence and criminality. Four prominent theoretical approaches include (1) social learning theory, (2) stress theory, (3) subculture of violence theory, and (4) mental illness theory. Explanations of causal correlates and factors of serious and violent juvenile offending are more fully explored in Part II.

Social Learning Theory

Social learning theorists view early childhood experiences as significantly associated with later patterns of juvenile violence (Flowers, 1990). Social learning theory posits that intrafamilial forms of violence such as child maltreatment and domestic violence are learned behaviors considered by the juvenile an appropriate response to or reaction to problems encountered. In a study of self-reported adolescent violent offending, Kratcoski (1984) found that youths who had been victims of parental violence or lived in households with weak family functioning were more likely to have exhibited violent behavior than youths without such negative intrafamilial experiences. Other researchers have found a similar association between violent youth and violent or dysfunctional backgrounds (Flowers, 1986; Sorrells, 1977).

Stress Theory

Advocates of stress theory regard youth violence as a way to cope with intolerable stress, which may occur when juveniles experience pressure from either a single traumatic incident or the gradual accumulation of numerous traumas (Flowers, 1990). The resultant violent acts are often unplanned or unintended. Mawson (1981) held that such violence may be directed toward family members or peers when the youth experiencing stress wishes to continue the intense emotional physical contact with the victim, even if the person is responsible for the stress. Hamparian's (1978) research further supported stress theory and juvenile violence, finding that violent delinquents tend to be characterized by weak impulse control, low self-esteem, lack of empathy toward others, rage, and little tolerance for frustration.

Subculture of Violence Theory

Marvin Wolfgang and Franco Ferracuti (1967) put forth a subculture of violence theory, postulating that juvenile violence is a reflection of lower-class norms and a learned response to the pressures encountered in lower-class living. According to subculture of violence theory, young males—particularly those living in households headed by females in socially disadvantaged neighborhoods—frustrated by the lack of self-esteem and access to material goods, resort to violent behavior as a means to achieve status. Though Wolfgang and Ferracuti acknowledged that some violent youths were "idiopathic" (a psychological disorder), they believed that more than 90 percent were "normatively prescribed violent delinquents," or goal-oriented youths who belonged to a subculture of violence (Ferracuti and Wolfgang, 1970, p. 71).

Mental Illness Theory

More focus has recently been put on mental illness perspectives on youth violence (Flowers, 1990; Howells et al., 1983; Marzuk, 1996). Many mental health professionals relate persistent youth violence to serious mental health problems (Office of Justice Programs, 1999). Some studies show that many violent juvenile offenders with serious mental illness are not being screened or receiving treatment (Woolard et al., 1992). Others question the validity of using mental illness as an excuse for juvenile violent behavior (Szasz and Alexander, 1968).

Some contemporary psychiatrists have combined traditional psychiatric principles and propositions with environmental correlates and causes in explaining youth violence. In a study of homicidally violent children ages three to twelve, the behavior was linked to psychomotor seizures, suicidal tendencies, psychiatric hospitalization of the mother, and a violent father (Flowers, 1990). Other psychiatric studies of violent youths age thirteen to nineteen indicated that the violence was related to neurological impairment, psychiatric symptoms, and a history of severe child abuse or witnessing severe violence (Collins, 1982).

Chapter 3

Kids, Drugs, and Crime

The use and abuse of drugs and alcohol by juveniles is strongly related to overall juvenile crime and delinquency. Numerous studies have documented this cause and effect correlation (Chaiken and Johnson, 1988; Flowers, 1999; Huizinga et al., 2000). Recent data indicate an increase in drug use among juveniles, as well as in arrests for drug-related violations (Federal Bureau of Investigation, 2000; Johnston, O'Malley, and Bachman, 2000b; U.S. Department of Health and Human Services, 2000). Youth and gang violence and drug-involved crimes such as drug dealing and teenage prostitution are commonly associated with substance abuse (Carpenter et al., 1988; Flowers, 1998, 1999; Howell and Lynch, 2000). The seriousness of drug use and alcohol consumption by youths under eighteen cannot be overstated in understanding delinquent behavior and its implications for society and our youth.

JUVENILES AND DRUG USE

The popularity of illicit drugs among juveniles has risen steadily in recent years. The rate of drug use by teenagers in the United States is the highest in the industrialized world (Flowers, 2000). According to a national survey conducted by the Parents Resource Institute for Drug Education (PRIDE), between 1998 and 1999 more than 40 percent of twelfth-grade students used at least one illicit drug in the previous year. Over 35 percent of students in grades nine to twelve and more than 16 percent of students in grades six to eight had used one or more drugs during the previous year. More than 20 percent of students in grades nine to twelve had used an illegal drug in the previous month (PRIDE Surveys, 2000).

Other studies have found that approximately 50 percent of all high school seniors have tried illicit drugs (Office of National Drug Control Policy, 1996; U.S. Department of Justice, 1999). According to the National Institute on Drug Abuse and the National Clearinghouse for Alcohol and Drug Information, the following facts on juvenile drug use have emerged:

- Marijuana is the most popular drug among teenagers.
- Cocaine is the second most commonly used drug.
- Marijuana and cocaine use by teens has increased.
- One-third of persons ages twelve to seventeen have used marijuana, while one in six are current users.
- More than nine out of ten students in grades four to six realize that crack or cocaine is an illicit drug.
- One in three sixth graders feel pressured by peers to use marijuana.
- Use of stimulants, such as Ritalin and amphetamines, and hallucinogens, such as LSD and PCP, among teenagers is on the rise (Flowers, 1999; Office of National Drug Control Policy, 1996).

The Youth Risk Behavior Surveillance System (YRBSS) reported from its national school-based survey of youth that, in 1999, 47.2 percent of all high school students in the United States had used marijuana during their lifetime, with 26.7 percent being current users. By comparison, approximately 16 percent of high schoolers had used cocaine, and 4 percent used it currently (U.S. Department of Health and Human Services, 2000).

Characteristics of Juvenile Drug Users

According to some studies, juvenile drug users are most likely to be male, Hispanic, white, and high school seniors (Flowers, 1999; Johnston, O'Malley, and Bachman, 2000b; Kann et al., 2000).

Table 3.1 shows reported drug use by high school seniors in the United States by sex, race, ethnicity, and grade level in 1999. Fifty-one percent of male students had used marijuana, compared to 43.4 percent of female students. Nearly 31 percent of males were current marijuana users compared to 22.6 percent of females. Almost 11 percent of male students had used cocaine compared to 8.4 percent

TABLE 3.1. High School Students and Drug Use, by Sex, Race, Ethnicity, and Grade Level, United States, 1999 (Percent Reporting Behavior)

	Total	Sex		Race, ethnicity			Grade level			
		Male	Female	White, non-Hispanic	Black non-Hispanic	Hispanic	9th grade	10th grade	11th grade	12th grade
Marijuana use, lifetime[a]	47.2	51.0	43.4	45.9	48.6	51.0	34.8	49.1	49.7	58.4
Marijuana use, current[b]	26.7	30.8	22.6	26.4	26.4	28.2	21.7	27.8	26.7	31.5
Cocaine use, lifetime[c]	9.5	10.7	8.4	9.9	2.2	15.3	5.8	9.9	9.9	13.7
Cocaine use, current[b]	4.0	5.2	2.9	4.1	1.1	6.7	3.4	3.7	4.5	4.8
Illegal steriod use, lifetime[a]	3.7	5.2	2.2	4.1	2.2	4.1	4.7	3.6	3.0	3.3
Injected illegal drug use, lifetime[d]	1.8	2.8	0.7	1.6	0.9	1.8	1.6	1.2	2.0	2.3
Methamphetamine use, lifetime[e]	9.1	9.9	8.4	10.3	1.7	11.3	6.3	9.3	10.1	11.5
Sniffed or inhaled intoxicating substances, lifetime[f]	14.6	14.7	14.6	16.4	4.5	16.1	16.5	16.0	13.4	11.3
Tried marijuana before age 13	11.3	14.5	8.0	9.4	14.8	13.9	12.7	12.6	9.5	9.5
On School Property										
Marijuana use[b]	7.2	10.1	4.4	6.5	7.2	10.7	6.6	7.6	7.0	7.3
Offered, sold, or given an illegal drug[g]	30.2	34.7	25.7	28.8	25.3	36.9	27.6	32.1	31.1	30.5

Source: Constructed from L. Kann et al., "Youth Risk Behavior Surveillance—United States 1999," CDC Surveillance Summaries, *Morbidity and Mortality Weekly Report* 49 No. SS-5 (Washington, DC: Government Printing Office, 2000), pp. 52, 60, 63, 66, 69, 72.

a Ever used.
b One or more times during the thirty days preceding the survey.
c Ever tried any form of cocaine (i.e., powder, crack, or freebase).
d Ever injected illegal drugs.
e Ever used methamphetamines (also called speed, crystal, crank, or ice).
f Ever sniffed glue or breathed the contents of aerosol spray cans or inhaled any paint sprays or became intoxicated.
g During the twelve months preceding the survey.

of female students. Males were also more likely than females to have used steroids, injected illicit drugs, used methamphetamines, or tried marijuana on school property. Male and female students were almost equally likely to have sniffed intoxicating substances.

Fifty-one percent of Hispanic students had smoked marijuana at least once in their lifetime, compared to 48.6 percent of black students and 45.9 percent of white students. Hispanics were more likely to be currently using marijuana or cocaine than non-Hispanic whites or blacks. Black high schoolers were significantly less likely than Hispanic or white students to be current users of cocaine or illegal steroids, or have used methamphetamines, or sniffed intoxicating substances. However, black youths were more likely than white or Hispanic youths to have tried marijuana before the age of thirteen.

More than 58 percent of twelfth graders had used marijuana and more than 31 percent were current users. The levels of lifetime marijuana users declined with each grade level; however tenth-grade students were more likely to be current marijuana users than eleventh graders. Nearly 14 percent of twelfth-grade students used cocaine at some point in their lives, with almost 10 percent of tenth and eleventh graders ever using cocaine. Tenth graders were more likely than eleventh and twelfth graders to use steroids illegally, inhale substances, or smoke marijuana before the age of thirteen.

On school property, males, Hispanics, and tenth graders were most likely to be offered, sold, or given an illicit drug. Nearly 40 percent of Hispanics, almost 35 percent males and over 30 percent tenth to twelfth graders fit into this category.

Trends in Drug Use Among Juveniles

Drug use by juveniles is on the increase, according to self-report surveys and other data. The National Household Survey on Drug Abuse reported that between 1992 and 1995, teens using drugs rose by 78 percent (Flowers, 1999). Cocaine use among teenagers climbed 166 percent, marijuana use by 37 percent, and use of LSD and other hallucinogens by 54 percent.

The YRBSS found that from 1991 to 1999, high school students' lifetime use of marijuana rose almost 16 percent and current use increased 12 percent (U.S. Department of Health and Human Services, 2000). Over the course of the nine years, students' lifetime use of cocaine increased more than 3 percent and use in the previous thirty days increased by 2 percent—more than doubling the percent of high schoolers using cocaine in 1991.

In the most recent Monitoring the Future Study, although researchers found that the overall use among secondary school students of such drugs as amphetamines, hallucinogens, tranquilizers, and barbiturates had remained steady, a dramatic increase was reported in teen use of the drug known as ecstasy (Johnston, O'Malley, and Bachman, 2000a). The study showed that from 1999 to 2000, the proportion of twelfth-grade students using ecstasy increased from 5.6 percent to 8.2 percent, rising among tenth-grade students from 4.4 percent to 5.4 percent and climbing among eighth graders from 1.7 percent to 3.1 percent. Reported use of steroids also increased among tenth graders and use of heroin increased among twelfth-grade students.

Arrests and Juvenile Drug Use

Another indicator of the increased drug use among youth can be seen in arrest figures. Official data show 128,286 arrests of youths under eighteen for drug abuse violations in the United States in 1999 (Federal Bureau of Investigation, 2000). Almost six arrests of males occurred for every female arrest for juvenile drug abuse violations. A representative sample of male juvenile arrestees testing positive for drug use in nine U.S. cities, by type of drug, race, and ethnicity in 1999 can be seen in Table 3.2. Black youths were most likely to test positive for drug use in five of the nine cities, with percentages ranging from 45.7 percent of black arrestees in Birmingham to 74 percent in Phoenix, figures disproportionate to their population numbers. White juvenile arrestees had a higher overall percentage of testing positive in two cities, ranging from 41.7 percent in Portland to 63.8 percent in San Diego. Hispanic youths testing positive for drugs had the highest percentage of arrests in two cities, with a range of 38.9 percent in Cleveland to 68.8 percent in Phoenix.

Long-term arrest trends reveal that from 1990 to 1999, arrests of persons under eighteen for drug abuse violations increased more than 132 percent (see Figure 3.1). Female juvenile arrests for drug abuse violations increased more than 190 percent, compared to a more than 124 percent climb in male juvenile arrests.

TABLE 3.2. Drug Use by Male Juveniles Arrested or Detained in Nine U.S. Cities, by Type of Drug, Race, and Ethnicity, 1999 (Percent Testing Positive)

City	Any drug[a]			Cocaine			Marijuana			Opiates		
	Black	White	Hispanic	Black	White	Hispanic	Black	White	Hispanic	Black	White	Hispanic
Birmingham, AL	45.7	47.8	(b)	3.3	8.7	(b)	43.5	43.5	(b)	0.0	0.0	(b)
Cleveland, OH	67.3	54.7	38.9	11.1	4.0	11.1	64.1	54.7	38.9	0.5	0.0	0.0
Denver, CO	62.1	52.6	65.5	6.3	2.6	13.7	60.0	52.6	59.7	0.0	2.6	0.0
Los Angeles, CA	58.3	46.9	52.7	0.0	4.1	13.4	58.3	42.9	50.0	0.9	0.0	0.9
Phoenix, AZ	74.0	66.7	68.8	10.0	8.7	22.2	70.0	60.9	61.9	2.0	2.9	1.7
Portland, OR	55.9	41.7	48.0	8.8	0.8	4.0	55.9	39.4	40.0	2.9	1.5	8.0
San Antonio, TX	57.9	54.2	57.0	10.5	4.2	7.3	57.9	50.0	53.6	0.0	0.0	3.4
San Diego, CA	56.3	63.8	56.6	2.1	2.9	2.9	56.3	60.9	50.7	0.0	0.0	0.7
Tucson, AZ	51.5	49.6	61.2	12.1	7.6	14.9	48.5	47.1	57.9	0.0	0.8	0.8

Source: Adapted from U.S. Department of Justice, National Institute of Justice, 1999 Annual Report on Drug Use Among Adult and Juvenile Arrestees (Washington, DC: Department of Justice, 2000), pp. 90-98.
a Includes cocaine, marijuana, opiates, methamphetamines, and phencyclidine (PCP).
bBase figure is less than ten cases.

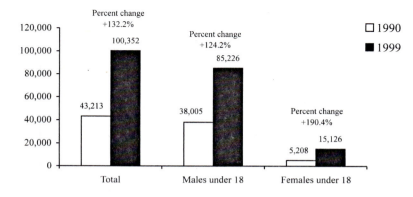

FIGURE 3.1. Juvenile Arrest Trends for Drug Abuse Violations, by Sex, 1990-1999. (*Source:* Derived from Federal Bureau of Investigation, *Crime in the United States: Uniform Crime Reports 1999*, Washington, DC: Government Printing Office, 2000, pp. 216-217.)

JUVENILES AND ALCOHOL USE

Juveniles use and abuse of alcohol has been a persistent problem over the years and is strongly associated with more serious offenses such as violent crimes, property crimes, drug crimes, and sex offenses (Carpenter et al., 1988; Flowers, 1990, 1998; Johnson, 1992). Although the purchase, possession, and use of alcohol by minors is prohibited by law, recent studies indicate that increasing numbers of youths are obtaining and drinking alcoholic beverages (Flowers, 1999; Office of National Drug Control Policy, 1997). The Monitoring the Future Project's self-report survey of high school seniors found that 80 percent had used alcohol and more than 50 percent had used alcohol within the last thirty days (Johnston, O'Malley, and Bachman, 1999).

According to the National Council on Alcoholism, the average age of initial alcohol use is twelve (Flowers, 1999). Almost one-third of students nationwide have used alcohol before the age of thirteen (Office of National Drug Control Policy, 1997). Four million teenagers are alcohol dependent (Geller and MacLean, 1993). In the PRIDE survey, nearly 75 percent of twelfth graders used alcohol during the past year (PRIDE Surveys, 2000). More than 68 percent of students in grades nine to twelve, and over 41 percent of the students in grades six to eight have used alcohol within the preceding twelve months.

Further evidence of the high rate of drinking among youth can be seen in the YRBSS survey, which reported that in 1999 half of all high school students were current alcohol users, while nearly 30 percent were episodic heavy drinkers who had five or more drinks on at least one occasion during the past thirty days (U.S. Department of Health and Human Services, 2000).

Studies of alcohol use by minors have revealed the following:

- By grade four, more than one-third of students feel pressured to drink alcohol.
- Over half of sixth grade students feel pressured to drink alcohol.
- Children left at home alone for eleven or more hours per week are nearly twice as likely to consume alcohol as children with adult supervision.
- Over one-third of high school seniors are considered binge drinkers.
- The relationship between peer group use of alcohol and an individual juvenile's use is significant. (Flowers, 1999)

Characteristics of Juvenile Alcohol Users

Among high school seniors, males, whites, and Hispanics are most likely to be alcohol-involved. Johnston, O'Malley, and Bachman (1999) reported in their national survey of drug use by high school seniors that 57.3 percent of males, 57.7 percent of whites, and 49.8 percent of Hispanic youths used alcohol within the previous thirty days. Comparatively, 46.9 percent of females and 33.3 percent of male students had used alcohol during the year.

However, when looking at all high school students and alcohol use, some data suggest that there may be actually more female drinkers in lifetime use (Kann et al., 2000). As shown in Table 3.3, in 1999, 81.7 percent of female students in the United States ever used alcohol, compared to 80.4 percent males. But males were more likely to be current users, episodic heavy drinkers, alcohol users before age thirteen, and consumers of alcohol on school property.

TABLE 3.3. High School Students and Alcohol Use, by Sex, Race, Ethnicity, and Grade Level, United States, 1999 (Percent Reporting Behavior)

| | Total | Sex | | Race, ethnicity | | | Grade level | | | |
		Male	Female	White, non-Hispanic	Black, non-Hispanic	Hispanic	9th grade	10th grade	11th grade	12th grade
Alcohol use, lifetime[a]	81.0	80.4	81.7	82.0	74.8	83.4	73.4	83.2	80.8	88.3
Alcohol use, current[b]	50.0	52.3	47.7	52.5	39.9	52.8	40.6	49.7	50.9	61.7
Episodic heavy drinking[c]	31.5	34.9	28.1	35.8	16.0	32.1	21.1	32.2	34.0	41.6
Drank alcohol before age 13[d]	32.2	37.4	26.8	29.9	35.2	35.1	40.4	35.6	26.2	24.3
On School Property										
Alcohol use[e]	7.2	10.1	4.4	6.5	7.2	10.7	6.6	7.6	7.0	7.3

Source: Constructed from L. Kann et al., "Youth Risk Behavior Surveillance—United States, 1999" CDC Surveillance Summaries, *Morbidity and Mortality Weekly Report* 49 No. SS-5 (Washington, DC: Government Printing Office, 2000), pp. 52, 60, 63, 66, 69, 72.

a Ever had at least one drink of alcohol.
b Drank alcohol on one or more of the thirty days preceding the survey.
c Drank five or more drinks of alcohol on at least one occasion on one or more of the thirty days preceding the survey.
d More than a few sips.
e On one or more of the thirty days preceding the survey.

More than 80 percent of Hispanic, white, and tenth through twelfth grade students ever used alcohol. Hispanics were the most likely current users, while white students were the most likely episodic heavy drinkers. Black high schoolers were more likely than Hispanic or white students to have used alcohol before the age of thirteen. High school seniors had the highest percentage of current use and episodic heavy drinking. Hispanic youths were more likely than whites or blacks to use alcohol on school property.

Arrests and Juvenile Alcohol Use

Juvenile arrests for alcohol-related offenses appear overall to be on the decline, according to official figures (Federal Bureau of Investigation, 2000). In 1999, 131,619 youths under the age of eighteen were arrested for the alcohol-related offenses of driving under the influence, liquor law violations, and drunkenness in the United States (see Table 3.4). Most of these arrests were for liquor law violations. Male juveniles were far more likely than female juveniles to be arrested for alcohol-related offenses, with a 2.5 to 1 ratio.

As seen in Figure 3.2, between 1990 and 1999, arrests of persons under the age of eighteen for drunkenness declined by more than 20 percent, and dropped a fraction for driving under the influence. However, juvenile arrests for liquor law violations rose more than 9 percent during this period. A further sign of a possible rise in drinking among youths is the increase in youth arrests over the ten-year period for offenses typically related to teenage drinking, including drug abuse violations, disorderly conduct, and curfew and loitering law violations (Federal Bureau of Investigation, 2000).

TABLE 3.4. Juvenile Arrests for Alcohol-Related Offenses, by Sex, 1999

Offense charged	Total	Male	Female
Driving under the influence	13,803	11,449	2,354
Liquor laws	1,037,334	71,530	32,204
Drunkenness	14,082	11,327	2,755
Total arrests	131,619	94,306	37,313

Source: Constructed from Federal Bureau of Investigation, *Crime in the United States: Uniform Crime Reports, 1999,* (Washington, DC: Government Printing Office, 2000), pp. 222, 224, 226.

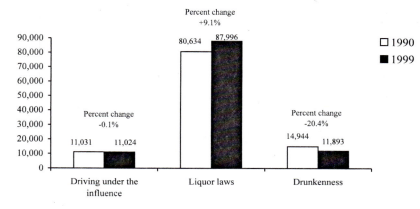

FIGURE 3.2. Juvenile Arrest Trends for Alcohol-Related Offenses, 1990-1999. (*Source:* Constructed from Federal Bureau of Investigation, *Crime in the United States: Uniform Crime Reports 1999,* Washington, DC: Government Printing Office, 2000, p. 216.)

JUVENILE SUBSTANCE ABUSE AND OTHER DELINQUENT BEHAVIOR

Aside from the illegality of juvenile drug and alcohol use, substance abuse by minors has been strongly associated with more serious forms of delinquency and criminality (Flowers, 1990, 1999; Huizinga et al., 2000). Official data, self-report surveys, and juveniles in custody information reveal that most serious juvenile crimes often involved drug and/or alcohol use by the offender (Federal Bureau of Investigation, 2000; Flowers, 1990; Hawkins et al., 2000; U.S. Department of Justice, 1999). The use of drugs or alcohol by juveniles in the commission of violent, property, drug, or sex offenses has been shown to relate to child abuse and neglect, sexual abuse, drug dependency, school problems, peer pressure, mental problems, and other factors (Elliot, Huizinga, and Menard, 1989; Elliot, Huizinga, and Ageton, 1985; Flowers, 1990, 1998).

Violent Crimes

The literature is replete with studies that correlate juvenile drug and alcohol use and violent offending (Carpenter et al., 1988; Chaiken,

2000; Johnson, Wish, and Huizinga, 1986; U.S. Department of Health and Human Services, 1997). Serious juvenile crime and delinquency, including homicide, aggravated assault, rape, and gang violence, typically involve substance abuse on the part of the perpetrator (Flowers, 1986, 1990). Violent juvenile offenders have been shown to be habitual users of marijuana and alcohol, and users of cocaine, speed, and hallucinogens to a lesser degree (Carpenter et al., 1988; Flowers, 1999).

Boys who commit serious juvenile offenses are much more likely to be substance abusers than girls who perpetrate serious offenses (Chaiken, 2000; Riley, 1997). Studies on drug use and serious delinquency in Denver, Rochester, and Pittsburgh found that 50 percent of male juvenile drug users and 20 percent of female juvenile drug users were consistently involved in serious delinquent behavior (Huizinga et al., 2000). In Pittsburgh, 70 percent of male juvenile drug users were serious offenders. The research also found that 38 percent of male youths engaging in serious delinquency were drug users, whereas just under 50 percent of the serious female delinquents were drug users.

Marijuana and alcohol use has been significantly more prevalent than other drugs among delinquent males involved in serious offending (Chaiken, 2000; National Governors' Association, 1999). Use of hard liquor, particularly by boys, was strongly related to serious offenses such as violent crimes, whereas use of marijuana was associated with offenses such as property crimes and drug dealing.

Property Crimes

Juvenile drug and alcohol use has been most strongly linked to property crimes (Flowers, 1990, 1995; Kozel and DuPont, 1977). Researchers have found this association reflected in two key factors: (1) the need or desire for drugs or alcohol, and (2) obtaining property, including money, which can be used to purchase alcohol or drugs.

Carpenter and colleagues (1988) reported that theft by juvenile substance abusers was motivated primarily by a desire to acquire cash or valued goods such as clothing or stereo equipment in order to be popular among peers, rather than as a means to purchase drugs or alcohol, per se. Other studies have generally supported this contention (Chaiken, 2000; Elliot, Huizinga, and Ageton, 1985).

However, research has also shown that alcohol and drug dependency are strong motivators for committing property crimes among adolescents or adults (Flowers, 1990, 1999). Young female thieves who are also drug or alcohol addicted have commonly been found to commit property offenses, including theft of drugs, to support habits (Campbell, 1981; Flowers, 1986, 1990, 1995).

Drug Dealing

Juvenile drug users often become drug dealers, usually as a means to support their habit or to make money for other purposes in what may be considered a low-risk occupation (Flowers, 1990). Many are drawn into the business by other young substance abusers who deal drugs (Chaiken and Johnson, 1988; Flowers, 1999). An estimated 10 percent of juveniles are involved in illegal drug transactions (Carpenter et al., 1988; Johnson, 1973). Researchers have found that many types of juvenile drug dealers exist, rather than one specific type (Chaiken, 2000; Chaiken and Johnson, 1988). An interrelationship exists between juvenile substance abuse, drug dealing, carrying weapons, and serious offending including homicide (Blumstein, 1996; Felson and Messner, 1996; Flowers, 1999).

Johnson, Wish, and Huizinga (1986) found that drug dealing by youths is highly concentrated. Their national sample of juveniles revealed that though less than 3 percent were cocaine users, nearly 60 percent of this group sold illicit drugs. Twenty-five percent of the drugs sold were other than marijuana. Carpenter and colleagues (1988) found that the majority of adolescent drug dealers used the same drug they sold, and that many regularly smoked marijuana and drank alcohol.

Marijuana is the most commonly used and sold drug by juveniles (Flowers, 1990). However, other drugs such as crack are easily accessible, affordable, and sold by juveniles around the country (Flowers, 1999). Most young drug dealers obtain, sell, and distribute drugs for both personal use and for profit.

While juvenile drug dealers are predominantly male, young females are increasingly becoming more involved in drug dealing, often to support a habit (Bartollas, 1985; Flowers, 1990).

Sex Crimes

The correlation between young drug and alcohol users and sex offenses has been well documented in a number of studies (Amir, 1971; Flowers, 1998, 2001b). In half of all rapes, the rapist was under the influence of alcohol or drugs (Flowers, 1999).

Many teenage date rapists used alcohol or drugs prior to committing the offense (Flowers, 2001b). Some also use popular "date-rape drugs" such as Rohypnol or "Roofies" to subdue the victim (Flowers, 1999).

A high percentage of child prostitutes use drugs and/or alcohol (Johnson, 1992; James, 1980; Weisberg, 1985). Almost 75 percent of teen streetwalkers use alcohol regularly, and as many as 67 percent of all young female prostitutes are habitual drug users (Flowers, 2001b; Goldstein, 1979). Many young prostitutes are also intravenous drug users and vice versa (Flowers, 1998; Plant, 1990).

Chapter 4

School Crime and Violence

School crime and violence have attracted considerable attention in recent years in the wake of a rash of school killings across the United States (Flowers and Flowers, 2001; U.S. Departments of Education and Justice, 2000). The link between fatal school violence and illegal firearms has been clearly established (Flowers and Flowers, 2001; Lizotte et al., 1994; Office of Justice Programs, 1999). Most experts in juvenile delinquency agree that such incidents often indicate other problems, including child abuse, family violence, substance abuse, and additional forms of youth violence and criminal behavior (Flowers, 1994, 2000; Howell and Lynch, 2000; Office of Juvenile Justice and Delinquency Prevention, 1998).

Criminologists have long studied delinquency and youth violence in relation to the school (Cernkovich and Giordano, 1992; Esbensen and Huizinga, 1993; Hindelang, Hirschi, and Weis, 1981; Liska and Reed, 1985; Rhodes and Reiss, 1969). A number of school-related variables are believed to play a central role in affecting antisocial behavior in juveniles at risk, including school failure, labeling, peer group problems, race, bullying, fighting, and victimization (Bjerregaard and Smith, 1993; Elliot and Voss, 1974; Kelly, 1971; Liska and Reed, 1985; Olweus, 1993; Thornberry, Moore, and Christenson, 1985).

Another important factor in school crime and violence is the presence of or involvement in youth gangs (Flowers, 1990; Howell, 1998; National Youth Gang Center, 1999; Office of Justice Programs, 1999). Studies show that gangs in school are closely related to school violence, guns in school, drug possession and sales, and student fears and victimization (Curry and Spergel, 1992; Lopez, 1989; Moore, 1978; Office of Juvenile Justice and Delinquency Prevention, 1998; Wang, 1995).

SHOOTINGS AND FATALITIES AT SCHOOLS

The number of fatal shootings at schools and school-related violent deaths in the United States since the late 1980s has been a wake-up call to the nation about the accessability of firearms to unstable, high-risk youth and their potential to create mass harm and havoc. Examples of recent killings at schools follow:

- On April 20, 1999, Eric Harris, eighteen, and Dylan Klebold, seventeen, orchestrated the country's deadliest massacre at a school when they entered Columbine High School in Littleton, Colorado, with semiautomatic weapons and opened fire, killing fifteen, including themselves, while wounding twenty-five others.
- On March 24, 1998, Mitchell Johnson, fourteen, and Andrew Golden, twelve, dressed in camouflage, began shooting students and teachers at Westside Middle School in Jonesboro, Arkansas, killing four students and a teacher, and injuring ten others.
- On May 21, 1998, Kip Kinkel, fifteen, walked into Thurston High School in Springfield, Oregon, and started shooting, killing two students and wounding twenty-five. A day earlier, Kinkel had shot and killed his parents.
- On February 19, 1997, armed with a shotgun, Evan Ramsey, sixteen, entered Bethel Regional High School in Bethel, Alaska, and began firing, killing the principal and a student, while wounding several others.
- On December 1, 1997, Michael Carneal, fourteen, went on a shooting rampage at Heath High School in West Paducah, Kentucky, killing three students and injuring five others. He had been inspired by the movie *The Basketball Diaries* in which the main character entered a classroom and shot five classmates.
- On February 2, 1996, Barry Loukaitis, fourteen and an honor student, arrived at Frontier Junior High School in Moses Lake, Washington, armed with a high-powered rifle and two handguns. He went on a shooting spree, killing two students and a teacher.
- On March 2, 1987, Nathan Ferris, twelve, took his father's .45 caliber pistol to his school in Missouri and shot and killed an-

other boy who had teased him, before killing himself (Flowers and Flowers, 2001).

According to government data, sixty school-related violent deaths occurred in the United States between July 1, 1997, and June 30, 1998 (U.S. Departments of Education and Justice, 2000). Forty-seven of the deaths were classified as homicide, twelve as suicide, and one as the result of a police shooting in the line of duty. Thirty-five of the forty-seven school-related homicide victims were school children, while seven of the twelve school-related suicide victims were school children. Firearms were used in the majority of school-associated homicides.

In spite of these sobering statistics, relatively few violent deaths of children occur at school or in association with school. As shown in Figure 4.1, from 1997 to 1998, of a total of 2,752 murders of persons ages five to nineteen in the United States, 2,717 occurred away from school and only thirty-five at school. Similarly, in Figure 4.2, between 1997 and 1998, there were 2,061 suicides in the country in-

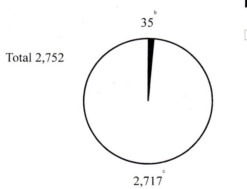

■ At school

□ Away from school

35[b]

Total 2,752

2,717[c]

FIGURE 4.1. Number of Murders of Students at School and Youths Ages Five to Nineteen Away from School, 1997-1998[a]. (*Source:* Derived from U.S. Department of Education and Justice, *Indicators of School Crime and Safety 2000*, (Washington, DC: Offices of Educational Research and Improvement and Justice Programs, 2000), p. 2.
[a] "At School" includes on school property, on the way to or from school, and while attending or traveling to or from a school-sponsored event.
[b] Student murders at school, July 1, 1997 to June 30, 1998.
[c] Murders of youth ages five through nineteen away from school, July 1, 1997 to June 30, 1998.

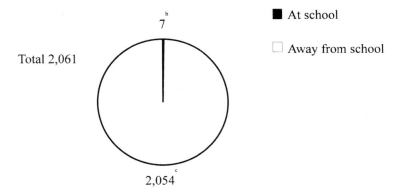

FIGURE 4.2. Number of Suicides of Students at School and Youths Ages Five to Nineteen Away from School, 1997-1998[a]. (*Source:* Derived from U.S. Department of Education and Justice, *Indicators of School Crime and Safety 2000,* Washington, DC: Offices of Educational Research and Improvement and Justice Programs, 2000, p. 2.)
[a] "At School" includes on school property, on the way to or from school, and while attending or traveling to or from a school-sponsored event.
[b] Student suicides at school, July 1, 1997 to June 30, 1998.
[c] Suicides of youth ages five through nineteen away from school, during calendar year 1998.

volving youths five to nineteen years of age. Although 2,054 occurred away from school, seven suicides took place on school property, on the way to or from school, or were otherwise school-associated.

Experts on youth school violence have identified warning signs for at-risk children. These include:

- Depression
- A history of temper tantrums
- A history of truancy, school suspensions, or being expelled
- Background of school or home disciplinary problems
- Background of substance abuse problems
- Preoccupied with firearms or explosives
- Displays cruelty to animals
- Fascinated with violence in games, movies, books, or other entertainment
- Obsessed or associated with Internet hate groups or antigovernment organizations
- Has experienced child abuse or witnessed family violence
- Has an excessive need for attention

- Is part of a gang or group of antisocial youth
- Has threatened to commit suicide or harm others
- Bullies fellow students or younger children, or been victimized by bullies
- Involved with ritualistic or satanic cults
- Easily blames others for self-caused problems

THE EXTENT OF SCHOOL CRIME

Though school crime in general is on the decline and constitutes only a fraction of crimes committed away from school, crime and violence in schools continues to be a major issue in this country, affecting offenders, victims, and communities. To put this in context, consider the following recent data on school crime from the Centers for Disease Control and Prevention's Youth Risk Behavior Survey (U.S. Department of Justice, 1999):

- Almost 40 percent of high school students were in a physical fight within the previous year.
- Almost 50 percent of male students were involved in a school fight within the previous year.
- Fifteen percent of high school students nationwide had fought on school property in the previous year.
- Minority students were more likely to be in school fights and to suffer injuries than white students.
- More than twice as many male students were likely to have been in a fight within the previous year as female students.
- Forty percent of high school students stayed away from school at least once in the previous month out of fear of crime or victimization.
- Nearly 20 percent of high school students carried a weapon to school in the previous month.
- Almost 6 percent of students carried a gun in the previous month.
- Seven percent of high school students were threatened or injured at school with a weapon in the previous year.
- High school seniors using drugs were more likely to be victims of a violent crime than seniors who did not use drugs.

- Thirty-three percent of high school students were the victims of property crime or vandalism in the previous year.
- More than 50 percent of middle and high schools across the country reported at least one episode of fighting or unarmed assault during the previous year.
- Approximately 20 percent of middle and high schools reported at least one serious crime of violence during the previous year.
- Violent school crime was more than twice as likely in cities than rural areas, and more than three times as likely as in small towns.

Various other government sources further illustrate the incidence and seriousness of school crime and violence. According to the *National Crime Victimization Survey Report* (U.S. Department of Justice, 2000), there were 1,239,267 crimes of violence inside school buildings or on school property in the United States in 1995 (see Table 4.1). More than 956,000 of these involved attempted or threatened violent crimes.

Perhaps the most comprehensive account of school crime is the annual *Indicators of School Crime and Safety* (U.S. Department of Education and Justice, 2000). It reported that in 1998 an estimated 2,715,600 school crimes in the country involved student victims twelve to eighteen years of age (see Table 4.2). Of these, 252,700 were classified as serious violent crimes, including rape, sexual assault, robbery, and aggravated assault. Violent crimes and theft victimizations were roughly equal.

School crime victims were most likely to be male, ages twelve to fourteen, white non-Hispanic, suburban, with household incomes of $50,000 or more. However, student victims of school crime were well represented in every characteristic.

From 1996 to 1997, at least one serious violent offense on school property was reported to law enforcement authorities by 10 percent of all public schools, including murder, rape, sexual battery, fights with weapons, robbery, and suicide. Reports of less serious crimes or nonviolent offenses were reported to police by 47 percent of public schools.

Middle and high schools were more likely to report any school crime or violence than elementary schools. The most frequently reported offense from 1996 to 1997 was physical assault or fight, with-

TABLE 4.1. School Violent Crime, by Type of Crime, 1995

Type of crime	Number of incidents	Inside school building/ on school property (%)
Crimes of violence	8,727,230	14.2
Completed violence	2,515,470	11.1
Attempted/threatened violence	6,211,770	15.4
Rape/sexual assault[b]	335,450	4.0[a]
Robbery	1,039,490	5.7
Completed/property taken	673,440	5.1
With injury	196,880	0.0[a]
Without injury	476,560	7.2
Attempted to take property	366,050	6.7
With injury	87,610	12.8[a]
Without injury	278,440	4.8[a]
Assault	7,352,290	15.8
Aggravated	1,622,360	6.4
Simple	5,729,920	18.5
Purse snatching/pocket picking	362,100	14.2
Motor vehicle theft	1,653,820	2.0
Completed	1,098,280	1.9[a]
Attempted	555,540	2.2[a]
Theft	22,006,050	13.3

Source: Derived from U.S. Department of Justice, *Criminal Victimization in the United States 1995: A National Crime Victimization Survey Report* (Washington, DC: Government Printing Office, 2000b), p. 71.

[a] Estimate is based on about ten or fewer sample cases.
[b] Includes verbal threats of rape and threats of sexual assault.

out the use of a weapon. Theft crimes tended to occur more often in high schools than middle schools (U.S. Departments of Education and Justice, 2000).

Trends in School Crime and Violence

In spite of the significant levels of school crime, violence, and victimization noted, overall serious criminality associated with schools

TABLE 4.2. Number of School Crimes Against Students Age Twelve to Eighteen, by Type of Crime and Student Characteristics, 1998[a]

Student characteristics	Total	Theft	Violent	Serious violent[b]
Total	2,715,600	1,562,300	1,153,200	252,700
Gender				
Male	1,536,100	814,900	721,300	144,200
Female	1,179,400	747,500	431,900	108,400
Age				
12-14	1,475,100	769,300	705,800	162,200
15-18	1,240,500	793,000	447,400	90,500
Race/ethnicity				
White, non-Hispanic	1,824,300	1,038,800	785,500	157,100
Black, non-Hispanic	464,000	265,700	198,200	48,100
Hispanic	315,100	185,900	129,200	42,600
Other, non-Hispanic	105,700	67,600	38,100	4,900[c]
Urbanicity				
Urban	865,000	503,600	361,400	99,100
Suburban	1,319,500	771,000	548,400	91,700
Rural	531,100	287,700	243,400	61,900
Household income				
Less than $7,500	136,500	69,900	66,700	21,100[c]
$7,500-14,999	242,600	95,700	146,900	30,400[c]
$15,000-24,999	428,700	218,300	210,400	35,400
$25,000-34,999	351,100	173,000	178,200	52,100
$35,000-49,999	361,500	239,100	122,400	27,200[c]
$50,000-74,999	497,400	306,700	190,600	45,000
$75,000 or more	453,000	303,500	149,500	23,800[c]

Source: Derived from U.S. Department of Education and Justice, Indicators of School Crime and Safety 2000 (Washington, DC: Offices of Educational Research and Improvement and Justice Programs, 2000), p. 49.

[a]Includes crimes occurring inside or on school property, as well as on the way to or from school.
[b]Serious violent crimes are also included in violent crimes.
[c]Estimate based on fewer than ten cases.

Note: Serious violent crimes include rape, sexual assault, robbery, and aggravated assault. Violent crimes include serious or violent crimes and simple assault. Total crimes include violent crimes and theft. "At school" includes inside the school building, on school property, or on the way to or from school. Because of rounding or missing data, detail may not add to totals. Numbers are rounded to the nearest 100.

has dropped in recent years. According to *Indicators,* between 1992 and 1998, the victimization rate for violent crime in schools dropped from 4.8 percent to 4.3 percent for students twelve to eighteen years of age. The percentage of students reporting being crime victims at school during the period declined from 10 percent to 8 percent (U.S. Departments of Education and Justice, 2000).

Other trends in school crime include the following:

- Between 1994 and 1998, teachers were the victims of 1,755,000 nonfatal school crimes, including 668,000 crimes of violence.
- Between 1994 and 1998, 12 percent of all teachers were threatened with physical injury by a student.
- Between 1993 and 1997, the percentage of ninth to twelfth grade students reporting bringing a weapon onto school property dropped from 12 percent to 9 percent.
- Between 1995 and 1999, the percentage of twelve- to eighteen-year-old students avoiding places at school due to fear fell from 9 to 5 percent.
- Between 1995 and 1999, the percentage of students reporting a gang presence at school dropped from 29 percent to 17 percent.
- Between 1993 and 1997 the percentage of students being offered, sold, or given illicit drugs on school property increased 8 percent. In 1997, 33 percent of students in grades nine through twelve reported the availability of drugs.

DYNAMICS OF SCHOOL CRIME

Gang Presence at School

Youth gangs are often associated with youth violence, weapons possession, and drug dealing on school property (Battin et al., 1998; Esbensen and Huizinga, 1993; Flowers, 1990; Howell and Lynch, 2000; National Youth Gang Center, 1999; Wang, 1995). According to the *Indicators* report, almost 20 percent of schools had a gang presence in the United States in 1999. Public schools were almost five times more likely to have gangs than private schools. Twenty-five percent of urban students reported the presence of street gangs at their schools. Hispanic and black students were more likely than white students to report that there were gangs in school. Overall, the reported presence of gangs at school dropped 11 percent between 1995 and 1999 (U.S. Departments of Education and Justice, 2000). See Chapter 5 for further discussion on youth gangs, delinquency, and violence.

Bullying at School

Bullying by and against youths has been shown to be an at-risk factor for juvenile violence and other antisocial behavior (Office of Juvenile Justice and Delinquency Prevention, 1998; Olweus, 1993). *Indicators* reported that in 1999, approximately 5 percent of students twelve to eighteen years old reported themselves as victims of bullying in the previous six months. Students in lower grades were more likely to report being bullied than students in higher grades. Generally the rate of bullying was relatively equal for males and females, as well as for racial and ethnic groups (U.S. Departments of Education and Justice, 2000).

Students Carrying Weapons at School

The relationship between students, weapons, and school violence has been strongly supported in the research (Bjerregaard and Lizotte, 1995; Flowers and Flowers, 2001; Office of Juvenile Justice and Delinquency Prevention, 1998). According to *Indicators,* in 1997, 18 percent of students admitted carrying a knife, gun, or other weapon in the previous thirty days. Approximately 10 percent of students reported carrying a weapon to school in the previous month. Males were three times more likely to carry weapons onto school property than were females. Students in lower grades were more likely to come to school with weapons than students in higher grades. From 1993 to 1997, the percentage of students who reported carrying weapons to school dropped approximately 3 percent (U.S. Departments of Education and Justice, 2000).

Property Crimes at School

Property crimes at school are a fairly common occurrence (Flowers, 1994; U.S. Department of Justice, 1999). Approximately 33 percent of ninth- to twelfth-grade students reported having property stolen or damaged in 1997, according to the *Indicators* study. This included cars, clothing, money, and books. Males were generally more likely than females to report theft victimization, as were lower grade students compared to students in higher grades (U.S. Departments of Education and Justice, 2000). Juvenile property crimes have been associated with other delinquent behavior such as violent crime and substance abuse (Carpenter et al., 1988; Flowers, 1999; U.S. Department of Justice, 1999).

Alcohol and Drug Use at School

Juvenile substance abuse is frequently related to more serious juvenile offenses such as violent criminality and drug dealing (Chaiken, 2000; Flowers, 1990; Huizinga et al., 2000; Office of Juvenile Justice and Delinquency Prevention, 1998). A high rate of alcohol and drug use can be found at schools across the country. *Indicators* reported that in 1997, more than 50 percent of the students in the ninth through twelfth grades had at least one alcoholic beverage in the previous month, and 6 percent of students had used alcohol on school property. Male youths were more likely than female youths to use alcohol either at or away from school (U.S. Departments of Education and Justice, 2000).

Approximately 25 percent of ninth- to twelfth-grade students reported using marijuana within the previous month in 1997. Almost 10 percent of students had used marijuana at school in the previous thirty days. Males were more likely than females to smoke marijuana on school property and away from school. The percentage of male and female students using marijuana grew between 1993 and 1997, from 21 to 30 percent and 15 to 21 percent, respectively.

The availability of drugs, including alcohol, on school property contributes to student substance abuse, youth drug dealing, and other criminal activity (Flowers, 1999; U.S. Department of Justice, 1999). In 1997, almost 33 percent of ninth- to twelfth-grade students reported being offered, given, or sold an illegal drug at school (U.S. Departments of Education and Justice, 2000). See Chapter 3 for further discussion of kids, drugs, and crime.

Chapter 5

Youth Gangs, Criminality, and Violence

The issue of violent and delinquent juvenile gangs has often been exaggerated by the media, based largely on highly publicized gang shootings, drug dealing, and turf wars. This notwithstanding, youth criminal gangs, as differentiated from nonviolent youth gangs, pose a serious problem in our society. The relationship between juvenile gangs and serious and violent offending has been well documented (Cohen, 1955; Esbensen and Huizinga, 1993; Flowers, 1990; Howell, 1998; Miller, 1975).

Many experts have found that youth involvement in gangs and gang delinquency has proliferated in recent years, giving cause for concern (Maxson and Klein, 1990; Miller, 1992; National Youth Gang Center, 1999; Office of Juvenile Justice and Delinquency Prevention, 1998). Especially troublesome is the link between juvenile gang homicides and firearms (Decker and Van Winkle, 1996; Hutson et al., 1995; Sheley and Wright, 1993). Drug-related criminality is seen as a primary activity of delinquent youth gangs and often reflects on other aspects of gang life (Howell, 1998; Meehan and O'Carroll, 1992; National Drug Intelligence Center, 1996; Waldorf, 1993).

WHAT IS A YOUTH GANG?

Defining what constitutes a youth or juvenile gang, much less a delinquent or criminal youth gang, has proven problematic for experts in the field. Sociologist Frederick Thrasher was one of the first to define the youth gang in the 1920s as

> an interstitial group originally formed spontaneously and then integrated through conflict. It is characterized by . . . meeting face to face, milling, movement through space as a unit, conflict, and planning. The result of this collective behavior is the

> development of tradition, unreflective internal structure, esprit de corps, solidarity, morale, group awareness, and attachment to local territory. (Thrasher, 1927, p. 57)

Various sources have attempted to define youth gangs as groups of individuals involved in territorial claims and often antisocial or violent behavior (Howell, 1998; Miller, 1975; Spergel and Bobrowski, 1989). The 1996 National Youth Gang Survey defined youth gangs as "a group of youths or young adults . . . that (the respondent) or other responsible person in [the] agency or community are willing to identify or classify as a 'gang'" (National Youth Gang Center, 1999, p. 7).

> In *The Adolescent Criminal,* the delinquent youth gang was defined as: a loosely organized or disorganized group of juveniles distinguished by colors, race and ethnicity, neighborhood, and principles; and whose delinquent and criminal activities relate to status, respect, revenge, celebrity, satisfaction, and profit, and include murder, gang wars, and drug dealing. (Flowers, 1990, p. 99)

THE EXTENT OF YOUTH GANGS
AND THEIR MEMBERSHIP

How many youth gangs exist in the United States today? How large is the membership? Studies indicate that a rapid growth in juvenile gangs and membership has occurred since the 1970s when Miller (1980) estimated that there were approximately 2,200 gangs nationwide with 96,000 members in over 300 communities. He concluded that these gangs were responsible for approximately 33 percent of all violent crimes and terrorized whole communities, including many inner city schools. Other researchers later estimated youth gangs to number between 8,600 and 9,000, with members ranging from 375,000 to 400,000 (Curry, Ball, and Decker, 1996; Klein, 1995).

More recently, the 1996 National Youth Gang Survey found the number of gangs and members to be much higher (see Table 5.1). In designing its survey to be more representative of the entire country than earlier studies, it estimated that there were almost 31,000 gangs with more than 846,000 members in approximately 4,800 jurisdictions in the United States in 1996.

TABLE 5.1. Reported and Extrapolated Number of Gangs and Gang Members in the United States, 1996

	Reported number		Extrapolated number	
Area Type	Gangs	Gang members	Gangs	Gang members
Large city	11,495	469,267	12,841	513,243
Small city	315	3,618	8,053	92,448
Suburban county	6,897	195,205	7,956	222,267
Rural county	533	5,000	1,968	18,470
Total	19,240	673,090	30,818	846,428

Source: National Youth Gang Center, *1996 National Youth Gang Survey* (Washington, DC: Office of Juvenile Justice and Delinquency Prevention, 1999), p. 13.

Youth gangs were most likely to be found in large cities with an estimated 11,495 reported gangs and 469,267 members. Extrapolating these numbers nationwide, there were approximately 12,841 gangs in large cities with 513,243 members. This represented roughly 42 percent of all gangs and 61 percent of gang membership in the United States.

CHARACTERISTICS OF YOUTH GANG MEMBERS

Age and Gang Membership

Studies show that the majority of youth gang members fall between the ages of ten and twenty-four (Flowers, 1990; Klein, 1995; National Youth Gang Center, 1999). Miller (1975) found that 82 percent of gang members arrested in the four largest cities with gang problems were between fourteen and nineteen years of age. Just over 4 percent were under fourteen. The average age of youth gang members is approximately seventeen to eighteen (Curry and Decker, 1998; Howell, 1998).

As seen in Figure 5.1, according to the Youth Gang Survey—after accounting for the number of gang members as reported in each jurisdiction—more than 34 percent of gang members nationwide fell between the ages of fifteen and seventeen in 1996. Sixteen percent were

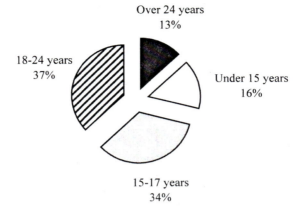

FIGURE 5.1. Age of Gang Members (Weighted for Number of Gang Members) in the United States, 1996. (*Source:* National Youth Gang Center, *1996 National Youth Gang Survey,* Washington, DC: Office of Juvenile Justice and Delinquency Prevention, 1999, p. 16.)

younger than fifteen years of age. Roughly 50 percent of all gang members were age eighteen and older.

Gender and Youth Gang Involvement

According to most studies, youth gangs are predominantly male (Bjerregaard and Smith, 1993; Flowers, 1990; Miller, 1992; National Youth Gang Center, 1999). Miller (1975) found that at least 90 percent of the gang members in his research were male youths. Other studies have estimated the number of female members of gangs as anywhere from 3 to 10 percent (Curry, Ball, and Fox, 1994; Klein, 1995; Miller, 1992).

However a number of researchers believe that females constitute a much greater number of youth gang members, with estimates of anywhere from 25 percent to 33 percent of gang membership (Brown, 1970; Curry and Decker, 1998; Flowers, 1995; National Youth Gang Center, 1999). In a study of institutionalized female delinquents, Giorando (1978) found that more than half reported being in a gang. Brown (1970) contended that female gang members are more likely to be in sexually integrated gangs than autonomous female gangs.

Although the general view holds that female members of gangs tend to perform less serious forms of gang delinquency (Klein, 1995;

Miller, 1975; Spergel, 1995), some research suggests female gang members do participate in serious and violent youth gang activity (Adler, 1975; Flowers, 1995; Hardman, 1969). Campbell (1991) advanced the theory that female youth gang members have the capacity to commit acts of violence more quickly than their male counterparts.

Racial and Ethnic Makeup of Youth Gangs

Most studies indicate that youth gangs in the United States are predominantly comprised of racial and ethnic minorities—primarily African Americans and Hispanics (Flowers, 1990; Klein, 1995; Miller, 1992). In a recent law enforcement survey, the national composition of gang membership was found to be 48 percent African American and 43 percent Hispanic, with 5 percent of members white, and 4 percent Asian youths (Curry, 1996).

According to the 1996 Youth Gang Survey, after adjusting for the number of gang members reported in every jurisdiction, the makeup of gang membership nationwide can be seen in Figure 5.2. Hispanics represented 44 percent of youths in gangs, African Americans 35 percent, Caucasians 14 percent, Asians 5 percent, and others—such as American Indians and Polynesians—2 percent. Some studies have

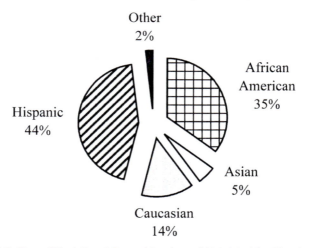

FIGURE 5.2. Race/Ethnicity of Gang Members (Weighted for Number of Gang Members) in the United States, 1996. (*Source:* National Youth Gang Center, *1996 National Youth Gang Survey,* Washington, DC: Office of Juvenile Justice and Delinquency Prevention, 1999, p. 24.)

found that the overrepresentation of black and Hispanic youths in official gang data is a reflection of different law enforcement standards and labeling, as well as racial or ethnic minority prejudices (Flowers, 1986, 1988; Miller, 1974; Spergel, 1995).

Researchers have found that certain offenses are more linked to particular racial or ethnic juvenile gangs. For instance, black gangs appear more likely to be involved in drug-related crimes, Hispanic gangs are more associated with territorial violence, and Asian and white gangs tend to commit more property offenses (Block et al., 1996; Moore, 1978; Spergel, 1990).

Recent findings indicate that white youth involvement in juvenile gangs is increasing (Curry, Ball, and Fox, 1994; Miller, 1970; National Youth Gang Center, 1999). In an examination of the Gang Resistance Education and Training Program, Esbensen and Osgood (1997) found that white youths comprised 25 percent of self-reported members of gangs. The increasing numbers of gang members in suburban and rural America are more likely to be white than nonwhite youths (Flowers, 1990; Hardman, 1969; Myerhoff and Myerhoff, 1964).

An estimated 46 percent of youth gangs are believed to be a mixture of different racial and ethnic group members, according to the Youth Gang Survey of 1996 (National Youth Gang Center, 1999).

YOUTH GANGS, CRIME, AND VIOLENCE

Youth gangs are often associated with criminal and violent activities (Cohen, 1955; Howell, 1998; Miller, 1966; National Young Gang Center, 1999; Sante, 1991; Yablonsky, 1962). Studies show that while not all gang involvement is delinquent or criminal, members of youth gangs are more likely to be involved in criminal behavior than youths who are not gang-affiliated (Curry and Decker, 1998; Esbensen and Huizinga, 1993). For example, in a Rochester study, seven times as many serious and violent offenses were perpetrated by youth gang members as nongang members (Bjerregaard and Smith, 1993).

The amount of gang criminality and violence can vary from jurisdiction to jurisdiction, city to city, or even neighborhood to neighborhood (Block and Block, 1993; Miller, 1974; Moore, 1988). In a self-report survey in Denver, the disproportionate level of youth gang involvement in antisocial behavior can be seen in the fact that more than 50 percent of all street crimes were committed by gang members (Esbensen and Huizinga, 1993). In Rochester, nearly 90 percent of serious offenses and approximately 70 percent drug and property crimes were committed by members of youth gangs (Thornberry, 1998).

Youth Gangs and Homicide

The relationship between youth gangs and homicides is significant (Block, 1993; Klein, 1995; Maxson, Gordon, and Klein, 1985). Although the overall rate of murders committed in the United States continues to decline, a high percentage of homicides are gang related. As shown in Figure 5.3, in 1996, gang members were blamed for an estimated 2,364 homicides occurring in large cities and 561 murders in suburban counties in the United States.

Deadly gang violence is attributed to possession and use of firearms (Bjerregaard and Lizotte, 1995; Block and Block, 1993; Howell, 1998). Studies have shown that illegal gun possession by members of violent youth gangs is directly related to an increase in gang-perpetrated homicides (Decker and Van Winkle, 1996; Sheley and Wright, 1993). In some cities, gang-related drive-by shootings have been on the rise (Hutson, Anglin, and Eckstein, 1996). Researchers have found

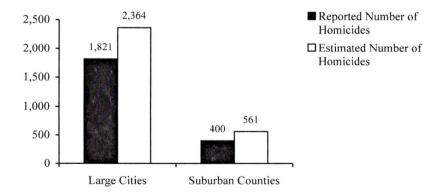

FIGURE 5.3. Gang Member Homicides, by Area Type, 1996. (*Source:* National Youth Gang Center, *1996 National Youth Gang Survey,* Washington, DC: Office of Juvenile Justice and Delinquency Prevention, 1999, p. 33.)

some association between drug trafficking by gangs and homicides (Inciardi, 1986; Maxson and Klein, 1996).

Youth Gangs and Drug Offenses

Youth gang participation in drug-related offenses has been examined in numerous studies on delinquency in gangs (Esbensen and Huizinga, 1993; Flowers, 1988; Klein, 1995; National Youth Gang Center, 1999). A relationship has been shown between youth gangs and various aspects of drug involvement including drug abuse, drug sales, drug distribution, and drug trafficking (Decker and Van Winkle, 1994; Flowers, 1999; Howell, 1998; Maxson, 1995; Moore, 1990; Waldorf, 1993).

According to data from the 1996 National Youth Gang Survey (1999), the following percentages have been reported by jurisdictions for youth gang involvement in drug offenses:

- Forty-three percent of drug sales.
- Twenty-nine percent control of more than 50 percent of the drug distribution.
- African-American gangs controlled 59 percent of gang drug distribution.
- One in three gang members controlling all of the drug distribution are between fifteen and seventeen years of age.
- In approximately three in ten Midwestern and Southern regions, gang members participated in a high level of drug sales.

Drug-related gang delinquency is typically associated with other forms of youth gang antisocial behavior, including violent, property, and sex crimes (Flowers, 1999, 2001b; National Youth Gang Center, 1999).

Youth Gangs and School Crime

The correlation between juvenile gangs and school crime and violence has been well documented (Chandler et al., 1998; Gottfredson and Gottfredson, 1985; Howell and Lynch, 2000). Chandler and associates (1998) found that between 1989 and 1995, gang presence at schools, which almost doubled from 15 percent to 28 percent, was related to firearms and drugs on school property. Youth gangs were more than twice as likely to be present in public schools as private schools.

In an examination of youth gangs in schools by Howell and Lynch (2000), 37 percent of students reported the presence of gangs. More than 67 percent of the students reported that gang members were involved in school violence, selling drugs, and/or gun possession.

Schools with a gang presence are more likely to have student violence than schools without gangs. According to the U.S. Justice Department (1999), the violent victimization rate of students in schools with a gang presence is nearly three times greater than in schools with no reported gangs. Research indicates a significant relationship exists between school violence and property crime victimization and crimes that occur in the home and elsewhere (Flowers, 1994, 2000; Howell and Lynch, 2000).

YOUTH GANG THEORIES

A number of theories have been advanced to explain youth gangs. Among the most influential are reaction-formation theory, opportunity theory, and lower-class culture theory. More general theories on juvenile gang delinquency and youth crime are discussed in Part II.

Reaction-Formation Theory

Reaction-formation theory of gang delinquency was first proposed by Albert Cohen in the 1950s. According to the theory, lower-class youth enter into gang delinquency as a group response to the failure to acquire status as measured by middle-class norms and values. Since lower-class youths are disadvantaged in institutional settings such as school, they lack the means and opportunities to attain culturally prescribed goals. Cohen theorized that such youths exhibit "status frustration" in competition with middle-class youths, causing them to band together in a delinquent gang subculture where their values are opposite those of the middle class (Cohen, 1955; Cohen and Short, 1958).

Although Cohen is credited as one of the first to relate the school system to delinquency, his theory has been criticized as unvalidated empirically. Further, there is little evidence to support the notion that lower-class youths reject middle-class values. Finally, in reaction-formation theory, too little attention is given to the relative weight of such correlates as family, biology, and sociodemographic character-istics in explaining youth gangs and delinquency.

Opportunity Theory

Opportunity theory was advanced in the 1960s by Richard Cloward and Lloyd Ohlin in explaining youth gang delinquency (Cloward and Ohlin, 1960). The theory posits that juvenile gang delinquency re-flects a disparity between the culturally prescribed goals lower-class youths aspire to and the lack of legitimate means for achieving these goals. Thus opportunity theory assumes that this disparity results in deep frustration, causing youths to turn to illegitimate means.

According to Cloward and Ohlin, there are three primary types of lower-class youth gangs or subcultural reactions to blocked access to legitimate (or illegitimate) avenues for success:

- *Criminal gang*—develops criminal values and skills to acquire through illegitimate means power, material gain, and prestige.
- *Conflict gang*—develops when both legitimate and illegitimate opportunities for success are blocked. Membership allows youths to achieve status, prestige, and a reputation for toughness among peers.
- *Retreatist gang*—develops when youths are denied or reject success through legitimate and illegitimate means. Retreatist youths often turn to drug abuse and secondary crimes such as drug dealing to support habits.

Opportunity theory has been criticized for focusing too much on lower-class gang delinquency and inadequately explaining individual delinquency or that existing in other classes. In addition, the theory fails to account for why some communities have more than one type of delinquent gang. Further, some critics question whether lower-class youths truly aspire to middle-class values (Flowers, 1990; Miller, 1958).

Lower-Class Culture Theory

Lower-class culture theory was put forth in the 1950s by Walter Miller in relating youth gang delinquency to the lower-class culture (Miller, 1958, 1975). Rather than postulating that lower-class gang delinquency results from a rejection of middle-class values, Miller argues that it is a reflection of positive attempts by youths to attain goals established by the values or focal concerns present in the lower-class culture.

The criminologist identifies six such focal concerns of lower-class youths:

- *Trouble*—circumstances resulting in unwanted involvement with the police.
- *Toughness*—associated with masculinity, physical superiority, bravery, and daring.
- *Smartness*—the ability to outsmart, outwit, or con others while avoiding the same.
- *Excitement*—the desire for thrills, risks, and avoiding boredom.
- *Fate*—beliefs related to luck, fortunes, and jinxes.
- *Autonomy*—a desire to be in control of one's own destiny and life.

According to lower-class culture theory, the delinquent gang serves as a social context in which youths can achieve prestige through actions related to lower-class focal concerns.

A number of critics have rejected the theory that lower-class youths do not adhere to culturally prescribed goals (Flowers, 1990; Hirschi, 1969). Also, lower-class culture theory does not explain the origination of these focal concerns or differentiate between lower-class offenders and nonoffenders.

More recent contributions by Miller in studying youth gangs have sought to clarify and improve upon his earlier propositions (Miller, 1966, 1974, 1992).

Chapter 6

Dating Violence

Since the early 1980s, researchers have put greater focus on dating violence as another form of intimate violence—much like domestic violence (Jasinski and Williams, 1998; Levy, 1998; Roscoe and Callahan, 1985). Teen violence in dating relationships has proven a persistent and serious problem in the United States (Flowers, 2000; Kantor and Jasinski, 1998; Koss, Gidycz, and Wisniewski, 1987). Along with physical aggression, many youths involved in dating violence also perpetrate and experience sexual aggression (Bateman, 1998; Flowers, 2000; Odem and Clay-Warner, 1998). This disturbing pattern of behavior by juveniles and young adults often occurs unchecked, shrouded in secrecy and shame, or otherwise diminished in its impact on the individuals involved and the greater society. Studies have found that dating violence among teens typically involves substance abuse (Flowers, 2000; Tontodonato and Crew, 1988), and is often a reflection of family violence, date rape, and other signs of aggression or dysfunction (Bergman, 1992; Flowers, 2001b; Makepeace, 1989; Thompson, 1986).

THE DYNAMICS OF DATING VIOLENCE

Dating violence emerged as a major social issue in the study of youth violence in the 1980s and 1990s (Brustin, 1995; Levy, 1998; Matthews, 1984; O'Keefe, Brockopp, and Chew, 1986; Peters, Kochanek, and Murphy, 1998), due to the extensive literature on violence between intimates, including battered women and marital rape (Brownmiller, 1975; Flowers, 1994; Russell, 1990; Straus and Gelles, 1990; Walker, 1984). Sociologists, criminologists, psychologists and others recognized the relationship between and similarities of dating violence and domestic violence (Carlson, 1987; Dobash and Dobash,

1979; Kanin, 1957; Keseredy, 1988; Rouse, Breen, and Howell, 1988; Walker, 1979). Further, the correlation between dating violence and a cycle of intrafamilial and intimate family violence has been documented (Flowers, 2000; Langley and Levy, 1977; Steinmetz, 1977; Straus, Gelles, and Steinmetz, 1980; Wolak and Finkelhor, 1998).

Studies show that both male and female youths are involved in dating violence (Gamache, 1998; Roscoe and Callahan, 1985); however, young women are far more likely to receive the brunt of intimate violence (Lane and Gwartney-Gibbs, 1985). Adolescents who are at greatest risk to become victims of dating violence include those who are pregnant, young women of color, and teenage lesbians (Levy and Lobel, 1998; McFarlane, 1989; Rich, 1980; Waterman, Dawson, and Bologna, 1989; Yoshihama, Parekh, and Boyington, 1998).

Relationship and dating violence has been shown to include not only serious assaultive behavior but also mental and verbal abuse and intimidation (Flowers, 2000; Kantor and Jasinski, 1998; Levy, 1998). Jealousy and anger are seen as the most significant factors in abusive dating relationships (Flowers, 2000; Levy, 1998). Sexual aggression such as date rape and sexual assault is commonly associated with dating violence as a cause-and-effect correlate (Flowers, 2001b; Goodchilds and Zellman, 1984; Koss, Gidycz and Wisniewski, 1987; Muehlenhard and Linton, 1987).

Substance abuse often acts as a precipitator or intensifier of dating violence (Flowers, 2000; Kantor and Asdigian, 1996; Taylor and Chermack, 1993). Perpetrators in violent teenage relationships are prone to display other forms of violent behavior, including family violence, school violence, and homicidal violence—which can often continue into adulthood (Flowers, 1990, 1994; Flowers and Flowers, 2001; Hershorn and Rosenbaum, 1985; Hughes, 1988; Powell, 1998; Sousa, 1999).

THE CHARACTERISTICS OF TEEN
DATING VIOLENCE

Defining Dating Violence

Dating violence, like domestic or intimate violence, is a means used by the perpetrator to control and dominate the victim through intimidation, threats, and physical, emotional, sexual, and verbal abuse (Flowers, 2000; Sousa, 1999). The abuser uses aggression to impose his or her will on the victim by releasing frustrations, jealousies, or other pent up negative energy and lashing out (Makepeace, 1981; Sugarman and Hotaling, 1998).

Researchers have defined dating violence in terms of type of violent acts perpetrated, weapons used, and even in interpreting whether or not nonphysical force should be included in the definition (Carlson, 1987; Makepeace, 1988; Puig, 1984; Thompson, 1986). Some definitions exclude sexual violence in defining dating violence (Bernard and Bernard, 1983; Billingham and Sack, 1987; Lane and Gwartney-Gibbs, 1985), preferring to focus on the physical violence, per se, as a separate issue in the context of dating relationships. Other definitions emphasize sexual violence in dating relationships (Lundberg-Love and Geffner, 1989; Sugarman and Hotaling, 1998).

A number of studies have focused on the broader definition of domestic violence in defining relationship violence to include physical, psychological, sexual, and verbal aggression and intimidation irrespective of the perception of those involved (Sugarman and Hotaling, 1998).

Teen dating violence is seen as a facet of the cycle of intrafamilial violence and other violent behavior young people are surrounded by (Flowers, 1990; Sousa, 1999). They then use this experience of victimization to manifest a state of mind to offend others, including dates, acquaintances, family, and strangers (Flowers, 2000). Only in recent years has dating violence been recognized as deviant behavior that must be addressed.

The Nature of Teen Dating Violence

Teen dating violence affects individuals from all racial and ethnic groups, religions and cultural backgrounds, socioeconomic levels, and parts of the country. Many teenage offenders in violent relationships were victims of child abuse or family violence (Flowers, 1994). Ten percent of teens experiencing intrafamilial violence become perpetrators of dating violence (Sousa, 1999). Similar to the dynamics of domestic violence, relationship violence is often repetitive and intensifies as long as the relationship remains intact. In the battered woman's syndrome (Walker, 1979; Walker, 1984), most victims endure apologies and false promises to end the battering by the abusive mate before a renewed cycle of violence commences. This pattern can escalate when the victim seeks to terminate the relationship (Levy, 1998; Sousa, 1999).

Dating violence in teen relationships coincides with adolescent development and the parallel occurrence can result in confusion, normative problems, gender role issues, and other concerns alongside the process of physical, emotional, moral, intellectual, and social development. Studies show that young male and female attitudes about violence in dating situations are that physical or sexual aggression may be expected and even considered normal behavior (Goodchilds and Zellman, 1984; Malamuth, 1981). Consequently, such violence may not be regarded as criminal violence by the victim, and thus not a reportable offense.

Sex role issues can further complicate the situation. Since many adolescents grow up in abusive households or environments with males the usual aggressors and females the passive victims, they come to believe this is normal behavior within their individual sex roles. Hence, adolescent males may act out on aggressions toward dates in the manner they have witnessed peers or adult males do and adolescent females may expect abusive treatment as a normal part of relationships as a result of seeing other female family members or friends victimized.

With societal and peer pressures on teenagers to date and mate, sex role expectations and physical aggression can be exacerbated as a result of territorial claims, jealousies, obsessions, frustrations, and violent tendencies inherited from generation to generation (Osmond and Martin, 1975; Riggs, O'Leary, and Breslin, 1990; Roscoe and Callahan, 1985; Spence, Helmreich, and Stapp, 1975).

The Scope of Teen Violence in Dating Relationships

Teen dating violence has become an epidemic in the United States, according to much of the research. Both incidence and prevalence studies indicate the extent of the problem (Jasinski and Williams, 1998; Kuehl, 1998; Peters, Kochanek, and Murphy, 1998; Sugarman and Hotaling, 1998). Consider the following statistics on teen violence in dating relationships:

- Between 25 percent and 40 percent of all teenagers have been the victims of dating violence.
- Approximately 80 percent of the incidents involve pushing, slapping, hitting, shoving, and grabbing.
- More than 70 percent of pregnant or parenting teens suffer from physical relationship violence.
- Twenty-five percent of teens will be in a violent relationship.
- More than half the restraining orders against teens in Massachusetts in 1994 were due to dating violence (Sousa, 1999).
- A high percentage of dating violence occurs at school.
- More than 80 percent of school dating violence is physical.
- Rates of high school dating violence range from 9 to 41 percent (Avery-Leaf, 1997).
- Nearly 10 percent of all homicides are murders committed by a current or former mate or date (Flowers, 2000).

It is estimated that as many as 33 percent of youth of high school and college age are involved in intimate or dating violence (Levy, 1998). In a self-report survey of dating violence in three Midwestern high schools, almost 16 percent of the girls and almost 8 percent of the boys had experienced physical violence in a dating relationship (Roscoe and Callahan, 1985).

Anywhere from 10 percent to over 50 percent of high schoolers in this country have experienced relationship violence (Gamache, 1998; Flowers, 2000), and approximately 22 percent of college students have been the victims of violence in a dating relationship (Cate et al., 1982; Henton et al., 1983). Other studies found prevalence rates of lifetime teen and young adult dating violence to range from 9 percent to 60 percent (Makepeace, 1981; McKinney, 1986a; Roscoe and Callahan, 1985).

Research on the relationship between dating violence and the nature of the relationship reveals that between 47 percent and 86 percent of acts of dating violence take place while the couple are "going steady" or seriously involved (Makepeace, 1989; Plass and Gessner, 1983; Roscoe and Kelsey, 1986). Laner (1989) found the highest levels of male dating aggression in the most serious dating relationships. Other studies have shown higher rates of violent behavior by males in dating situations as the level of commitment to the relationship increased (Arias, Samios, and O'Leary, 1987; Burke, Stets, and Piroz-Good, 1989; Marshall and Rose, 1987).

Gender and Teen Dating Violence

With respect to gender and teenage dating violence, the literature indicates that at least as many young females as young males exhibit violent behavior in a dating relationship (Gamache, 1998; Girschick, 1993). In one study of students who had ever dated, physical violence was reported in a dating relationship by 36.4 percent of the girls and 37.1 percent of the boys (Molidor and Tolman, 1998). Some studies have reported significantly higher rates of male-perpetrated dating violence (McKinney, 1986b; Sigelman, Berry, and Wiles, 1984; Sousa, 1999); while most studies have yielded higher rates of female-perpetrated violence in dating relationships (Bernard and Bernard, 1983; Billingham and Sack, 1987; O'Keefe, Brockopp, and Chew, 1986).

Most experts agree that males tend to inflict much more severe violence in dating relationships than females (Lane and Gwartney-Gibbs, 1985; Roscoe and Callahan, 1985). Conversely, teenage girls are more likely to be the victims of serious physical or sexual violence than their male counterparts in a dating relationship (Gamache, 1998). In a study of 500 female adolescents at the Young Women's Resource Center in Des Moines, Iowa, it was found that during a six-month span virtually all the respondents had been victims of dating violence (Flowers, 2000). Thirty-three percent of females will experience violence at the hands of a dating partner before reaching the age of eighteen (Kuehl, 1998).

TEEN DATE RAPE

Date rape by teenagers is a serious consequence and correlate of dating violence in the United States. Many studies have documented the magnitude of the problem (Bateman, 1998; Deal and Wampler, 1986; Gray and Foshee, 1997; Koss, Gidycz, and Wisniewski, 1987; Parrot and Bechhofer, 1991; Sanday, 1990). Ageton (1983) found that date rape constituted 67 percent of the sexual violence reported by adolescent girls and young women. An estimated 50 percent of all rapes are committed against adolescent victims, with most of these falling within the date or acquaintance rape category (Bateman, 1998). To put youth date rape in this country in its proper perspective, one need only look at the following figures and victim characteristics:

- Nearly 90 percent of female sexual assaults are perpetrated by dates, acquaintances, or friends.
- Sixty percent of rapes reported to rape crisis centers were committed by dates or acquaintances of the victim.
- The majority of date or acquaintance rape victims are between the ages of fifteen and twenty-five.
- Fifty percent of females raped were victimized during a first date, casual date, or other romantic occasion.
- More than 12 percent of females are date rape victims.
- Twenty percent of female college students are victims of an attempted or completed rape.
- The majority of nonstranger rapes take place during the evening or at night.
- Rape victims are less likely to take protective measures when the offender is a date or acquaintance rather than a stranger (Flowers, 1994; Flowers, 2000).

As far back as the late 1950s, a survey of women found that 62 percent had been victims of sexual aggression as high school seniors (Kanin, 1957). Forty-four percent of the respondents identified their assaulters as fiancés or boys they were going steady with. More than 20 percent were victims of attempted or completed sexual intercourse. Kanin and Parcell (1977) later found that 83 percent of female college students reported being victimized by male sexual aggression. Sixty-one percent had been victims since starting college, while 24 percent had been date raped.

More recently, Koss (1988) surveyed 6,159 female college students and found that 25 percent reported being rape or attempted rape victims. Eighty-four percent of the assailants were described as acquaintances, and 57 percent of these were dates. Rapaport and Burkhart (1984) found that 15 percent of the male college students surveyed admitted to having forced sexual relations with females in dating situations. In a study by Briere and Malamuth (1983), 60 percent of the male college student respondents admitted to raping or having forced sexual relations with females.

Although youth date rape is largely a male perpetrator/female victim phenomenon, young males can also be victims of forced sexual aggression (Bateman, 1998). However, studies have found that reports of female-perpetrated sexual dating violence are rare (Sigelman, Berry, and Wiles, 1984; Straus, 1979). According to Makepeace (1986), eight times as many females believed themselves to be victims of forced sexual relations as males. It is estimated that 38 percent of date-rape victims are young females between fourteen and seventeen years of age (Warshaw, 1988).

Perception and Teen Date Rape

In spite of its prevalence, date rape of teenage females has a low rate of reporting (Bateman, 1998; Koss, Gidycz, and Wisniewski, 1987). Experts attribute this, in part, to the inability by many young women to recognize that a rape has occurred. In a study conducted by *Ms.* magazine, nearly three out of four young rape victims, as legally defined, did not identify their experience as rape (Koss, 1988).

Similar to dating violence in general, many young people involved in sexual violence are often confused over sex role expectations, stereotypes of what constitutes violence, and peer norms in their perceptions of rape and other inappropriate sexual conduct (Koss, 1985; Levy, 1998; McKinney, 1986b; Silverstein, 1994; Warshaw, 1988). This can lead to sexual aggression that both the perpetrator and victim may somehow view as acceptable or permissible.

Miller (1988) found that 56 percent of the adolescent females surveyed believed that forced sex was acceptable in certain situations. Almost 17 percent of young female respondents in another study reported feeling that when a man was sexually aroused, nothing could be done to prevent him from sexual aggression to fulfill his desires (Miller and Marshall, 1987). More than 25 percent of the females disclosed participation in undesired sexual relations due to psychological pressures from the males they were dating.

Other studies have found that many males believe it is up to females to satisfy their sexual needs, thus justifying rape and other sexual violence (Bateman, 1998; Koss and Leonard, 1984; Mahoney, Shively, and Traw, 1985).

Date-Rape Drugs

The illicit use of so-called date-rape drugs such as Rohypnol, Ketamine, and GHB is becoming increasingly popular by adolescent and young adult males in rendering young females helpless as rape victims (Flowers, 2001b). Commonly found at clubs and parties where young people hang out, these drugs are often taken unknowingly by targeted females, leaving them vulnerable to and often unaware of rape victimization. Some victims have become comatose or died from an overdose of a so-called date-rape drug (Flowers, 1999).

Many teens use GHB or "Liquid X," Rohypnol or "Roofies," and other drugs to get high, compounding the dangers from the drugs and making adolescent women more susceptible to rape and sexual assault. More than 100 cases of date rape involving these illicit drugs have been reported across the country (Gorman, 1996). Recent legislation has toughened laws against possessing, manufacturing, or distributing date-rape drugs (Flowers, 2001b).

WHAT CAUSES DATING VIOLENCE?

Dating violence cannot be attributed to a single factor or condition, but rather to a series of variables and circumstances, often interrelated. Many studies have identified the importance of childhood violence to perpetrating violence in dating situations (Bernard and Bernard, 1983; Laner and Thompson, 1982; Marshall and Rose, 1987). Some have focused on sex-role expectations and attitudes (Arias and Johnson, 1989; Deal and Wampler, 1986), and others have looked at self-concept and additional personality issues with offenders in dating violence (Burke, Stets, and Piroz-Good, 1989; Riggs, O'Leary, and Breslin, 1990; Sigelman, Berry, and Wiles, 1984).

Many researchers have found a strong correlation between male aggressor alcohol use and dating violence (Brodbelt, 1983; Laner, 1983; Matthews, 1984). Studies have also shown that dating violence is more likely to occur when the persons involved are in a steady or serious relationship (Henton et al., 1983; Plass and Gessner, 1983; Roscoe and Kelsey, 1986).

Finally, some examinations into relationship violence have pointed out the inequality of the partners in terms of power and resources as important variables in the likelihood of partner violence (Sigelman, Berry, and Wiles, 1984; Sugarman and Hotaling, 1998). The literature suggests that the rate of relationship violence would be lower in a partnership more balanced in power and resources.

Chapter 7

Family Violence

Juvenile delinquency and criminal behavior typically begin in the home and continue into the greater community. Many experts believe that kids who either witness or participate in violence in the home are much more likely than those from nonviolent homes to engage in similar conduct elsewhere (Flowers, 2000; Haskell and Yablonsky, 1974b; McCord, 1958; Schmitt and Kempe, 1975) or perpetuate violence later in life (Flowers, 1994; Straus, 1992; Wolak and Finkelhor, 1998). Conversely, juvenile perpetrated family violence is seen by others as another indication of kids out of control in a society where growing juvenile violence knows no boundaries and even the home is open territory for adolescent assaultive behavior (Flowers, 1990, 2000; Straus, Gelles, and Steinmetz, 1980).

What is clear is that juvenile serious offending is closely interrelated in more ways than one with family violence.

DYNAMICS OF FAMILY VIOLENCE

Intrafamilial violence involving spouses, children, parents, grandparents, or other relatives is a major problem in the United States. Every year over one million children are the victims of family violence (Flowers, 2000) and four million spouses are beaten annually (Commonwealth Fund, 1993; Flowers, 2000). Thirty-three percent of intrafamilial assaults involve the use of a weapon or result in serious injury (U.S. Department of Justice, 1994) while 23 percent of patients admitted to emergency rooms across the country were victims of family violence (U.S. Department of Justice, 1997b). Family violence is directly responsible for thousands of deaths every year (Flowers, 2000) and indirectly related to tens of thousands of other deaths (Federal Bureau of Investigation, 2000; Flowers, 1994).

According to the Justice Department's National Crime Victimization Survey (NCVS)—seen as the most comprehensive victimization survey—in 1995, 876,530 violent crime victimizations occurred in which the offender was related to the victim. The breakdown by relationship can be seen in Table 7.1. Spouses, ex-spouses, parents, and children accounted for 613,860 of the victimizations. The majority of the offenses involved assaults and attempted or threatened violence. Nearly 12 percent of the single-offender victimizations and over 2 percent of the multiple-offender victimizations were perceived as perpetrated by family members, including spouses, ex-spouses, and children (U.S. Department of Justice, 2000).

The magnitude of family violence is such that professionals and researchers commonly break it down into categories including child abuse, intimate violence, battered women, elderly abuse, and parent abuse. Each of these typologies in and of itself reveals the nature of intrafamilial violence (Flowers, 1989; Gelles, 1972; Straus, Gelles, and Steinmetz, 1980) and its characteristics in identifying the problems (Flowers, 2000; Jasinski and Williams, 1998).

Child Abuse

Child abuse is believed the most common form of family violence (Flowers, 1994) and seen as having the most direct impact on juvenile crime and violence (Cyriaque, 1982; Haskell and Yablonsky, 1974a; Hunner and Walker, 1981). The National Child Abuse and Neglect Data System estimates that over two million reports of child abuse and neglect occur each year in the United States (U.S. Department of Health and Human Services, 1998). Other sources place the number at as many as three million reported cases of child maltreatment (Chalk and King, 1998; Leventhal, 1999). Child protective services substantiates around one million cases of child maltreatment each year (U.S. Department of Health and Human Services, 1998).

According to the American Humane Association (1994), most child abuse comes in the form of neglect, as shown in Figure 7.1. Almost 60 percent of child abuse cases are for neglect. However, almost 30 percent of child maltreatment reports involve physical or sexual child abuse and more than 10 percent of cases involve emotional abuse.

TABLE 7.1. Family Violence Victimizations, by Type of Crime and Victim-Offender Relationship, 1995

Type of crime	Total number of victimizations[a]	Number of victimizations by relatives					
		Total[a]	Spouse	Ex-spouse	Parent	Own child	Other relatives
Crimes of violence	9,604,570	876,530	333,400	125,390	86,150	68,920	262,670
Completed violence	2,785,570	345,960	178,650	24,520	38,720	16,440c	87,630
Attempted/threatened violence	6,819,000	530,580	154,750	100,870	47,430	52,480	175,040
Rape/sexual assault[b]	340,380	40,840	20,260c	4,330c	11,910c	0c	4,340c
Robbery	1,141,820	53,430	23,840c	9,200c	1,760c	3,960c	14,660c
Completed/property taken	744,810	38,080	21,500c	2,710c	1,760c	0c	12,120c
Attempted to take property	397,010	15,340c	2,340c	6,500c	0c	3,960c	2,550c
Assault	8,122,370	782,270	289,300	111,850	72,480	64,960	243,670
Aggravated	1,882,810	160,280	56,190	12,710c	3,040c	11,330c	77,010
Simple	6,239,560	621,990	233,120	99,140	69,440	53,630	166,660

Source: Derived from U.S. Department of Justice, *Criminal Victimization in the United States, 1995: A National Crime Victimization Survey Report* (Washington, DC: Office of Justice Programs, 2000), p. 41.

a Detail may not add to total shown because of rounding.
b Includes verbal threats of rape and threats of sexual assault.
c Estimate is based on about ten or fewer sample cases.

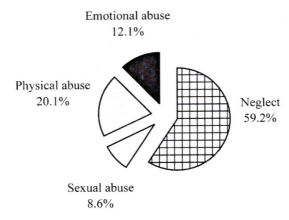

FIGURE 7.1. Types of Child Maltreatment. (*Source:* American Humane Association, *Child Abuse and Neglect Data: AHA Fact Sheet #1,* Englewood, CO: American Humane Association, 1994, p. 1.)

Females are more likely than males to physically abuse children (Flowers, 2000; U.S. Department of Health and Human Services, 1998); whereas males are much more likely to sexually abuse children (Flowers, 1986, 1994; U.S. Department of Health and Human Services, 1998). Overall, studies have shown that females or mothers tend to be perpetrators of child maltreatment more often than males or fathers (Flowers, 2000; Gelles, 1972; Steele and Pollock, 1968).

Most child abuse victims are young children, with the abusive parents also young and often themselves child abuse victims (Flowers, 1986). Researchers such as Solomon (1973) and Flowers (1994) have identified the characteristics of abusive families as follows:

Abusive Parent

- Most are married and living together at time of abuse.
- The average age of abusive father is thirty years old.
- The average age of abusive mother is twenty-six years old.
- The mother perpetrates the most serious abuse.
- A hairbrush is the most common instrument used to inflict abuse.
- Thirty to 60 percent of abusers were themselves abused as children.

Abused Child

- Average age is less than four years old.
- The majority are under two years of age.
- Average age of death by abuse is under three years of age.
- The average span for being exposed to abusive treatment is one to three years.

In addition, the dynamics of abusive families have been found to include marriages at a young age or forced marriages, unwanted or illegitimate pregnancies, emotional and financial problems, and social and family isolation (Flowers, 2000).

Children at Risk for Child Abuse

All children are potential victims of child abusers. However, studies have identified some children at particular risk for abuse (Gelles, 1978; Gil, 1970; Helfer, 1975; Justice and Justice, 1976; Light, 1973). These include children from large families, those characterized as "difficult," and children in families facing crises such as pregnancy, financial burdens, and retirement. Bishop (1971) found six groups of children at special risk for child maltreatment:

- Congenitally malformed babies
- Babies born premature
- Illegitimate children
- Twins
- Children conceived while the mother was depressed
- Children of mothers experiencing frequent pregnancies or excessive workloads

KIDS AND DOMESTIC HOMICIDES

Murder in the family is predominantly reflected in intimate fatalities (Federal Bureau of Investigation, 2000; U.S. Department of Justice, 1998). Thousands of deaths recorded annually involve husbands, wives, ex-spouses, boyfriends, and girlfriends (Ewing, 1997; Flowers, 2000; Wilson, 1993). However, children are well-represented in intrafamilial homicide figures as both victims and offenders. Over 1,000 children are killed in the United States as a result of child maltreatment each year (U.S. Department of Health and Human Services, 1998). An estimated 600 cases of female-perpetrated filicide, or mothers killing their children, occur annually (Flowers, 2000). Morales (1998) estimated that 3,000 children die from abuse in the country each year. Other figures place the number at 5,000 annually (Flowers, 1986).

A juvenile committing murder within the family is relatively rare but it does occur. According to the FBI, in 1999 there were 1,743 intrafamilial murders committed in the United States (see Table 7.2). Of these, 549 were committed by a son, daughter, brother, or sister. Juvenile killers may be reflected in the 262 homicides attributed to other family members. The majority of child-perpetrated domestic homicides were the nonfelony type, most often involving an argument.

Recent years have seen a number of cases of juvenile intrafamilial killers such as:

- On March 21, 1996, in Massachusetts, James Gilligan, fourteen, shot to death his two-year-old brother.
- In February 1996, fifteen-year-old Josh Jenkins bludgeoned to death his parents and grandparents with a hammer in California. The next day, he purchased an axe and killed his ten-year-old sister with it.
- On June 23, 1995, a nine-year-old boy in Oregon shot to death his five-year-old sister with a hunting rifle owned by their father.
- On March 2, 1995, in Pennsylvania, sixteen-year-old Jeffrey Howorth murdered his parents with a gun.
- On July 12, 1993, in Oklahoma, fifteen-year-old Herman Dutton and his twelve-year-old brother, James, used a deer rifle to shoot to death their abusive father while he slept.
- In February 1988, sixteen-year-old David Brom killed his parents, his brother, and sister with an axe at their home in Minnesota.

Unfortunately, such cases of parricide, fratricide and sororicide are occurring in this country with alarming regularity (Ewing, 1997; Flowers and Flowers, 2001).

TABLE 7.2. Homicides in the Family, by Type, 1999

Type	Total	Husband	Wife	Mother	Father	Son	Daughter	Brother	Sister	Other relative
Total	1,743	156	542	99	135	221	224	78	26	262
Felony type	127	1	12	10	10	28	33	2	4	27
Nonfelony type	1,415	138	480	69	107	178	160	71	20	192
Argument	777	106	311	39	76	37	23	50	15	120

Source: Adapted from Federal Bureau of Investigation, *Crime in the United States: Uniform Crime Reports 1999* (Washington, DC: Government Printing Office, 2000), p. 19.

Why do kids kill within the nuclear family? Sargeant (1971) proposed that juvenile killers are the unwitting lethal agents of an adult, often a parent, whose wishes they carry out. According to Bender and Curran (1940), the most common factor in child intrafamilial killings or attempted murder is the child identifying with aggressive parents and their own violent behavior.

Some researchers have found that intrafamilial juvenile killers' violent aggression was encouraged and condoned by parents (Easson and Steinhilber, 1961). Others have attributed patricide and other forms of family homicides to severe physical abuse or child sexual abuse (Flowers and Flowers, 2001; King, 1975; Tooley, 1975). Handgun availability, profit, drug abuse, and mental illness are also frequently cited as factors in intrafamilial fatalities perpetrated by juveniles (Ewing, 1997; Heide, 1992; Mones, 1991).

SIBLING VIOLENCE

Juvenile intrafamilial violence also manifests itself through other forms of aggression, particularly sibling violence. The NCVS reported that in 1995 approximately 102,024 single-offender victimizations and nearly 4,300 multiple-offender victimizations occurred in which the perpetrator was a brother and/or sister (U.S. Department of Justice, 2000).

FBI figures indicate that juvenile arrests for family violence are on the rise. According to the Uniform Crime Reports, between 1991 and 1999 persons under the age of eighteen arrested for offenses against the family and children (including abuse and attempted abuse) increased by more than 143 percent (see Figure 7.2). For females under eighteen, the number of persons arrested rose by nearly 165 percent (Federal Bureau of Investigation, 2000).

During the late 1970s the first major empirical study was conducted on sibling violence. Steinmetz (1977) found that nearly all the respondents reported verbal aggression against siblings and 70 percent engaged in physical violence toward siblings to resolve conflicts. In their study of family violence, Straus, Gelles, and Steinmetz (1980) found that 75 percent of the families sampled with children between three and seventeen years of age reported sibling violence. The researchers estimated that 138,000 children nationwide had used a weapon on a sibling the year the survey was conducted. The findings further estimated that based on "ever happened," some 8.3 million children in this country have been "beaten up" by a sibling, with 2.3 million using a gun or knife on a brother or sister.

Parental neglect or lack of recognition of sibling violence can actually promote, encourage, or increase sibling aggression (Flowers, 2000). Wiehe (1997) notes that sibling violence is typically mistaken for sibling rivalry, contributing to its underreporting or misinterpretation.

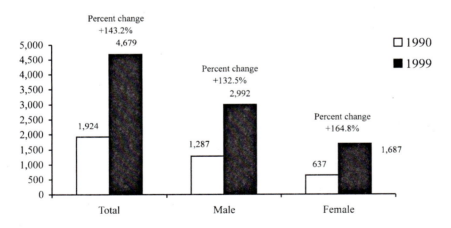

FIGURE 7.2. Arrest Trends for Persons Under Eighteen for Offenses Against Family and Children, 1990-1999. (*Source:* Adapted from Federal Bureau of Investigation, *Crime in the United States: Uniform Crime Reports 1999,* Washington, DC: Government Printing Office, 2000, pp. 216-217.)

PARENT BATTERING

Another form of domestic violence—the abuse by children of their parents—has risen in recent years (Flowers, 2000). It is estimated that 2.5 million parents are beaten by their children each year in the United States (Peterson, 1983). Of these acts of violence, approximately 900,000 parents experience severe violence, including being a victim of a knife or gun attack. Ten percent of parents are physically assaulted by a child annually (Straus, Gelles, and Steinmetz, 1980).

Many experts see parent abuse as the next wave of family violence in the exploration of family dysfunction. In a study of teenage parent batterers, Warren (1978) identified three primary reasons why the violence occurs:

- Violence in response to alcohol use by the victim
- Violence as a response to goals being blocked
- Violence as a resource

Parent batterers are typically described as the recipients of weak models of social behavior and very stressful social conditions (Flowers, 2000). The strong correlation between abusive parents and the risk of becoming an abused parent has been documented (Flowers, 1986; Freeman, 1979; Straus, Gelles, and Steinmetz, 1980).

The characteristics of parent batterers and battered parents are seen as follows:

- Teenage sons are the most frequent parent batterers.
- Mothers are the most likely victims of parent abuse.
- Battered parents typically feel embarrassment, shame, guilt, and failure as parents.
- Middle-aged victims tend to be least likely to seek help, primarily due to fear of the batterer.
- In order to maintain family unity, parent victims and their juvenile abusers typically live in denial and secrecy. (Flowers, 1986)

GRANDPARENT BATTERING

Many grandparents and elderly parents today are also at risk for battering and other violence at the hands of juvenile grandchildren and adult children (Flowers, 2000). Commonly known as "granny bashing," the physical and mental abuse of grandparents and aging parents is believed by many to be the most neglected form of family violence. An estimated one million senior citizens are the victims of intrafamilial battering annually in the United States (Wolfe, 1998). McCabe and Gregory (1998) found that almost 30 percent of elderly abuse victims were beaten by their children. The researchers also reported that more than 15 percent of elderly abuse was perpetrated by juvenile grandchildren and other relatives.

Grandparent abuse is often difficult to detect because of the isolation and fear of many victims. It is also commonly misdiagnosed as injuries or conditions sustained due to accidents, illness, and the normal aging process. The maltreatment of grandparents usually reflects a reversal of dependency between elderly victims and their abusers and the inability of senior citizens to either recognize or prevent their victimization (Flowers, 1994).

Studies have shown that grandparent abuse, similar to parent abuse, is often rooted in a family cycle of violence in which the victim was once the offender and now, in a weakened state, becomes the target of similar mistreatment (Flowers, 1986; Freeman, 1979). Batterers of aging parents or grandparents are commonly characterized as being drug or alcohol dependent, financially dependent on the elderly victim, under stress, mentally ill, and having a history of intrafamilial violence (Arbetter, 1995; Flowers, 2000).

CAUSES OF FAMILY VIOLENCE

Family violence theories on causation are generally reflected in three primary categories: (1) psychiatric-psychological theories, (2) social-structural theories, and (3) social-cultural theories.

Psychiatric-Psychological Theories

Psychiatric-psychological theories often focus on personality traits of offenders and victims of intrafamilial violence. Some researchers have found a correlation between family violence and such mental conditions as depression, psychosis, and schizophrenia (Flowers, 1994; Zalba, 1966). Other studies have linked violence in the family to psychotic and neurotic tendencies (Flowers, 2000; Weinberg, 1966). Further studies have shown a relationship between violent homes, substance abuse, and severe mental dysfunction (Flowers, 1989; Steele, 1976).

Social-Structural Theories

Social-structural theories regard family violence as caused by external and societal factors adversely affecting the family or individuals within (Gelles and Straus, 1979). Stress, communication problems, and intergenerational violence are reflected in this school of thought. The socialization of aggression theory, for example, holds that children tend to be more aggressive toward family when punished more severely by parents, thereby perpetuating a cycle of family violence (Danield, Gilula, and Ochberg, 1970). Other theories, such as general systems theory, learning theory, and the exchange theory further apply social-structural concepts in exploring family dynamics and values in relation to intrafamilial violence (Flowers, 1989; Straus, 1973).

Social-Cultural Theories

Social-cultural theories examine domestic violence as due to inequalities in the social structure and cultural norms on abuse, violence, and relations in the family (Abrahamsen, 1970; Flowers, 1989). Gil (1970) explored societal power struggles and their relationship to family violence. Other criminologists have interrelated social and cultural theories in studying violence in the home and among relatives (Flowers, 2000; Gelles, 1972). Subculture of violence theory and structural-functional theory are two important social-cultural theories with respect to family violence (Flowers, 1994).

PART II:
EXPLAINING JUVENILE CRIME

Chapter 8

Biological Perspectives
on Delinquent Behavior

The biological school of thought regarding delinquency represents the earliest means of attempting to understand deviant juvenile behavior. Biological or biogenic theories advance that juvenile delinquency is a reflection of certain hereditary traits or genetic anomalies that predispose the individual to criminal behavior (Fishbein, 1996; Flowers, 1990; Loeber and Dishion, 1983; Lombroso, 1918; Schulsinger, 1980). These propositions blame many violent and habitual criminal tendencies on biological conditions rather than sociological factors. Most early biological theories of delinquent behavior have been discredited by modern criminologists as biased and methodologically weak.

Recent biological approaches in the study of youth crime have been more promising. Behavioral scientists from various disciplines, including biochemistry, neuroscience, and psychophysiology, have taken a multidisciplinary stance in associating biology with criminal behavior (Dorfman, 1984; Hippchen, 1978; Mednick, Moffitt, and Stack, 1987). These approaches incorporate biological variables with psychological and sociological variables in explaining juvenile deviant behavior.

EARLY BIOLOGICAL THEORIES ON DELINQUENCY

Atavistic Theories

Italian physician Cesare Lombroso (1918) is the recognized pioneer of the biological school of thought in the study of criminality. Referred to as the "father of positivist criminology," it was in his 1876 book, *Criminal Man,* that Lombroso first advanced his theory of atavism (Lombroso and Ferrero, 1972). He believed criminals were biological degenerates or throwbacks to primitive genetic forms, referring to them as *homo delinquens*. Lombroso asserted that certain people were biologically predisposed to commit crimes or were born criminals and identified these types by particular physical traits.

Greatly influenced by the writings of Charles Darwin, including his book, *The Origin of Species* (Darwin, 1995; Richards, 2000), Lombroso derived his own proposals through scientific examination of Italian prisoners and army personnel. He advanced that criminals and delinquents could be distinguished by certain stigmata, including big lips and ears, flattened nose, skull shape, superior strength on the left side, and ability to withstand pain. Other propositions indicative of a predisposition to criminal behavior included a predilection for tattoos and orgies.

Lombroso later modified some of his hypotheses, but they were nevertheless mostly rejected as unscientific and biased. Goring (1913) refuted Lombroso's atavistic theories by comparing physical measurements of 3,000 English prisoners to an equal number of nonprisoners, finding the differences inconsequential.

Lombroso's work was also attacked for the small prison sample, lack of control groups in the general population, and an inability to consider biological determinants of criminality other than heredity. However, Lombroso is still recognized for his contribution to the biological-positivistic school of criminology.

Body Type Theories

The debate over the relationship between body type and deviant behavior was revived in the late 1930s by Ernest Hooton (1939) with the publication of his book, *Crime and the Man*. An advocate of Lombroso's theroies, Hooton studied the physical characteristics of thousands of prisoners and nonprisoners, concluding that the majority of criminals were both physically and mentally inferior to noncriminals. Hooton posited that criminals could be identified by certain physical traits, including reddish hair, mixed eye color, and long necks typecasting criminals based on these characteristics. For example, he believed that heavy, tall men were more likely than others to be murderers (Flowers, 1990).

It was not until the 1940s that research showed a systematic relationship between body types and juvenile delinquency. In collecting and comparing a substantial number of physical measurements, Sheldon (1942) identified three basic body types or somatypes, relating these to personality or temperamental characteristics: (1) *endomorphic,* (2) *ectomorphic,* and (3) *mesomorphic.*

The endomorphic was described as fat, soft, round, extroverted, and seeking comfort. The ectomorphic was seen as thin, weak, fragile, introverted, shy, and sensitive. The mesomorphic was characterized as muscular, hard, assertive, aggressive, and active. Sheldon believed that mesomorphics were the most likely to become juvenile delinquents. He further proposed that there were particular somatype and personality differences between delinquent and nondelinquent youth.

Glueck and Glueck (1956) also studied body types in their research on delinquents. Applying Sheldon's principles, they found mesomorphs to be disproportionately represented among the institutionalized delinquents studied. Mesomorphic types constituted 60.1 percent of the delinquents, compared to only 30.7 percent of the nondelinquents. More recently, Cortes and Gatti's (1972) study of adolescents supported the Gluecks' findings of proportionately more mesomorphic juveniles within the delinquent group.

Body type theories have been dismissed as credible approaches to explaining delinquency. The primary drawbacks lie in the absence of a physiological relationship between body type and delinquent behavior, methodological weaknesses, and that many of the same traits found in delinquents can also be found in nondelinquent youth.

Heredity Theories

The role heredity plays in delinquent and criminal behavior has long been studied by biological criminologists in attempting to relate criminality to genetics (Flowers, 1990; Gottfredson and Hirschi, 1996; Mednick, Gabrielli, and Hutchings 1987). The notion that various forms of abnormal behavior such as delinquency, mental illness, and alcoholism are inherited characteristics has received support (Glueck and Glueck, 1968; McCord, 1958; Ounsted, Oppenheimer, and Lindsay, 1975).

Early theorists such as Dugdale (1877) and Goddard (1914) documented the long histories of deviance in some families, including delinquency, prostitution, idiocy, feeblemindedness, and fornication. Although such research has generally been rejected for its lack of scientific basis and biases in the methodology, a strong interest in the possibility of genetic transmission of delinquent tendencies and other biological predisposition to certain types of human behavior continues today (Denno, 1988; Fishbein, 1996; Hutchings and Mednick, 1977; Mednick, Gabrielli, and Hutchings, 1984). However, most modern researchers tend to relate biological factors in criminality and delinquency to multiple causes including sociologically based factors (Flowers, 1986; Rojek and Jensen, 1996).

CONTEMPORARY BIOLOGICAL RESEARCH ON DELINQUENCY

Twin Studies

Research into the genetic influences of delinquent behavior has resulted in the study of twins. Criminologists have analyzed the patterns and prevalence of crime among twins developed from a single egg—monozygotic (MZ twins)—or identical twins as compared to twins coming from separately fertilized eggs—dizygotic (DZ) twins—or fraternal twins. The theory is that if deviant tendencies were hereditary, then identical twins would be more similar in their behavior than fraternal twins.

Concordance refers to the degree in which twins or related pairs of subjects both exhibit a particular behavior or condition. Some early studies, such as one by Lange (1931) of Bavarian inmates, have found a higher concordance rate of criminal behavior between identical twins than with fraternal twins.

More recent advanced research has also indicated a higher concordance rate of criminality between identical twins; however not as much as in earlier studies. For instance, in a study of 444 pairs of twins born in Denmark between 1870 and 1910 and reaching fifteen years of age, Christiansen (1977) found that the rate of concordance for MZ or identical twins was more than three times the rate of DZ or fraternal twins. By comparison, the concordance rate of identical twins in the Lange study was more than six times that of fraternal twins.

In a review of twin research, Eysench (1973) found that the consistent differential in concordance rates between identical and fraternal twins indicated that heredity played a very important part in development of criminal behavior. Some researchers are not convinced. In a study by Dalgaard and Kringlen (1976), no significant differences were found in the concordance rates of identical and fraternal twins. Other studies have supported this contention (Flowers, 1990).

Adoption and Fosterling Studies

Heredity and delinquent behavior has also been examined through adoption and fosterling studies, giving weight to the argument of a genetic basis for criminality (Ellis, 1982; Gottfredson and Hirschi, 1996; Hutchings and Mednick, 1977). Such research generally studies the association between the delinquency of adopted or foster children and the criminal behavior of their biological and adoptive parents. The implication is that should such children display behavior more resembling that of their biological parents, then a stronger case can be made for inherited deviant tendencies than were the behavior more similar to the adoptive parents.

One of the first adoption studies was conduced in Denmark. In comparing the incidence of "psychopathy" in the biological families of adoptees, Schulsinger (1972) found that 3.9 percent of the biological family members of psychopathic adoptees could be classified as psychopathic. By comparison, only 1.4 percent of the control groups' biological relatives fit into this category. The findings were criticized due to definitional and methodological shortcomings.

A more advanced adoption study of the relationship between genetics, environment, and delinquent behavior was undertaken by Hutchings and Mednick (1975). In examining 1,145 male adoptees and the same number of nonadoptees—controlling such variables as age, gender, and occupation of the fathers—the researchers found that nearly twice as many adoptees had criminal records as nonadoptees. They also found a strong relationship between the criminality of the adoptees and that of their fathers.

The adoptees' biological fathers were more than three times as likely to be involved in criminality than either the adoptive fathers or the fathers of the nonadopted control group. The adoptees' criminality was twice as high when the biological father had a criminal record and the adopted father did not, than the other way around. When both the biological and adoptive parents had criminal records, the chances that the adoptee would become delinquent were much higher.

In one of the most comprehensive studies of adoptees, genetics, and crime, Mednick, Gabrielli, and Hutchings (1984) compared the conviction records of 14,427 adoptees to conviction records of both their biological and adoptive parents. They concluded that a relationship did exist between the criminal convictions of biological parents and those of their adoptee children, and further that the genetic transmission of deviant tendencies by parents who are criminals increased the probability of their children manifesting criminal behavior.

Other researchers have generally supported these findings in adoption studies and genetics with respect to heredity and juvenile antisocial behavior (Brodzinsky, 1987; Cloninger and Gottesman, 1987; Ellis, 1982; Loehlin, Willerman, and Horn, 1987; Rowe and Osgood, 1984). However, some have disputed the relationship between adoptees and inherited criminality (Wilson and Herrnstein, 1985). Most biological criminologists, including Hutchings and Mednick (1975), agree that even with the genetic factor environmental variables may play an even greater role in delinquent behavior.

The XYY Chromosome and Criminality

Another genetic perspective on criminality and delinquency that has drawn much interest and controversy pertains to the XYY chromosomal pattern in males (Flowers, 1990; Witkin et al., 1977). In the early 1960s, researchers discovered a genetic abnormality present in some males. The normal human chromosome count is forty-six, with XY the male configuration and XX the female. The finding that some males possess an extra Y set chromosome, or a configuration of XYY, led researchers to link this abnormality to aggressive and violent behavior. Most studies of males with the XYY complement have been of tall, institutionalized prisoners and mentally retarded persons (Flowers, 1990). These XYY males have been found to be in disproportion to the population in general (Sandberg et al., 1961).

In a cohort study of tall men in Denmark, Witkin and colleagues (1977) found that XYY males had a higher rate of criminal behavior than XY males of similar height, age, and social status. However, the researchers found no evidence that the XYY group was more prone to violence than the XY group.

Recent research has failed to yield results in support of the relationship between XYY chromosomal pattern and criminal behavior (Flowers, 1990; Gottfredson and Hirschi, 1996). On the contrary, some have argued that XYY individuals have a lower rate of criminality or aggressive behavior than those with a normal chromosomal configuration; whereas others have rejected the notion that XYY prisoners are significantly disproportionate to XYY individuals in the general public (Flowers, 1988).

Brain Disorder Studies

In recent years more biological research on the relationship between delinquency and brain disorders and dysfunction has been conducted. Some evidence suggests that delinquent youths have a higher rate of epilepsy, in which seizures can affect self-control (Pollock, Mednick, and Gabrielli, 1983). Other research has revealed abnormal electroencephalogram (EEG) readings of the brain activity in delinquents and criminals, relating this to aggressive and violent behavior, destructiveness, poor social adaptation, and limited impulse control (Flowers, 1990).

Brain dysfunction has also been linked to learning disabilities such as dyslexia, hyperactivity, and aphasia, which some researchers believe predisposes one to delinquent behavior, rejection, and poor educational achievement (Holzman, 1979; Murray, 1976). Research has also related violent criminal behavior to brain tumors (Kletschka, 1966).

Other Biological Research

Current biological study of juvenile delinquency and criminal behavior is focusing on research efforts in multiple fields including heredity, biochemistry, immunology, neuroscience, and endocrinology (Fishbein, 1996; Lewis, Shanok, and Balla, 1979; Mednick, Moffitt, and Stack, 1987). This multidisciplinary study of biology and deviance is seen as important in establishing a better understanding of the overall forces that can increase or decrease susceptibility to biological influences on criminality. For instance, recent biochemical research on delinquent behavior has studied the problem in terms of nutritional deficiencies, allergies, hypoglycemia, and the role of environmental contaminants on the mind and body (Dorfman, 1984; Hippchen, 1978).

Chapter 9

Psychological Perspectives on Delinquency

As with biological approaches to delinquent and criminal behavior, the psychological or psychogenic perspective in explaining youthful antisocial behavior has been around a long time. Developed by psychiatrists, psychologists, and other mental health experts, psychologically based theories tend to relate delinquency to a variety of mental, emotional, and personality disorders and dysfunctions (Crason, 1943; Flowers, 1986, 1990; Freud, 1933; Hirschi and Hindelang, 1977; Quay, 1983). Though such theories are often criticized for their methodology, lack of empirical strength, and other weaknesses, psychological explanations of crime and delinquency generally have more support in the criminological community than biological research. Current psychological perspectives on delinquency also tend to factor in the influences of family and environmental variables in explaining delinquent behavior.

PSYCHOANALYTIC THEORIES AND DELINQUENCY

Psychoanalytic theories regard the deviant behavior of youths as a result of unresolved instincts and drives within the human psyche. When these are in conflict, delinquent or other aberrant behavior may occur.

It was Sigmund Freud (1933) who pioneered psychoanalytic research in explaining delinquency. Freud posited that the personality is made up of three integral parts: (1) the *id,* (2) the *ego,* and (3) the *superego.* These function as follows:

- The id is the source of instinctive energy and biological drives.
- The ego is the part of the psyche that experiences and reacts to the surrounding world.
- The superego acts as the conscience of the psyche, interceding between the id and moral values.

To treat these behavioral problems, Freud relied on psychoanalysis, which consisted of delving deep into the individual's past experiences to uncover and resolve unconscious conflicts.

While Freud is recongized as having established a relationship between delinquent behavior and personality formation, especially the unconscious sense of guilt developed during childhood, it was the work of August Aichorn (1935) that is regarded as most responsible for applying psychoanalytic principles to criminality. In his study of juvenile delinquents, Aichorn postulated a psychological predisposition to committing criminal and delinquent acts. He referred to this as latent delinquency, present in youths whose personalities compelled them to act on impulse, instincts, and, for self-satisfaction, absent of guilt feelings.

More recently, Schoenfeld (1975) postulated that most acts of delinquency are caused not by criminal tendencies but rather a weak or defective superego unable to sufficiently control the primitive and strong early childhood urges, resulting in deviant behavior.

Psychoanalytic theories have been rejected as a reliable means for understanding delinquency as they cannot be tested empirically (Flowers, 1986; Sheley, 1985). Indeed, some fear that psychoanalysis can hamper more reliable approaches to discovering delinquency and treating delinquents.

PERSONALITY DISORDER THEORIES
AND DELINQUENCY

Personality disorder theories tend to explain juvenile delinquency in terms of personality flaws and emotional disorders not necessarily related to unconscious conflicts. The most common feature of personality disorder theories is the reliance on personality tests, such as IQ and Rorschach inkblot tests, often given to youths labeled delinquent. Personality theories use test results to develop a delinquent personality profile based on inferred personality traits derived through test results.

Personality theories have little support in the study of delinquency. For instance, Schuessler and Cressey (1950) found in their review of personality studies that no single personality trait differentiated delinquent from nondelinquent youth. However, in examining one test—the Minnesota Multiphasic Personality Inventory (MMPI)— Waldo and Dinitz (1967) found that delinquents and nondelinquents could be differentiated in more than 80 percent of the studies using the test. But the researchers admitted that the overall test results were still inconclusive in identifying delinquent youth.

Emotional Disturbances

Since the early 1900s, psychologists, psychiatrists, and other researchers have examined the relationship between emotional problems and delinquent behavior. In the 1930s, Burt (1938) found that 85 percent of the delinquents studied were emotionally impaired. Similarly, in a comparison of 105 delinquents and nondelinquents, Healy and Bronner (1936) found that over 90 percent of the delinquents were unhappy, discontented, and severely emotionally disturbed, compared to 13 percent of the nondelinquents.

Critics have since dismissed, by and large, the link between emotional disturbances and delinquency, finding fault with both the methodology and subjectivity in defining problems as emotionally-based. Waldo and Dinitz (1967) found no relationship between emotional troubles and delinquent behavior. In his study of research findings on emotional troubles among adolescent delinquents, Hakeem (1958) concluded that the results were more likely a reflection of psychiatric biases than delinquent characteristics.

Today emotional problems among troubled youth have been recognized and identified by researchers in the study of violent juveniles, teenage prostitutes, and young substance abusers (Flowers, 1999, 2000; Johnson, 1992; James, 1980). However, the same problems also often exist in nondelinquent youth, which reflects more of an issue of child development than relating to delinquency, per se.

Psychopathic Theory

The psychopathic personality theory has received a great deal of attention as an explanation of juvenile delinquency. The psychopath or sociopath is defined as a person who is mentally unstable, antisocial, amoral, hostile, insensitive, egocentric, and fearless, while having limited social ties (Crason, 1943; Flowers, 1990). According to psychopathic theory, the psychopathic personality lacks normal feelings to conform to societal norms; the psychopath is considered to be without moral constraints in acting impulsively and freely, and out of touch with reality (Erikson, 1962; Flowers, 1986; Scheff, 1966).

After conducting extensive research on psychopaths, McCord and McCord (1964) identified two traits in particular that distinguish the psychopath from others: (1) guiltlessness and (2) lovelessness. The researchers advanced that the psychopathic personality originated in brain damage, physical trauma, and severe childhood emotional deprivation.

In an attempt to link psychopathic personalities to juvenile delinquency and adult criminality, Robins (1966) did a follow-up study of 524 patients at a child guidance clinic thirty years after they were treated at the clinic. He also tracked them with a control group of 100 normal children. According to Robins, more than 70 percent of the clinic juveniles had been referred by the juvenile court for delinquent behavior. He found that the majority of these youths continued to have troubled lives in adulthood, marked by frequent arrests for serious crimes as well as other problems such as drunkenness, psychiatric problems, divorce, unstable work patterns, and dependency on the welfare system.

The study concluded that the clinic group was much more likely to be involved in serious criminality through adulthood than the control group. For instance, 44 percent of the delinquent youths had been arrested for a serious crime compared to only 3 percent of the control group.

Psychopathic personality theories have been criticized as unreliable, with little empirical evidence to support their propositions with respect to delinquency (Erikson, 1962; Flowers, 1990). Some experts contend that juveniles would need to commit far more and a greater variety of crimes in order to fit into the psychiatric definition of psychopathy (Matza, 1964; Scheff, 1966). Most evidence suggests that psychopaths comprise only a very small percentage of delinquents and criminals. Quay (1983), who has examined the personality patterns of delinquents, pointed out that as adult psychopaths constituted less than 25 percent of all criminals, juvenile psychopaths were proportionality that much smaller in the offender community.

Criminal Personality Theory

A more recent approach to the delinquent personality is the criminal personality theory. Developed by Yochelson and Samenow (1976) after years of studying violent criminal patients, the researchers advanced that patterns of deviant thinking existed in all the subjects. They found that violent offenders saw normal interaction with family and others as dull and they sought excitement, with criminality representing the greatest form of excitement. This abnormal pattern of behavior often developed in early childhood (Samenow, 1984). Yochelson and Samenow dismissed explanations of delinquency and criminality that relied on causal agents outside the individual, such as poverty and environment. However, they do note that most violent offenders indicate being victims of family violence or other abuses.

Criminal personality theory falls flat for many in understanding violent behavior, due to its inability to satisfactorily explain how criminal behavior comes into being, and the lack of a control group with which to compare the clinical findings. A further criticism is the rejection of the strong body of research that supports environmental and social causes of delinquent behavior (Flowers, 1990).

Intelligence Quotient Theories

The relationship between intelligence and delinquency has been examined by researchers, applying both psychological and biological hypotheses (Flowers, 1990; Hawkins, 1996; Loeber and Dishion, 1983). Some early criminologists firmly believe that a lower-than-average intelligence quotient (IQ) among delinquents and criminals was both inherent and a primary cause of antisocial behavior (Healy and Bronner, 1936). Most contemporary criminologists have rejected IQ theories as biased, methodologically weak, and short on significant findings.

However, some researchers have given credence to the correlation between delinquent behavior and intelligence. The most significant is a review of IQ research by Hirschi and Hindelang (1977), who found a strong relationship between delinquency and IQ, independent of other variables such as social class and race. The researchers postulated that a low IQ affects school performance, which in turn produces failure and incompetence, leading to juvenile delinquency.

Loeber and Dishion (1983) supported these findings through their own review of the literature. Similarly, a relationship between intelligence and youth antisocial behavior has been found in other studies (McMichael, 1979; Simonton, 1985). The implication is that IQ plays a role in the process of becoming delinquent in combination with other factors such as family life, peer group pressure, substance abuse, and environment (Flowers, 1986, 1998).

PSYCHIATRIC THEORIES AND CONCEPTS OF DELINQUENCY

Psychiatric perspectives have often related delinquency to mental illness, using such psychiatric terminology as suffering from delusions, schizophrenia, and hallucinations (American Psychiatric Association, 1987). However, most experts in delinquency and criminality believe that delinquents suffering from mental illness are in the minority. In one study of juvenile delinquents referred to the juvenile court, 75 to 80 percent were classified as "normal delinquents," with only 12 to 17 percent diagnosed as emotionally or psychologically disturbed (Haskell and Yablonsky, 1974b). Similarly, in a government report, between 5 and 17 percent of children ages three to fifteen suffered from a persistent, socially interfering mental illness (President's Commission on Mental Health, 1978). Roughly the same percentage of juveniles with mental problems exist in the delinquent population (Flowers, 1990).

One of the most prominent psychiatric theories of delinquency is the "superego lacunae" theory. Johnson (1949) focused on middle-class delinquency in proposing that inconsistent discipline in many normal middle-class families fosters delinquent conduct. The superego lacunae theory posited that such children have gaps or lacunae in their superego and become scapegoats in families where parents project their own difficulties onto them, receiving vicarious pleasure from the delinquent acts of the child (Johnson and Burke, 1955).

Eissler (1949) held that not only is such delinquency fostered by the parents of delinquents, but society fosters delinquent conduct as a societal scapegoat; suggesting that society actually interferes with programs seeking to prevent delinquency. Matza and Sykes (1961) advanced that many values of the delinquent are, in fact, subterranean values held by particular segments of society.

The superego lacunae theory has been criticized as being unscientifically supported, based only on cases brought forth by the theorists, in which emotional disturbance is the primary problem and delinquent behavior only a secondary problem (Hakeem, 1958).

Chapter 10

Sociological Perspectives
on Delinquent Behavior

The sociological school of thought in explaining juvenile delinquency has received the most support among criminologists, scholars, and other delinquency experts in understanding youth antisocial behavior (Agnew, 1992; Austin, 1980; Hawkins, 1996; Rojek and Jensen, 1996; Shaw, 1929; Sutherland, 1939). Unlike biological and psychological theories on delinquency that seek to define and show causation in terms of individual abnormalities and character flaws, sociological theories are more concerned with the social and economic structure, environment, social life, and other cultural factors that relate to the formation of crime and delinquency (Burgess and Akers, 1966; Cloward and Ohlin, 1960; Farnworth and Leiber, 1989; Mueller, 1983; Sellin, 1938; Wolfgang and Ferracuti, 1967).

Sociological theorists commonly regard delinquency as "normal" behavior within the delinquent's social and cultural setting and conditions that create juvenile deviance (Flowers, 1986, 1990). Within the sociological perspective of delinquency, most theories fall under four primary areas: (1) social control, (2) strain, (3) cultural transmission, and (4) a radical approach. Each of these plays an important role in criminological theorizing on delinquency and criminality in relation to society.

SOCIAL CONTROL THEORIES AND DELINQUENCY

Social control theories argue that all individuals have the potential and opportunity to perpetrate delinquent or criminal offenses, but most refrain from such because of fear and social constraints. This perspective explains juvenile delinquency as a reflection of inadequate external social control and internalized social values for some youths, creating a freedom in which delinquent conduct may occur (Frazier, 1976; Linden and Hacker, 1973; Matza and Sykes, 1961). Control theorists are not as concerned with what motivates youths to deviate from the norm as with the social institutions that create conditions favorable to either violating the laws or refraining from doing so.

Social control theories seek to explain the patterns of delinquent behavior by identifying those social situations in which the ties are weakest and sanctions the least likely to be experienced subjectively by the youth. Various contributors to this field have focused on different aspects of control over individuals in society, and the circumstances under which the controls are ineffective (Glueck and Glueck, 1950; Hagan, Gillis, and Simpson, 1985; Hirschi, 1969; Matza, 1964; Nye, 1958).

Social control theory has been successful in explaining how to understand the episodic delinquency of most juveniles, and why even the most habitual or serious delinquents commit offenses only under certain conditions. The primary criticism of the control perspective is that it fails to sufficiently explain the role of internalized norms and values. Empirical examinations have supported the basic premise of control theory (Flowers, 1986; Frazier, 1976).

Social Disorganization Theory

Social disorganization perspectives relate to the inability of social institutions and communities to adequately socialize and control its youth. The concept of social disorganization was developed in the 1960s by members of the University of Chicago's sociology department that became known as the Chicago School. Social disorganization was a term used to describe the breakdown in conventional social structures within the community characterized mostly by transitory, economically disadvantaged, and heterogeneous people, and the failure of family, organizations, groups, and individuals as part of that community to adequately solve its problems (Bursik and Grasmick, 1996; Farrington, 1996; Flowers, 1986; Rojek and Jensen, 1996). Researchers found that this social disorganization or inadequate social controls in certain areas corresponded with their having the highest delinquency rates (Flowers, 1990; Shaw, 1929; Thrasher, 1927).

The theory of social disorganization was given serious attention with the zonal model of urban ecology developed by Park and Burgess (1925). In studying the ecological pattern of delinquency and crime in Chicago, the researchers found that delinquency rates were highest in the central cities, and decreasing the greater the distance from the center. This high rate of inner-city crime and delinquency was blamed on the high concentration of social and physical conditions commonly linked to criminality. Shaw and McKay (1969) were the first to apply this zonal model systematically. Their findings supported the concept of social disorganization in inner-city neighborhoods and the inverse correlation between delinquency rates and distance from the city center.

In a study of 1,313 Chicago gangs, Thrasher (1927) found that youth play groups existed in all neighborhoods; however these groups differed in socially disorganized neighborhoods by the social institutions' failure to control the delinquency patterns of these groups. Thrasher posited that in the absence of social control, juveniles do not need to be motivated to commit delinquent acts, as deviant behavior represented a more exciting alternative to conventional behavior.

Despite the findings from the early applications of social disorganization hypotheses, it was not until the work of the Chicago School was later modified that social-disorganized control theories became more effective in explaining why juveniles in socially disorganized communities committed delinquent acts.

Social Bonding Theory

One of the most influential social control theories was put forth by Travis Hirschi (1969) who advanced the theory that a social bond ties youth to the social order. This social bond is made up of four components: (1) attachment, (2) commitment, (3) involvement, and (4) belief. These are described as follows:

- *Attachment* relates to ties to others such as family and peers.
- *Commitment* is the devotion to social conformity.
- *Involvement* in legitimate activities.
- *Belief* refers to attitudes towards conformity.

The degree and strength of these components on an individual's conformity to the societal values and norms vary from individual to individual.

According to Hirschi, the less an individual believes he or she should conform to social convention, the more likely the individual is to not conform or become antisocial. Under social bonding theory, juvenile delinquents are without the intimate attachments, goals, and moral standards that tie people to the norms and values of society, therefore they are free to perpetrate acts of crime and delinquency.

Critics of social bonding theory argue that it falls short in accounting for the variance in the frequency of delinquent offenses. Also questioned is the assertion that attachment can help prevent delinquency, even if the attachments are themselves delinquents. Hirschi later contended that a weakened social bond and delinquent attachments were directly related to youthful misconduct.

Containment Theory

Containment theory was developed by Walter Reckless (1970). This social control theory posited that juveniles are restrained from perpetrating delinquent acts by a combination of inner containment and outer containment as follows:

Inner Containment

- Positive self-concept
- Self-components
- Well-developed superego
- High tolerance level
- Positive goal orientation

Outer Containment

- Positive social ties
- Strong parental supervision
- Institutional support of the juvenile's positive self-concept

According to Reckless, these containments act as buffers against the influences of delinquent conduct, including delinquent subculture, temptations, and additional delinquent environmental factors. Although both inner and outer containments were seen as the most effective measures to counter delinquency, strong inner containment could compensate for weak or defective outer containment, and vice versa.

Containment theory has been attacked as a theory of delinquency for its methodological failings and doubts about the validity of self-concept measures. In all, it appears that outer containment variables may be more prominent in explaining youth participation in delinquent acts than inner containments (Flowers, 1990; Jensen, 1973).

STRAIN THEORIES AND DELINQUENCY

Strain theories also reflect concepts originated from the Chicago School. These theories explain the delinquency of youths as a response to a lack of socially approved opportunities (Bernard, 1987; Durkheim, 1933; Merton, 1938; Miller, 1975). Strain theorists regard juvenile antisocial behavior as caused by the frustrations of lower-class youth when they find themselves unable to achieve the material success expected of the middle class (Cloward and Ohlin, 1960; Cohen, 1955; Cohen and Short, 1958; Kluegel and Smith, 1986). This frustration and inability to meet such expectations makes some youths participate in acts of delinquency and crime as another means of acquiring money, material items, and prestige socially (Flowers, 1986; Hawkins, 1996; Rowe, 1996). The concept of strain is viewed as a common problem of adjustment originating from a social position shared by a group of people (Agnew, 1996; Averill, 1982; Flowers, 1990; Greenberg, 1977; Zillman, 1979).

Many contemporary criminologists have rejected strain theory in relation to delinquency and criminality as empirically weak and ineffective (Bernard, 1984; Cole, 1975; Farnworth and Leiber, 1989; Johnson, 1979; Thornberry, 1987). Others have sought new perspectives in applying the theory to such areas as juvenile stress and aggression (Agnew, 1985; Bernard, 1987; Elliot, Ageton, and Canter, 1979).

Anomie Theory

The concept of anomie was established by Emile Durkheim (1933) in reference to a condition of relative normlessness that existed within a group or society. Durkheim, a sociologist, saw this anomie as occurring when the existing social structure was unable to control the desires of people. Anomie generally was attributed to social disruption caused by natural or human-created disasters such as economic depression and war.

Robert Merton (1957) adapted the anomie theory to societal conditions and cultural values existing in the United States. He sought to associate certain types of behavior to the social position of those involved. According to Merton, delinquent behavior is caused by the anomie interaction of two elements in society: (1) culturally defined goals, and (2) the structured means for achieving them. Since people have unequal access to socially approved means, some are prevented from achieving societal goals unless they deviate from the norm.

Merton identified five modes of adaptation to societal goals and means. The two most applicable to juvenile delinquency are *innovation* and *retreatism*. These are described as follows:

- *Innovation* relates to the acceptance of culturally prescribed goals of success without following the institutional means of attainment.
- *Retreatism* relates to the rejection of both culturally prescribed goals and the conventional means of achieving them.

An example of juvenile innovation may be the theft of an expensive pair of Nike shoes as a common desire and status symbol of youth that may occur because the juvenile did not have the money or means to acquire them legally. A retreatist delinquent may turn his back on conventional goals and the means of attainment, drifting instead into an escapist lifestyle such as drug addiction.

Anomie theory has been attacked for its principles. For instance, it fails to explain why some innovators choose theft and others assault, or why some retreatists turn to drugs and others to another form of retreat. Questions arise as to whether all Americans share the same goals and expectations of success. Further, while anomie explains the delinquency of the have-nots, it does not account for either delinquency and criminality of the upper class or different patterns of delinquent conduct.

Shortcomings aside, Merton's theory is credited as among the most influential in subsequent theoretical perspectives on the association between criminal behavior and differential economic opportunity (Clinard, 1964; Cohen, 1965; Flowers, 1990; Short, 1964).

Subculture Theories

Subculture theories were developed in the 1950s and 1960s through the study of juvenile gangs (Cohen, 1955; Miller, 1975; Short, 1964; Yablonsky, 1962). Most influential was the work of Cloward and Ohlin (1960), who developed the delinquent subculture theory to explain delinquent behavior, positing that a delinquent opportunity structure exists alongside a legitimate opportunity structure. The basic tenet of the theory lies in the structural conditions that result in lower-class gang delinquency. The researchers also attempt to explain the development of other delinquent youth subcultures.

Subculture theory defines a delinquent subculture as a group fostering beliefs that legitimize delinquent activities. The theory advances that the goals, strategies, and culture of the lower class or subgroups within are significantly different from those existing in the middle class. According to Cloward and Ohlin, lower-class youths have their own lifestyles, traditions, and focal concerns attaching importance to "toughness," "living by one's wits," and "hustle." Conforming to this lifestyle reflects a deviation from middle-class standards.

The main criticism leveled against subculture theory is the argument that lower-class youths have different goals and norms from the middle class. In contrast, many professionals believe that lower-class youths tend to adopt the goals of material, educational, and occupational success of the middle class (Flowers, 1990). The theory has further been attacked for its lack of applicability in explaining the delinquency of most youths, as well as in accounting for the fact that the majority of young lower-class gang members tend to reject the delinquent lifestyle in adulthood, turning instead to more conventional norms. (See also Chapter 5.)

CULTURAL TRANSMISSION THEORIES AND DELINQUENCY

Cultural transmission theories postulate that delinquency is learned behavior or reflecting of norms, values, beliefs, and behavioral characteristics taken from those with whom the delinquent interacts (Freedman, 1986; Patterson, 1986; Robinson and Jacobson, 1987;

Rowe and Osgood, 1984). Theorists of the cultural transmission school hold that juvenile delinquency is caused by youth conformity to the behavioral norms of a culture or subculture that are contrary to conventional values and norms which favor abiding by the law (Hawkins, 1996; Jensen and Brownfield, 1983; Luckenbill and Doyle, 1989; Patterson, 1996; Sellin, 1938). Delinquent norms are further viewed in this perspective as intergenerational in both the socialization process and techniques of perpetrating delinquent acts (Curtis, 1963; Flowers, 1990; Lane and Davis, 1987; Rutter, 1977; Widom, 1989).

Cultural transmission theorists (Boyd and Richerson, 1985; Cavalli-Sforza and Feldman, 1981; Hawkins, 1996) have identified three primary ways in which deviant behavior can be transmitted through the learning process: (1) vertical transmission, (2) horizontal transmission, and (3) oblique transmission. These are described as follows:

- *Vertical transmission:* intergenerational transmitting of deviant behavior from parents to offspring
- *Horizontal transmission:* learning juvenile deviance from peers of the same generation
- *Oblique transmission:* intergenerational transmitting of delinquent behavior from non-parental adults to children

Transmitting antisocial behavior to juveniles can cross between transmission types and often does, increasing the likelihood of juvenile susceptibility to a delinquent lifestyle (Flowers, 1986; Geismar and Wood, 1986; Howing et al., 1990; Wright and Wright, 1996).

Differential Association Theory

The most influential cultural transmission theory has been the differential association theory. First introduced by Edwin Sutherland in his 1939 text, *Principles of Criminology,* differential association attempted to explain the reasons for the delinquency and crime rate among various groups and why a particular individual participates in or refrains from criminal or delinquent behavior (Cressey, 1979; Short, 1957; Sutherland, 1939; Sutherland and Cressey, 1978; Tittle, Burke, and Jackson, 1986).

The theory advances that the probability of delinquent behavior varies in relation to the frequency, priority, duration, and intensity of an individual's contacts with delinquents and deviant behavior and, inversely, with the individual's contacts with nondelinquents. Interaction with antisocial contacts tends to occur most often when individuals' perceptions of their circumstances are more supportive of law violations. Thus, the theory assumes that many types of nonconformity—such as delinquency and crime—are most likely to be centered in inner-city areas characterized by cultural traits that often alienate individuals from one another and from the norms of the middle class.

According to differential association theory, delinquency is a learned behavior. It outlines the general conditions under which there is likely to be more than less delinquency learned, leading to a higher probability that the youth will acquire a set of "definitions" more favorable to antisocial than to law-abiding conduct. The theory maintains that if most of the juveniles' contacts are with frequent violators of the law who express beliefs seeking to justify their behavior, then the juvenile is more likely to become delinquent than youths whose greater contacts are with those who disapprove of violating the law.

Most criminologists support Sutherland's differential association theory regarding its explanation of delinquent and criminal behavior. However, there has been some criticism of the theory (Flowers, 1990). The most glaring criticism has been its inability to be validated through empirical testing. Other shortcomings include the failure to explain how crime and delinquency originated and the lack of a greater explanation of the nature of the learning process or the basis for differential vulnerability to become delinquent for different persons.

Social Learning Theory

As a result of the limitations of differential association theory, some sociologists have sought to modify its learning proposition in explaining delinquency. The most prominent application was developed by Burgess and Akers (1966) with their social learning theory, originally known as differential association-reinforcement theory (Akers, 1985). Unlike some sociological theories more concerned with explaining sociodemographic variances in delinquency and criminality, social control theory addressed factors related directly to deviant behavior irrespective of socioeconomic variables (Catalano and Hawkins, 1996; Flowers, 1990; Rojek and Jensen, 1996).

Social learning theory seeks to establish functions in which deviance or conformity to societal norms either continue or desist. The theory proposes that youths learn to commit acts of delinquency or criminality through social interaction with persons who comprise their primary source of reinforcement. The researchers view these social reinforcements as symbolic and verbal rewards for supporting group expectations and norms. A lesser role is attached to nonsocial reinforcement, which is associated primarily to physiological variables that may be relevant for such offenses as drug abuse.

Critics of social learning theory argue that nonsocial reinforcements are, in fact, stronger than social ones in determining involvement in delinquent behavior. As with differential association theory, there is also skepticism as to whether or not the theory can be empirically evaluated.

Labeling Theory

Labeling theory has tenets of various sociological perspectives but is most often seen as a cultural transmission theory of delinquency (Cooley, 1902; Flowers, 1986; Lemert, 1967). Rather than focusing on the individual's response to or interaction with deviant norms of behavior, labeling theory addresses the societal response to such individuals, their behavior, and the results of the response (Becker, 1963; Flowers, 1990; Schur, 1972). According to labeling theorists, the onset of delinquency does not begin with a delinquent act per se, but rather by being labeled a delinquent by the juvenile or criminal justice system and society as a consequence. This labeling mechanism is seen as creating a negative reaction on the part of the labeled youth, thus causing them to engage in a delinquent lifestyle (Erikson, 1962; Flowers, 1986; Matza, 1964; Rausch, 1983).

Many believe that the delinquent labeling process is differentially applied by those in social power—such as lawmakers, law enforcement, and the judicial system—differentially affecting those occupying the low end of the socioeconomic strata with the least power to resist the stigmatizing effects of labeling.

While labeling theory continues to receive some support as a criminological explanation of juvenile delinquency, a number of studies have found it methodologically flawed and inconsistent in its proposals when examined (Hirschi, 1975; Mahoney, 1974; Tittle, 1975).

CRITICAL CRIMINOLOGY THEORIES AND DELINQUENCY

Critical or radical criminology theories tend to explain crime and delinquency in terms of the relationship between capitalism and criminal and juvenile justice (Flowers, 1988, 1990). Critical criminologists argue that the criminal laws primarily serve the interests of the ruling class who use these laws to exploit, control, and victimize the lower and working classes in order to maintain the economic and political system of capitalism. Since such laws are a product of the wealthy and capitalists, their socially harmful "crimes" such as exploitation and demoralization are generally not defined as offenses by the criminal justice system.

Critical theorists attribute the high rate of street crime to the economic functioning of the capitalist system that creates unemployment and underemployment allowing for conditions that produce delinquency and criminality. Greenberg (1977) found this especially true for juvenile criminality, which he suggests explains high rates of delinquency. In applying a radical perspective to delinquency causation, Greenberg proposed three key pressures faced by juveniles that account for the majority of delinquent conduct in capitalist societies:

- Deprivation of employment opportunities needed to finance social objectives stressed in peer norms
- Stigmatizing and degrading school experiences by individuals with a lesser stake in conformity (such as lower-class and unemployed youths), resulting in hostility, rebellion, and delinquency
- Fear of failure in achieving adult male status positions, resulting in violence and status defining behavior

Critical criminology has been attacked for its predictability, disregard for objective reality, and overstating its hypotheses (Flowers, 1990). In spite of that, its basic principles appear sound in the overall interpretation of the capitalist system as it relates to criminality, criminal laws, and defining crime and delinquency.

Chapter 11

Intrafamilial Causes and Correlates of Juvenile Delinquency

In addition to theoretical perspectives on youthful deviance, a variety of family-related causes and correlates of delinquent behavior have frequently been mentioned (Flowers, 1990, 2000; Helfer and Kempe, 1976; Wright and Wright, 1996). Most notably, juvenile antisocial conduct has been linked with such intrafamilial factors as child abuse (Hunner and Walker, 1981; Lane and Davis, 1987; Silver, Dublin, and Lourie, 1969; Welsh, 1976), a cycle of intrafamilial violence (Burgess, Hartman, and McCormack, 1987; Farrington, 1990; Flowers, 1994; Olweus, 1980), broken homes (Bowlby, 1951; McCord, 1982; Sroufe, 1986; Wadsworth, 1979), and family discord and dysfunction (Andry, 1962; Loeber and Stouthamer-Loeber, 1986; Riley and Shaw, 1985; Weinberg, 1958).

Recent research has incorporated within family dynamics the role television and movie violence may play in the onset and continuation of juvenile delinquency and violence (Belson, 1978; Kruttschmitt, Heath, and Ward, 1986; Milavsky et al., 1996; Rosenthal, 1986; Snyder, 1991).

Family circumstances and school variables have also shown relevance in the study of juvenile delinquency and youth violence (Brier, 1995; Cernkovich and Giordano, 1992; Howell and Lynch, 2000; Maguin and Loeber, 1996; Stinchcombe, 1964). The relationship between school and antisocial behavior by youth is examined more closely in Chapter 4.

CHILD MALTREATMENT AND DELINQUENCY

Child Abuse and Neglect

Strong documentation exists for a correlation between child abuse and neglect and juvenile delinquency (Flowers, 2000; Hunner and Walker, 1981; Schmitt and Kempe, 1975). More than one million children are abused or neglected annually in the United States (U.S. Department of Health and Human Services, 1998). Some experts believe the number of child abuse victims are double that estimate (Arbetter, 1995; Flowers, 1994; Gil, 1970).

Steele (1976) cited research that found more than 80 percent of a sample of juvenile offenders to be victims of child maltreatment. In a study of 653 delinquents, Adams, Ishizuka, and Ishizuka (1977) reported that 43 percent of the youths had ever been abused, neglected, or abandoned. Haskell and Yablonsky (1974a) noted that juvenile corrections facilities are filled with juveniles who were abused or mistreated.

Violence, in particular perpetrated by parents upon their children, is thought by criminologists to consciously or subconsciously encourage abused children to act out in aggressive or violent behavior what they have experienced (Curtis, 1963; Cyriaque, 1982; Siegel and Senna, 1991). Simmons (1970) held that brutal parents tend to have brutal offspring. Violently abused children represent a high percentage of child killers and other violent offenders (Flowers and Flowers, 2001; Widom, 1989). In a study of violent juvenile offenders receiving the death penalty, Lewis and colleagues found that 46 percent had been the victims of severe physical or sexual abuse (Lewis et al., 1988).

Researching official data on abuse, Howing and colleagues (1990) found the range of abused delinquents to be between 9 and 26 percent. Other studies of child abuse victims have reported delinquency rates varying between 14 and 20 percent (Bolton, Reich, and Guiterres, 1977; Silver, Dublin, and Lourie, 1969).

Self-report data have shown an even closer relationship between child abuse and juvenile delinquency, with numbers of abused delinquents ranging from 51 to 69 percent of the delinquent youth (Mouzakitis, 1981; Rhoades and Parker, 1981). The strong correlation between child maltreatment and delinquent behavior prompted

Schmitt and Kempe (1975) to suggest that stopping child abuse would prevent delinquency.

Child Sexual Abuse

The link between child sexual abuse and juvenile sex offenders such as rapists, child molesters, and prostitutes, may be even more persuasive than with child physical abuse (Burgess, Hartman, and McCormack, 1987; Flowers, 2001b; Silbert, 1982). According to the Justice Department, youthful offenders incarcerated for sexual assaults were more likely than any other type of inmate to report having been victimized by sexual or physical child abuse (U.S. Department of Justice, 1997a).

Young juvenile prostitutes are particularly likely to have been victims of sexual abuse or molestation (Flowers, 1998; Volkonsky, 1995). Most teenage prostitutes ran away from sexually or physically abusive homes (Flowers 2001a; Hersch, 1988; Office of Juvenile Justice and Delinquency Prevention, 1999c; Seng, 1989). In a Huckleberry House study, 90 percent of the prostitution-involved girls had been sexually abused (Harlan, Rodgers, and Slattery, 1981). Sixty-seven percent of the teenage female prostitutes in Silbert's study were incest and child abuse victims (Silbert, 1982). Boy prostitutes also have a high rate of sexual abuse in their childhoods (Flowers, 1998; Lloyd, 1976; Weisberg, 1985).

Child Discipline

Extreme child disciplinary practices by parents are related to juvenile antisocial behavior according to a number of studies (Button, 1973; Deykin, 1971; McCord, 1979; Shore, 1971). Longitudinal research has utilized both self-report and official data in finding a strong association between parental discipline and a likelihood of delinquent conduct on the part of severely disciplined youth (Olweus, 1980; Snyder and Patterson, 1987; West and Farrington, 1973).

Many researchers have discovered that, along with extreme physical discipline, lax or inconsistent disciplinary practices can also lead to delinquent behavior. Glueck and Glueck (1950) reported that lax or erratic discipline accounted for a higher percentage of delinquents than overly severe discipline. Slocum and Stone (1963) found the degree of fairness in disciplinary practices to be closely related to conformity by youths.

In a review of family factors and correlates of delinquent behavior, Snyder and Patterson (1987) found delinquency often a response to severe or inconsistent parental discipline, antisocial behavior by parents, and other intrafamilial variables. Other comprehensive reviews of studies linking delinquent conduct to disciplinary practices have yielded similar findings (Loeber and Stouthamer-Loeber, 1986; Utting, Bright, and Henricson, 1993). McCord, McCord, and Zola (1959) found that consistent discipline, whether or not punitive, significantly lowered the incidence of delinquency.

INTERGENERATIONAL VIOLENCE, CHILD ABUSE, AND DELINQUENCY

The transmission of violence and abuse from generation to generation as predictive of delinquent behavior has received strong support (DiLalla and Gottesman, 1991; Farrington, 1991; Flowers, 1990; Fontana, 1964; McCord, 1979). Ounsted and associates postulated that abusive parents typically came from families where violence and abuse was intergenerational (Ounsted, Oppenheimer, and Lindsay, 1975). Similarly, Polansky and colleagues' study of neglectful families reported finding that neglect and abuse were often passed between the generations (Polansky, DeSaix, and Sharlin, 1972).

In a retrospective study of more than 900 abused children, Widom (1989) found that children physically abused up to the age of eleven had a strong chance of becoming violent offenders themselves within the next fifteen years. Another study found that severe discipline and parental attitude when the youth was eight was predictive of violent and chronic criminality and delinquency up to the age of thirty-two (Farrington, 1978, 1991).

Other intergenerational research on violence has demonstrated that violent and abusive parents were often themselves victims of parental violence, abuse, and neglect (Flowers, 1986; Gibbons and Walker, 1956; Laury, 1970; Kempe and Helfer, 1972; Straus, 1973).

BROKEN HOMES AND DELINQUENT BEHAVIOR

The literature is replete with studies examining the impact of broken-home families on delinquent behavior (Bowlby, 1951; Brady, Bray, and Zeeb, 1986; Burt, 1925; Finkelhor, Hotaling, and Sedlak, 1990; Kolvin et al., 1988). The term "broken home" is typically defined as a home in which one or both parents are missing, usually due to divorce, separation, or desertion. The implication is that a home absent of a loving mother and father destabilizes the environment and reduces control mechanisms over the child, thereby increasing susceptibility to involvment in delinquent behavior.

Early studies produced conflicting results on the broken home factor of delinquency. For example, in a study of Chicago schoolboys and juvenile court cases in the 1930s, Shaw and McKay (1932) found only a weak correlation between high rates of delinquency and a high rate of broken homes. The findings were criticized as being unrepresentative and methodologically flawed.

Other researchers contradicted these findings. Burt (1925) found that more than twice as many delinquents came from broken homes as nondelinquents. Similarly, Glueck and Glueck (1962) reported that 60.4 percent of their delinquent sample came from broken homes compared to 34.2 percent of the nondelinquent control group. Other studies and reviews of early research also found the broken home correlated with high rates of delinquency (Rothman, 1990; Wadsworth, 1979; Weeks and Smith, 1939).

More recent studies on broken homes and single-parent families in relation to delinquency have also yielded contradictory findings (Blum, Boyle, and Offord, 1988; Gibson, 1969; LeFlore, 1988; McCord, 1982). In a study of 1,517 male youths and delinquency, Loeber, Weiher, and Smith (1991) found that children from single-parent families were more likely to increase their incidence of delinquency as they went through adolescence compared to children living in homes with both parents. McCord (1982) found a high rate of delinquent conduct for boys raised in broken homes absent of affection or with the presence of parental conflict. These studies have been supported in other research (Denno, 1985; Matsueda and Heimer, 1987; Wilkinson, 1980).

Other studies have suggested otherwise. In a review of fifteen studies of the correlation between broken homes and male delinquency over a forty-three year period, Rosen and Neilson (1978) found only a minimal relationship when race, age, and class were considered. Other researchers found no association between single parent homes and delinquency (Farnworth, 1984; Gray-Ray and Ray, 1990; Rosen and Neilson, 1982).

Some studies have shown a correlation between broken homes and delinquency in relation to variables such as age, sex, family structure, and substance abuse (Denno, 1985; Gove and Crutchfield, 1982; Toby, 1957). Yet for some criminologists, the relevance of the broken home on delinquent behavior remains inconclusive (Teeters and Reinemann, 1950; Wells and Rankin, 1986).

FAMILIAL FACTORS AND DELINQUENCY

Marital Discord and Conflict

Dissention and conflict in a marriage have been revealed as important factors in the onset of delinquency among youth—including domestic violence, marital dysfunction, divorce, and substance abuse (Farrington, 1996; Flowers, 2000; Wright and Wright, 1996). Glueck and Glueck (1950) found considerably more delinquents' than non-delinquents' parents had poor conjugal relations, with more family incohesiveness in the delinquent's home. Nye (1958) also found that consistent dissension within the marriage was a predictor of delinquency more than divorce or broken homes.

More recent studies have generally supported the link between marital discord and delinquency (Bane, 1976; Blechman, 1982; Emery, 1982; Loeber and Stouthamer-Loeber, 1986; Minty, 1988). However, the significance of this correlation has been found moderate in relation to other factors of delinquency (Snyder and Patterson, 1987; Widom, 1989). Some researches argue that the literature on this aspect of familial variables in delinquent behavior is inadequate (Koski, 1988; Wright and Wright, 1996).

Parental Affection and Parenting

Parental affection and parenting are seen by many as critical factors in the likelihood of juvenile involvement in delinquency. Glueck and Glueck (1950) found that every pattern of intrafamilial affection was important, with the most important being the father's affection for his son. This assertion has been supported by a number of researchers (Andry, 1962; Davids, 1977; Slocum and Stone, 1963).

Bandura and Walters (1959) noted that fathers of delinquents were more likely to reject than be affectionate with their offspring. Kroupa (1988) found that institutionalized girls were more likely to believe their parents had rejected them than noninstitutionalized girls. Loeber and Dishion (1984) related juvenile fighting at home or in school to parental rejection. Gray-Ray and Ray (1990) associated black male delinquency to rejection by parents. In other studies, parental rejection has been strongly associated with delinquency (Loeber and Dishion, 1984; McCord, McCord, and Howard, 1963; McCord, McCord, and Zola, 1959; Nye, 1958; Simons, Robertson, and Downs, 1989).

Positive parenting, on the other hand, appears to play a key role in preventing delinquency by encouraging the development of normative values and positive behavior in children (Flowers, 1990). Longitudinal research has documented the predictive relationship between positive parenting techniques and delinquent behavior (Farrington, Grundy, and West, 1975; Olweus, 1980; Wadsworth, 1979). Nonpositive parenting, such as parental rejection and indifference, has been shown through both self-report and official data associated with violent and property crimes committed by juveniles as well as recidivism of delinquency (Flowers, 1990).

Family Structure

The relationship between family structure and delinquency has been examined in a number of studies (Farrington, 1996; Flowers, 1986; Newson, Newson, and Adams, 1993; Wadsworth, 1979). Family size, in particular, has received attention as a predictor of delinquent behavior. Early studies by Glueck and Glueck (1950) and Nye (1958) suggested that delinquent youths were more likely to come from large families than small ones. In the Nye study, the results applied only to male delinquents.

Recent studies support this correlation. Large family size was found among the most significant factors contributing to juvenile delinquency in studies by Kolvin and colleagues (1988) and Newson, Newson, and Adams (1993). West and Farrington (1973) reported that the risk of a male juvenile delinquent being convicted doubled if he had four or more siblings by the time he turned ten. Self-report surveys of delinquency and conviction studies of juveniles and adults have shown large families to be significantly related to antisocial behavior (Farrington, 1996; Flowers, 1990).

Reiss (1961) found that psychiatric classifications such as weak ego and superego differentiated delinquents with respect to family size. Delinquents with weak superegos were more likely to come from families that were large. Some studies have found, however, that a large family size was not predictive of delinquent behavior in male youths, in particular (Ferguson, 1952; West and Farrington, 1973).

Other research on family structure has examined the ordinal position of the child within the family. For example, a study by Lees and Newson (1954) found that intermediates—children with younger and older siblings—were overrepresented among a group of delinquents. The researchers held that parental attention given to the youngest and oldest children often squeezed the intermediates out of the family and into delinquency.

Family structural dynamics have also been shown related to socioeconomic and family dysfunction factors such as divorce, unemployment, social class, and substance abuse, which, in turn, has a cause and effect relationship to delinquency (Flowers, 1990).

PART III:
JUVENILE CRIME
AND THE JUSTICE SYSTEM

Chapter 12

The Police and Juvenile Criminals

The relationship between the juvenile offender and the criminal justice system usually begins with the police (Federal Bureau of Investigation, 2000; Flowers, 1990; Snyder, 1999; U.S. Department of Justice, 1999). The dynamics of this contact are often determined by the nature of the offense, youth circumstances, police discretionary power, and departmental policies (Black and Reiss, 1979; Emerson, 1969; Flowers, 1988; McEachern and Bauzer, 1967). Juvenile due process rights limit to some degree the actions of police in arresting juvenile offenders, conducting searches and interrogations, fingerprinting, and photographing practices (Bartollas, 1985; Ferster and Courtless, 1969; Flowers, 1990; Hahn, 1984; U.S. Department of Justice, 1999).

Studies indicate that demographic characteristics, particularly race and ethnicity, play a major role in the involvement of law enforcement with youthful offenders (Dannefer and Schmitt, 1982; Hawkins et al., 2000; Smith, Visher, and Davidson, 1984; Snyder, 1999; Werthman and Piliavin, 1967). Violent juvenile offenders and those in delinquent gangs are the most likely to make contact with the police and other branches of the criminal justice system (Goldman, 1969; Hagan and Peterson, 1995; Hawkins, Laub, and Lauritsen, 1998; Sampson and Wilson, 1995).

The delicate interrelationship between the police, juveniles, and the community can affect attitudes, perceptions, and responses for all concerned which, in turn, is often reflected in police and juvenile violence, arrests, and police-community relations (Bouma, 1969; Flowers, 1990; Portune, 1971; Wilson, 1968).

POLICE AND JUVENILE ARRESTS

Police arrests of juvenile offenders are tracked through the Federal Bureau of Investigation's Uniform Crime Reports (UCR), as detailed in Chapter 1. In 1999, more than 1.5 million arrests occurred of persons under the age of eighteen in the United States (Federal Bureau of Investigation, 2000). Serious crimes, including murder, forcible rape, aggravated assault, robbery, and burglary accounted for 420,543 arrests.

Table 12.1 breaks down these juvenile arrests by age, sex, and race. More than 25 percent of juvenile arrests were for Crime Index offenses. Juvenile offenders were almost five times as likely to be arrested for a property crime as a violent crime.

Juvenile arrestees are predominantly male, white, and over sixteen years of age. Approximately 70 percent of youths under the age of eighteen arrested in 1999 for serious offenses were male or white, while more than 80 percent were age sixteen or seventeen. Black youths constituted nearly 30 percent of arrests for Crime Index offenses and 40 percent of the violent crime arrests, well in disproportion to their population figures.

According to the UCR, in 1999, only 19 percent of crimes involving juvenile offenders were cleared or solved by law enforcement agencies through an arrest. Juveniles were responsible for 12 percent of the violent crime clearances and 22 percent of property crimes cleared (Federal Bureau of Investigation, 2000).

Persons under age eighteen accounted for almost 20 percent of arrests in 1999, as shown in Figure 12.1. Almost 28 percent of all serious crime arrestees were juveniles, comprising almost 30 percent of the persons arrested for property crimes and more than 16 percent of those arrested for violent crimes.

Juvenile Arrest Trends

Juvenile arrests are on the rise. Figure 12.2 shows that from 1990 to 1999, overall arrests of juveniles nationwide climbed 11 percent. Arrests of female youths increased even more sharply, growing by nearly 32 percent, while male juvenile arrests rose almost 5 percent.

These trends notwithstanding, police arrests of juveniles for Crime Index offenses have been on the decline. Between 1990 and 1999,

TABLE 12.1. Juvenile Arrests for Serious Offenses in 1999

Type of Offense	Ages under 18	Ages under 15	Ages under 10	Percent distribution of total juvenile arrests				
				Male	Female	White	Black	Other[a]
Total Crime Index Arrests	**420,543**	**159,940**	**8,212**	**72.8**	**27.2**	**67.3**	**29.3**	**3.5**
Murder and nonnegligent manslaughter	919	114	1	92.4	7.6	47.0	49.0	4.0
Forcible rape	3,182	1,221	40	98.1	1.9	63.0	34.5	2.5
Robbery	18,735	4,888	133	91.3	8.7	43.3	54.4	2.3
Aggravated assault	45,080	16,139	830	77.6	22.4	62.2	35.2	2.7
Total Violent Crime	**67,916**	**22,362**	**1,004**	**82.6**	**17.4**	**56.8**	**40.6**	**2.6**
Burglary	64,481	24,561	1,486	88.7	11.3	72.6	24.5	2.9
Larceny-theft	249,100	100,635	4,871	64.3	35.7	69.8	26.4	3.8
Motor vehicle theft	33,255	8,508	108	83.7	16.3	57.2	38.9	3.9
Arson	5,791	3,874	743	88.5	11.5	79.8	18.2	2.0
Total Property Crime	**352,627**	**137,576**	**7,208**	**71.0**	**29.0**	**69.3**	**27.1**	**3.6**
Overall Arrests	**1,588,839**	**506,817**	**24,530**	**72.8**	**27.2**	**71.9**	**25.1**	**3.0**

Source: Adapted from Federal Bureau of Investigation, *Crime in the United States: Uniform Crime Reports 1999* (Washington, DC: Government Printing Office, 2000), pp. 222, 224, 226, 231.

aIncludes American Indians or Alaskan Natives and Asians or Pacific Islanders.

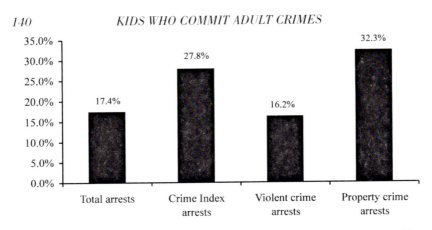

FIGURE 12.1. Juvenile Percentage of Total Arrests, 1999. (*Source:* Derived from Federal Bureau of Investigation, *Crime in the United States: Uniform Crime Reports 1999,* Washington, DC: Government Printing Office, 2000, p. 223.)

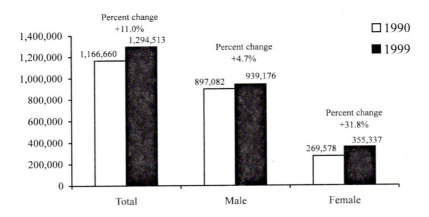

FIGURE 12.2. Juvenile Ten-Year Arrest Trends, 1990-1999. (*Source:* Derived from Federal Bureau of Investigation, *Crime in the United States: Uniform Crime Reports 1999,* Washington, DC: Government Printing Office, 2000, p. 217.)

arrests of persons under the age of eighteen for serious violent or property crimes decreased by more than 20 percent (see Figure 12.3). Studies of long-term arrest data indicate that the juvenile arrest rate for violent crime continues to decline, while the arrest rate increases substantially for drug abuse violations, family offenses, and other assaultive crimes (Federal Bureau of Investigation, 2000; U.S. Department of Justice, 1999).

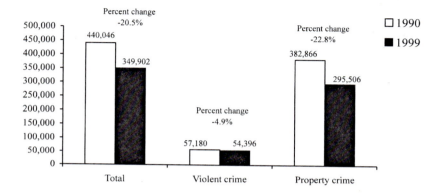

FIGURE 12.3. Juvenile Crime Index Arrest Trends, 1990-1999. (*Source:* Derived from Federal Bureau of Investigation, *Crime in the United States: Uniform Crime Reports 1999,* Washington, DC: Government Printing Office, 2000, p. 216.)

POLICE CONTACT WITH THE JUVENILE OFFENDER

Initial Police-Juvenile Interaction

Law enforcement officers typically become involved with juvenile offenders through two primary sources: (1) citizen complaints, and (2) direct observation of juveniles perpetrating delinquent or criminal acts, or otherwise acting suspicious. The vast majority of police-juvenile contacts are initiated by citizen complaints. In a study of 281 police encounters with adolescents in Chicago, it was found that 72 percent were initiated by citizens, who primarily reported delinquent behavior by telephone. Sixty percent of the complaints were for minor delinquent offenses such as rowdiness and mischief. Approximately 5 percent of the citizen complaints involved serious juvenile criminality (Black and Reiss, 1979).

Police Disposition of Juvenile Offenders

When police either witness a juvenile law violation or respond to a complaint of such, a number of formal and informal options are available for use at their discretion in disposing of the case. They are:

- Outright release at the scene after questioning.
- Admonish or reprimand on the street before releasing.
- Take the juvenile into custody for questioning, then release.
- Issue a citation to appear in juvenile court at a later date, then release to family.
- Issue a citation to the juvenile and take directly to the juvenile court.
- Refer to a diversionary program such as a runaway shelter with no court appearance or delinquency record.
- Refer the juvenile to the criminal court.

Studies indicate that in the majority of police-juvenile contacts, no arrests are made (Flowers, 1990). When arrests do occur, police disposition of the case often results in something other than a juvenile court referral. In a study of Illinois police-juvenile contacts, only 40 percent of the youths were referred to the juvenile court (Morris and Hawkins, 1970). The researchers found that only 20 percent were arrested in encounters in which police had sufficient grounds for an arrest.

When arrested, most juveniles are likely to be referred to the juvenile court jurisdiction. As shown in Table 12.2, more than 69 percent of juvenile offenders taken into custody in 1999 were referred to the jurisdiction of the juvenile court. Over 6 percent of the juveniles were referred to the criminal or adult court jurisdiction. More than 22 percent of the youths were handled within police departments, and then released. Less than 2 percent were referred to another police agency or a welfare agency.

Approximately 10 percent of juveniles arrested across the country are held in police lockups or temporary facilities for holding juvenile suspects (U.S. Department of Justice, 1999). Juvenile arrestees in smaller cities and rural counties are more likely to be referred to criminal court jurisdictions than juvenile offenders arrested in large cities. For instance, in 1999 law enforcement agencies referred just over 6 percent of juvenile arrestees in cities with a population of 250,000 or more to a criminal court compared to more than 10 percent of arrestees in cities with populations under 10,000 (Federal Bureau of Investigation, 2000).

TABLE 12.2. Police Disposition of Juvenile Offenders Taken into Custody, 1999

Disposition	Total agencies: 6,130; population 134,225,000		Total cities: 4,571; population 97,068,000	
	Number	Percentb	Number	Percentb
Totala	997,035	100.0	828,542	100.0
Handled within department and released	224,605	22.5	189,665	22.9
Referred to juvenile court jurisdiction	689,990	69.2	572,848	69.1
Referred to welfare agency	8,171	0.8	7,283	0.9
Referred to other police agency	10,140	1.0	8,196	1.0
Referred to criminal or adult court	64,129	6.4	50,550	6.1

(*Source:* Adapted from U.S. Department of Justice, *Juvenile Offenders and Victims: 1999 National Report,* (Washington, DC: Government Printing Office, 1999), p. 269.

a Includes all offenses except traffic and neglect cases.
b Because of rounding, the percentages may not add to total.

POLICE DISCRETION AND THE JUVENILE OFFENDER

Police have enormous discretionary powers regarding contact with juvenile offenders, although this is not as prevalent in cases of serious juvenile offenses. Often this use of discretion may reflect an officer's background, experiences, prejudices, nature and severity of the offense, departmental priorities, and other factors including the credibility and influence of the complainant or community pressures on the local police to control crime (Flowers, 1990).

The Severity of the Juvenile Offense

In general, the degree of severity is the most crucial factor in police discretion involving juvenile crime and delinquency. Studies have found that in 80 to 90 percent of police-juvenile contacts, the disposition is often little more than a warning to the youth (Wilson, 1968). However, for violent and other serious juvenile offenders, the disposition of the case is much more likely to result in arrest and referral to the juvenile court and, increasingly, the adult court (Flowers, 1990; U.S. Department of Justice, 1999). The probability of juvenile arrest and subsequent involvement in the juvenile or criminal justice system increases relative to the severity of the suspected offense (Black and Reiss, 1979).

The Citizen Complainant

The person initiating a complaint against a juvenile has been shown to significantly influence police discretion and disposition of the matter. Black and Reiss (1979) found that when a citizen initiates a complaint, is at the scene, and requests that a juvenile be arrested, the police will generally arrest the youth. Whereas when the complainant believed that an arrest was unnecessary, police were more likely not to make an arrest. Similar findings have been made in other studies (Emerson, 1969; Flowers, 1990).

The complainant's race has been found to affect police discretion in the disposition of a youthful offender. Research has indicated that the police were more likely to make an arrest if the complainant was white (Hawkins, 1995; Smith, Visher, and Davidson, 1984; Tonry, 1995).

Overall, the probability of a juvenile arrest is much higher as a result of a citizen complaint than in an encounter initiated by police (Emerson, 1969).

Gender and the Juvenile Offender

Serious male juvenile offenders are far more likely to be arrested and referred to the juvenile or criminal courts than their female counterparts (Flowers, 1990). According to official data, in 1999, nearly three males under the age of eighteen were arrested for Crime Index offenses for every one female under eighteen (Federal Bureau of Investigation, 2000). Studies show that girls are more likely to be arrested than boys for certain status offenses, such as running away (Flowers, 1998, 2001a; Johnson, 1992). This is generally seen as more indicative of a double standard related to sex role expectations and more lenient treatment of young females by the justice system, while taking a harsher stance toward male youths who commit more serious offenses (Flowers, 1986, 1998).

Racial and Ethnic Bias in Police Discretion

The race or ethnicity of a juvenile suspect appears to play a major role in police discretion and disposition of a delinquent case (Blumstein, 1995; Flowers, 1988; Hawkins et al., 2000; Rodriguez, 1988; Snyder, 1999). In a Philadelphia cohort study, Wolfgang, Figlio, and Sellin (1972) found that the most important factor considered by police when referring a juvenile to juvenile court jurisdiction rather than disposing of the case themselves was whether the youth belonged to a minority group. Another study comparing police and juvenile court dispositions of juvenile arrestees found that police exhibited a greater degree of racial bias in requiring a minority youth to appear before the court than there was racial bias in the court's disposition of the case (Dannefer and Schmitt, 1982).

Race and ethnicity seem especially relevant in cases of violent juvenile offending. Studies have shown that black and Hispanic youths are disproportionately more likely to be arrested for crimes of violence such as murder and robbery than white youths (Flowers, 1988; Hawkins et al., 2000; Valdez, Nourjah, and Nourjah, 1988; U.S. Department of Justice, 1999).

Some researchers question the notion of a racial or ethnic bias in juvenile arrests. Black and Reiss (1979) found that minority youths tended to be arrested more often than white youths partly because complainants who are minorities themselves were more likely to insist upon arrest than the complainants of white juvenile offenders. Wolfgang, Figlio, and Sellin (1972) found race and socioeconomic status of juvenile arrestees related to the frequency and severity of the crimes.

Interaction Between Police and Juveniles

The nature of police-juvenile communication and interaction is seen as an important factor in police discretion. Piliavin and Briar (1964) note that juveniles who are polite and respectful to police officers are much more likely to receive an informal disposition than belligerent and disrespectful youths. Werthman and Piliavin (1967) related the scorn and hostility of black juvenile gang members toward law enforcement with their high rate of court referral. According to a study by Lundman, Sykes, and Clark (1980), in the absence of physical evidence linking a youth to a crime, the youth's demeanor serves as the most important determinant of the police officer's discretionary powers and disposition of the situation.

Personality clashes between an officer and juvenile can also affect the outcome of a case. For instance, a confrontation involving an arrogant, racist policeman who may resent the youth's attitude, demeanor, or otherwise be at odds with, could result in a harsher or more formal disposition (Flowers, 1990).

Departmental Policies and Police Discretion

The policies, procedures, and objectives of a police department can greatly influence police discretion in dealing with juveniles. In general, the greater the degree of professionalism in a department (defined as high standards in administration, operations, and policing), the more likely it is to dispose of a juvenile case formally. Wilson (1968) found that the more professional police departments tended to refer greater numbers of juveniles to the juvenile court because they relied less on discretion than departments with less professionalism.

Police department policies toward juvenile offenders can vary considerably. In a study of juvenile arrests in four Pennsylvania communities, Goldman (1969) found that the proportion of arrests varied from 9 percent in one community to 71 percent in another. A study of 46 Southern California police departments revealed that although in some departments 80 percent of youths were referred to the juvenile court, in other police departments virtually all police-juvenile contacts resulted in a warning and release.

YOUTH ATTITUDES TOWARD POLICE

Juvenile attitudes toward police have generally been found positive. However studies show that attitudes vary, depending on factors such as police contacts, race, ethnicity, and gender. In a study of junior high school students in Cincinnati, Portune (1971) found that white students had a more positive attitude toward law enforcement than black students, female students were more likely to view police favorably than male students, and upper- and middle-class students viewed law enforcement in a more positive light than lower-class students. Similar results were produced in Bouma's (1969) self-report survey of 10,000 Michigan juvenile students. The majority of students found police to be nice, and indicated they would cooperate in a police investigation of a crime that did not involve a friend.

Some studies have found that juveniles with police contacts tend to have less positive attitudes toward law enforcement than juveniles with no police contacts. A study of students in seventeen high schools found that a strong relationship existed between police contacts and adolescent attitudes. Negative contacts had a greater influence on such attitudes than race, gender, social class, or residence (Winfree and Griffiths, 1977). Another study found that delinquent males had more negative feelings toward police officers than nondelinquent males (Bouma, 1969). Delinquent youths, in particular, have been shown to feel hostility toward law enforcement (Flowers, 1990; McEachern and Bauzer, 1967; Werthman and Piliavin, 1967).

Chapter 13

Juvenile Offenders and the Juvenile and Adult Courts

In spite of the current wave of adultlike violent and serious criminal behavior perpetrated by youth, most juvenile offender cases are handled by the juvenile justice system, (Flowers, 1990; Office of Juvenile Justice and Delinquency Prevention, 1999b). Indeed, more than 50 percent of the male youths and nearly 75 percent of the female youths who enter the juvenile court do not return once they pass through (U.S. Department of Justice, 1999).

This notwithstanding, many assert that the juvenile justice system is too soft on hardened, dangerous kids. This result has led most states to crack down on habitually delinquent, serious, and violent juvenile offenders. Today more such youths are being bypassed by the juvenile court in favor of the criminal or adult court, where it is believed that the punishment can more appropriately fit the serious and violent offenses.

However, some still view juvenile delinquents as troubled youth and victims of familial and societal circumstances and, as such, should not be held accountable for violent or serious criminal acts to the same degree as adults. As the debate rages on, the justice system appears to be shifting toward a get-tough policy with violent or seriously delinquent youth as a necessary measure of juvenile crime control and protection of the public.

THE ORIGINS OF THE JUVENILE JUSTICE SYSTEM

The development of the juvenile justice system is a relatively recent occurrence in American history. Until the late eighteenth century, juveniles as young as seven who violated the law received the same treatment as adult offenders, including standing trial and, if convicted, being sent to prison or even receiving a death sentence. Only children under the age of seven, who were considered incapable of criminal intent or distinguishing right from wrong, were exempt from being prosecuted or receiving punishment (Office of Juvenile Justice and Delinquency Prevention, 1999b).

In the nineteenth century, certain philanthropic organizations, supported by a general reform movement, began to advocate separating juvenile offenders from adult offenders. The reformers attributed the problems of society, and youth as a consequence, to rapid industrialization and urbanization.

They asserted that something must be done to save those children of the lower-class slums, who were often forced to work in sweatshops, factories, and mines where cheap, unskilled labor was much in demand. Reformers saw these deplorable conditions as largely responsible for the increase in juvenile delinquency and immoral behavior of many youths. In an attempt to offset this trend and its causes, backers of the child-saving movement started to take a hard look at the treatment and mistreatment of juvenile offenders by the criminal justice system (Flowers, 1990; Platt, 1968).

Parens Patriae

Though the "juvenile court" is uniquely an American invention, its roots can be traced to the English court of chancery, established in the thirteenth and fourteenth centuries (Flowers, 1990). The chancery court was the first to provide special consideration to juveniles as it related to equity and protection. Operating under the doctrine of *parens patriae,* or "father of his country," the king,

> acting through his representative, the chancellor of the court, could depart from the due process of law and, as a benevolent parent, not only exempt children from the penalties set for various criminal offenses, but also take control over children who had not committed crimes but were involved in vagrancy, idleness, incorrigibility, or association with undesirable persons. Under the concept of *parens patriae,* all children are regarded as subject to the benevolent protection of the courts. (Kratcoski and Kratcoski, 1986, p. 77)

In England, the chancery court was primarily concerned with disposing of or protecting the estates of children whose parents had passed away before the children reached mandatory age. In the late nineteenth century, American social philosophers applied the principles of *parens patriae* toward a new type of American court—one designed to respond only to the needs, behavior, treatment, and cases of juveniles.

Creation of the Juvenile Court

Near the turn of the twentieth century, a number of American cities began establishing special courts and procedures for handling juveniles, in spite of the view by some that such benevolence would only succeed in spoiling youths. The first formally established juvenile court was in Cook County, Illinois, in 1899. The Illinois Juvenile Court Act was a comprehensive child welfare law reflecting not only the earlier reforms in the treatment of children but—in the creation of the juvenile court—applied the doctrine of *parens patriae* philosophy in extending the flexible rules and procedures of equity jurisdiction to juvenile delinquents, dependent, and neglected children (Flowers, 1986).

The concept of the juvenile court was quickly established in other states. By 1910, juvenile court or probation provisions had been adopted in thirty-two states. By 1925, every state but two had enacted legislation creating juvenile courts. As of 1945, all states had established a juvenile court jurisdiction (juvenile court statutes were already in effect when Alaska and Hawaii became part of the Union).

Early juvenile courts were concerned primarily with helping and protecting children, particularly lower-class youth, from the undesirable influences believed to cause and promote antisocial behavior. This benevolent intent and the authority and enforcement power granted to juvenile courts in 1899, in effect stripped juveniles of their constitutional right to due process accorded to adults in criminal matters. It was to remain this way for the most part up until the mid-1960s. The courts, in their attempt to "straighten out children" and promote "moral development," even went so far as to identify "predelinquents"—children who had not exhibited antisocial behavior but were believed to be susceptible or inclined toward delinquent conduct.

Until the mid-1970s, juvenile courts by and large had exclusive original jurisdiction over all persons under the age of eighteen charged with criminal law violations. Only upon the juvenile court waiving its jurisdiction could the juvenile be transferred and tried in the criminal court as an adult (Office of Juvenile Justice and Delinquency Prevention, 1999b). In differentiating juvenile court proceedings and philosophy from that of the adult court, much of the language was changed. "Punishment" became "treatment," a "criminal complaint" became a "juvenile court petition," juvenile courts held "hearings" instead of "trials," "arraignments" became "initial hearings," juvenile violators of the law were now "offenders" instead of "criminals," "convictions came to be referred to as "findings of involvement," and "sentences" were changed to "dispositions" (Flowers, 1990). The intent of the new language with respect to juvenile offenders was to "restructure the proceedings [of the juvenile court] and to further the goal of investigation, diagnosis, and prescription of treatment rather than to adjudicate guilt or fix blame" (Flowers, 1986, p. 173).

U.S. SUPREME COURT CASES AND JUVENILE JUSTICE

Between the 1960s and 1980s, a series of landmark U.S. Supreme Court decisions had a dramatic impact on juvenile rights and the juvenile justice system. These decisions resulted in a shift from a juvenile court philosophy based on the *parens patriae* doctrine to an approach that gave equal consideration to guaranteeing juveniles their constitutional rights; responding to their need for treatment, guidance, rehabilitation, or punishment; and acting in the community's best interest.

Kent v. United States

In 1966, *Kent v. United States* became the first case brought before the Supreme Court regarding a juvenile's right to due process of law in juvenile court proceedings. The case concerned sixteen-year-old Morris Kent. In 1961, while on probation, he was charged with rape, robbery, and forcible entry into an apartment in Washington, DC. The juvenile court judge waived jurisdiction, transferring the case to the adult court without benefit of a hearing on the waiver of jurisdiction, conferring with the youth, his mother, or counsel. Kent was eventually convicted of forcible entry and robbery counts and sentenced to thirty to ninety years in prison.

In Kent's appeal before the U.S. Supreme Court as a denial of his constitutional rights due to being a minor, the Court held that he was entitled to a hearing, to be present when the court waived jurisdiction, and that the juvenile judge should have given a written statement explaining his reasons for the transfer. According to the Court:

> the child involved in certain juvenile court proceedings was both deprived of constitutional rights and at the same time not given the rehabilitation promised under earlier juvenile court philosophy and statutes . . . . There is evidence, in fact, that there may be grounds for concern that the child receives the worst of both worlds; that he gets neither the protection accorded to adults nor the solicitous care and regenerative treatment postulated for children. (*Kent v. United States*, 1966)

In re Gault

In 1967 in *In re Gault*, the Supreme Court went even further in recognizing the constitutional rights of a juvenile in handing down its first decision regarding juvenile court procedure. The case involved a fifteen-year-old Arizona youth, Gerald Gault, who while on probation was taken into custody along with a friend for making an obscene phone call to a neighbor. Gault was arrested without notifying his parents, advising him of his right to counsel and to remain silent, and without the appearance of the complainant at the adjudication hearing. Gault was committed to a state training school until the age of twenty-one for an offense that would have amounted to a maximum sentence for an adult of two months in jail or a fifty-dollar fine.

In its decision on Gault's appeal, the Supreme Court ruled that he had been denied due process and that in hearings that could lead to institutionalization, juveniles were entitled to the right to counsel, early written notification of the charge, to be able to confront and cross-examine their accuser, to remain silent, and protection against self-incrimination (*In re Gault*, 1967).

The ruling of the Court was based on the belief that rather than being helped by the juvenile court, Gault was being punished. *In re Gault*

thus upheld the juvenile's right to due process and procedural safe-
guards during adjudication proceedings.

In re Winship

In 1970, the Supreme Court ruled in *In re Winship* that juveniles
are entitled to the same "proof beyond a reasonable doubt" due process standards during adjudication proceedings as required in adult
criminal proceedings. The case involved a twelve-year-old New York
youth, Samuel Winship, charged with stealing $112 from a woman's
purse. Though some witnesses questioned the identification of Winship as the thief, he was adjudicated delinquent and committed to a
state training school for eighteen months or more. The commitment
was based on the "preponderance of evidence" standard required in
civil court.

On appeal, the Supreme Court held that when a juvenile is charged
with an offense that would be criminal if committed by an adult and
could result in confinement, the charges must be proven beyond a
reasonable doubt (*In re Winship,* 1970). The decision expanded on
the ruling in *In re Gault,* as well as reflected the Court's desire to protect minors during adjudication hearings in addition to maintaining
"the confidentiality, informality, flexibility, and speed of the juvenile
[court] process in the prejudicial and postadjudicative states" (Bartollas, 1985, p. 444).

McKeiver v. Pennsylvania

In 1971, *McKeiver v. Pennsylvania* was concerned with whether
the Fourteenth Amendment's due process clause guaranteeing the
right to a jury trial was applicable in the adjudication of a delinquency
case in juvenile court. The issue involved a sixteen-year-old Pennsylvania youth, Joseph McKeiver, charged with robbery, larceny, and receiving stolen goods—all felonies under state law, though the money
taken in the robbery amounted to only twenty-five cents and involved
as many as thirty youthful offenders. Following a denial for a request
for a jury trial, McKeiver was adjudicated a delinquent at a juvenile
court hearing and placed on probation.

In its decision on appeal, the Supreme Court upheld the right of a
juvenile to due process but rejected the right of a juvenile to a jury

trial in juvenile court, suggesting that the "fundamental fairness" due process standard applied. The Court held that allowing juveniles the right to jury trials would for all intents and purposes "remake the juvenile proceeding into a full adversary process and will put an effective end to what has been the idealistic prospect of an intimate, informal protective proceeding" (*McKeiver v. Pennsylvania*, 1971).

Breed v. Jones

In 1975, in *Breed v. Jones*, the issue of transferring jurisdiction of a juvenile case to the adult court, earlier looked at in *Kent v. United States*, was again brought before the Supreme Court. The case concerned whether a juvenile could be prosecuted in criminal court after receiving an adjudication hearing in juvenile court. The matter involved a seventeen-year-old California youth, Gary Jones, charged with armed robbery and adjudicated delinquent before the juvenile court on this charge and two additional robberies.

At his dispositional hearing, Jones was found unfit for treatment in the juvenile justice system and transferred to the adult court. At a preliminary hearing, he was bound over for criminal trial and subsequently convicted. In filing a writ of *habeas corpus*, his attorney argued that Jones's Fifth Amendment right against double jeopardy was violated as a result of the waiver to the criminal court.

On appeal, the Supreme Court ruled that Jones had been a victim of double jeopardy, as a juvenile court could not adjudicate a case and then transfer it to the criminal court. The Court further noted that jeopardy is applicable at the adjudication hearing when evidence in the case is first presented. The waiver cannot take place after the jeopardy is in effect (*Breed v. Jones*, 1975).

Schall v. Martin

In 1984, in *Schall v. Martin*, the issue of fundamental fairness in preventive detention of a juvenile was brought before the Supreme Court. The case involved fourteen-year-old Gregory Martin, arrested and charged with robbery, assault, and weapons possession after he and two other juveniles allegedly assaulted a youth with a loaded firearm and stole his sneakers and jacket. Martin was detained pending adjudication as a serious risk to commit another offense upon release.

After a lower court reversed the detention order of the juvenile court, arguing that it is, in effect, punishing the youth, the Supreme Court upheld the preventive detention statute's constitutionality. The Court held that it serves the objective of the state to protect the juvenile and society from pretrial criminality, and therefore is not meant as punishment. The Court also reaffirmed the *parens patriae* philosophy of the state in acting on behalf of the needs, welfare, and interests of children brought into the juvenile justice system (*Schall v. Martin,* 1984).

THE JUVENILE COURT
AND SERIOUS JUVENILE OFFENDERS

A get-tough policy toward seriously delinquent youths is reflected in the delinquency cases handled by the juvenile court. The number of serious, chronic, and violent youths being processed by the juvenile court has risen sharply in recent years. The Justice Department reported that between 1987 and 1996, the number of *person offense* delinquency cases—which include criminal homicide, forcible rape, robbery, aggravated assault, simple assault, other violent sex offenses, and other person offenses—involving males grew 87 percent, while climbing a staggering 152 percent for females. Cases involving drug offenses also increased considerably for males and females, at 149 percent and 123 percent, respectively. The case rate for person offenses rose 80 percent during the period, while climbing 120 percent for drug offenses (U.S. Department of Justice, 1999).

Overall, the rate of delinquency caseloads from 1987 to 1996 rose 34 percent. Increases in case rates were highest for fifteen- and sixteen-year-olds, but showed a significant rise for all ages between eleven and seventeen (see Table 13.1).

In 1996, 86 percent of delinquency cases were referred to the juvenile court by law enforcement agencies, according to the National Center for Juvenile Justice (1999). This included 86 percent of the person offense cases, 93 percent of the drug law violation cases, and 91 percent of the property cases.

As shown in Table 13.2, a total of 983,100 delinquency cases were formally processed (involving the filing of a petition in which an adjudicatory or waiver hearing is requested) by juvenile courts in 1996. This represented more than 50 percent of all delinquency cases

TABLE 13.1. Delinquency Case Rates, by Age Group of Juveniles, 1987-1996

Age at referral	Delinquency cases per 1,000 juveniles in age group		Percent change
	1987	1996	
All ages	46.2	61.8	34
10	5.7	6.0	6
11	9.7	11.6	19
12	18.0	24.8	38
13	33.9	47.8	41
14	53.7	74.8	39
15	70.4	101.9	45
16	84.0	119.8	43
17	89.1	119.0	34

Source: Adapted from U.S. Department of Justice, *Juvenile Offenders and Victims: 1999 National Report* (Washington, DC: Government Printing Office, 1999), p. 146.

disposed by juvenile courts. As opposed to informally handled or non-petitioned cases, formally processed or petitioned delinquency cases are more likely to involve serious, violent, and drug offenses; older youths; and juveniles with a history of court appearances. Fifty-nine percent of person offenses cases were formally handled by the juvenile courts including 91 percent of the criminal homicide cases, 79 percent of those for forcible rape, 87 percent of the robbery cases, and 61 percent of those for aggravated assault. More than 60 percent of the cases involving drug law violations were formally processed by the courts.

Male and black youths are disproportionately likely to be involved in serious delinquent offense caseloads of the juvenile court. In 1996, around 75 percent of person and property offense cases and nearly 90 percent of the drug cases handled by juvenile courts involved males, though they represent only half the juveniles in the general population.

As shown in Table 13.3, in 1996, black youths were involved in 38 percent of the person offense cases and 33 percent of the drug cases processed by juvenile courts, even though they constitute only 15 percent of the juvenile population. Overall, black juveniles were

TABLE 13.2. Formally Processed Delinquency Cases by Juvenile Courts in 1996

Most Serious Offense	Number of formally processed cases	Percent of total cases[a]
Total	**983,100**	**56**
Person Offense	**223,600**	**59**
Criminal Homicide	2,200	91
Forcible Rape	5,600	79
Robbery	32,700	87
Aggravated Assault	53,800	61
Simple Assault	110,400	51
Other Violent Sex Offense	6,700	75
Other Person Offense	12,200	63
Property Offense	**455,800**	**52**
Burglary	107,500	76
Larceny-Theft	173,000	41
Motor Vehicle Theft	38,000	73
Arson	5,000	56
Vandalism	59,500	50
Trespassing	26,500	41
Stolen Property Offense	22,400	68
Other Property Offense	23,900	71
Drug Law Violation	**109,500**	**62**
Public Order Offense	**194,200**	**60**
Obstruction of Justice	97,500	77
Disorderly Conduct	34,400	38
Weapons Offense	26,300	64
Liquor Law Violations	5,000	49
Nonviolent Sex Offenses	5,400	51
Other Public Order	25,500	54
Violent Crime Index [b]	**94,300**	**70**
Property Crime Index [c]	**323,500**	**52**

Source: Adapted from National Center for Juvenile Justice, *Juvenile Court Statistics 1996* (Washington, DC: Office of Juvenile Justice and Delinquency Prevention, 1999), p. 12.

[a] Detail may not add to totals because of rounding. Percent change calculations are based on unrounded numbers.
[b] Violent Crime Index includes criminal homicide, forcible rape, robbery, and aggravated assault.
[c] Property Crime Index includes burglary, larceny-theft, motor vehicle theft, and arson.

TABLE 13.3. Delinquency Cases, by Race and Most Serious Offense, 1996 (Percent)

Most serious offense	White	Black	Other races	Total[a]
Total Delinquency cases	66	30	4	100
Person	59	38	4	100
Property	70	26	4	100
Drugs	65	33	3	100
Public order	64	32	4	100
Juvenile population	80	15	5	100

Source: Adapted from U.S. Department of Justice, *Juvenile Offenders and Victims: 1999 National Report* (Washington, DC: Government Printing Office, 1999), p. 150.

[a] Detail may not add to totals because of rounding. Nearly all juveniles of Hispanic ethnicity are included in the white racial category.

involved in 30 percent of the delinquency caseload, while white juveniles were involved in 66 percent of the delinquency cases, and other races 4 percent. White youths and those of other races were underrepresented in juvenile court caseloads relative to their population figures.

Delinquency cases formally handled by juvenile courts are most likely to involve older youths and juveniles with a history of juvenile court involvement. In 1996, nearly 60 percent of cases involving juveniles fourteen years of age or older were formally processed. Less than half the cases that involved younger juveniles were handled formally (U.S. Department of Justice, 1999).

THE CRIMINAL COURT
AND SERIOUS JUVENILE OFFENDERS

Although the vast majority of juvenile offenders remain under the original jurisdiction of the juvenile court, recent trends in dealing with particularly serious, violent, and chronic youthful offenders have resulted in more being transferred to the adult criminal court. Since the 1980s, most states have toughened laws against serious juvenile offenders, allowing for more adult-like treatment in the juvenile justice system and less difficult transfer for some to the criminal justice system.

Between 1992 and 1997 alone, all but three states modified or created new laws dealing with serious juvenile offenders, including:

- Transfer provisions in forty-five states—laws making it easier to transfer juvenile offenders from the juvenile justice system to the criminal justice system.
- Sentencing authority in thirty-one states—laws allowing for expanded sentencing options in criminal and juvenile courts.
- Confidentiality in forty-seven states—laws modifying or removing traditional confidentiality provisions in juvenile court by allowing for records and proceedings to be more open.

Most states have established mechanisms for the transfer of juvenile cases to adult or criminal court, including *judicial waiver, concurrent jurisdiction* statutes, and *statutory exclusion*. Judicial waiver is the most common means of transfer, in which a juvenile court judge is authorized to waive juvenile court jurisdiction over a case, transferring it to the juvenile court. In concurrent jurisdiction, for certain juvenile cases the original jurisdiction is shared by both juvenile and criminal courts, allowing for prosecutor discretion in using either court to file such cases. The number of states with statutory-exclusion provisions in dealing with serious and violent juvenile crime is on the rise, whereby states statutorily exclude from the jurisdiction of the juvenile court juvenile offenders if they fall under certain offense or age criteria. These cases would automatically come under the jurisdiction of the criminal court.

Only 1 percent of petitioned delinquency cases were judicially waived to the criminal court in 1996 (National Center for Juvenile Justice, 1999). Cases most likely to be waived include those concerning person and drug offenses, both reflecting on the seriousness attached to these types of crimes and those committing them (U.S. Department of Justice, 1999). Between 1987 and 1996, petitioned person offense and drug offense delinquency cases judicially waived to the criminal court grew 125 percent and 124 percent respectively, as seen in Figure 13.1. Overall, petitioned delinquency cases waived to adult court rose 47 percent over the span.

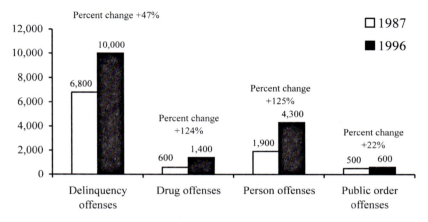

FIGURE 13.1. Petitioned Delinquency Cases Judicially Waived to Criminal Court, 1987-1996ᵃ. (*Source:* Adapted from National Center for *Juvenile Justice, Juvenile Court Statistics 1996,* Washington, DC: Office of Juvenile Justice and Delinquency Prevention, 1999, p. 13.)

ᵃDetail may not add up due to rounding.
Note: Delinquency offenses includes property offenses. These declined 2 percent during the span.

According to the Bureau of Justice Statistics, the following data reflect the characteristics of offenders and nature of offenses for juveniles transferred to adult courts from 1990 to 1994:

- Forty percent of juvenile transfers were age seventeen.
- More than half of juvenile transfers were fifteen to sixteen years of age.
- Males accounted for 92 percent of total juvenile transfers.
- Black males constituted nearly 70 percent of juvenile transfers charged with person offenses.
- White males accounted for more than 30 percent of juvenile transfers.
- White males represented more than 80 percent of juvenile burglary transfers.
- Juveniles of other races constituted 2 percent of transfers to adult court.
- Females accounted for 8 percent of all juvenile transfers.
- More than 70 percent of female transfers were charged with person offenses.

- Sixty-six percent of juvenile transfers to criminal court were charged with a felony person offense.
- More than 10 percent of juvenile transfers were charged with murder.
- Fourteen percent of transfers were charged with a drug offense. (U.S. Department of Justice, 1999)

As shown in Table 13.4, between 1990 and 1994 in the seventy-five largest counties in the United States 64 percent of the juvenile transfers to criminal court were convicted. Nearly 60 percent of transfers for person offenses, including murder, rape, robbery, and assaults resulted in a conviction. Seventy percent of juvenile transfers for drug offenses and nearly 75 percent for property offenses were convicted. More than 50 percent of all juvenile defendants transferred on felony charges pled guilty.

TABLE 13.4. Juvenile Transfers to Criminal Court in Seventy-Five Largest Counties, Percent Convicted, 1990-1994

Most serious offense	Total[a]	Felony			Misdemeanor
		Total	Plea	Trial	
All offenses	64	59	51	8	5
Person	59	56	47	9	4
Murder	58	56	37	19	3
Rape	54	54	54	0	0
Robbery	58	56	48	8	2
Assault	63	53	46	7	9
Property	74	61	59	3	13
Burglary	77	64	64	0	13
Theft	76	59	54	6	16
Drug	70	68	56	12	2
Public Order	91	91	91	0	0

[a]Detail may not add up to totals because of rounding.

Source: Adapted from U.S. Department of Justice, *Juvenile Offenders and Victims: 1999 National Report* (Washington, DC: Government Printing Office, 1999), p. 174.

Chapter 14

Juveniles in Custody
and Confinement

Increasing public concern about serious youth crime has resulted in stiffer laws, sentences, and punishment (Bureau of Justice Statistics, 2000a; Flowers, 1990; U.S. Department of Justice, 1999). More juveniles who commit violent and serious crimes are being tried and incarcerated as adults (Bureau of Justice Statistics, 2000b) and held for longer periods of time in juvenile correctional facilities (Office of Juvenile Justice and Delinquency Prevention, 1999b). Minority youths, in particular, are disproportionately represented among juveniles in custody and confinement (Bilchik, 1999; Flowers, 1988).

Issues concerning violence, victimization, health, and legal rights with respect to institutionalized youths are being addressed and examined by juvenile delinquency and juvenile justice professionals with an eye toward not only protecting the public from dangerous young offenders, but protecting juvenile inmates from each other and the problems within confinement facilities that can affect treatment, welfare, and recidivism (ABT Associates, Inc., 1994; Bartollas, Miller, and Dinitz, 1976; Flowers, 1990; Poole and Regoli, 1983; Volenik, 1978).

Noninstitutional approaches to treating juvenile offenders such as intensive aftercare and residential treatment programs, are seen by many professionals as more cost-effective than institutionalization and a more effective way to help turn troubled young lives around (Carter and Klein, 1976; Emerson, 1969; Office of Juvenile Justice and Delinquency Prevention, 1994; Wiebush, 1993). However, the current trend in dealing with habitual, serious, and violent juvenile offenders appears to be longer sentences of confinement in secure institutions.

JUVENILE OFFENDERS IN ADULT
CORRECTIONAL FACILITIES

Juveniles in Jail

Relatively few juvenile offenders are held in jails. According to the Annual Survey of Jails, less than 2 percent of the jail population in the United States consists of persons under the age of eighteen (Bureau of Justice Statistics, 2000a). As seen in Figure 14.1, in 1997 an estimated 9,105 juveniles were in jails nationwide. Of these, 7,007 were held as adults, while 2,098 were held as juveniles. Persons under the age of eighteen were more than three times as likely to be in jail as adults than as juveniles.

Since many juveniles are only detained in jail for a short while, it is believed that the actual number of juveniles to pass through adult jails in this country is much higher. It is estimated that as many as 600,000 persons under the age of eighteen spend some time in jail each year (Sarri, 1983; Wilson, 1978). Many such youths are placed in jail facilities because of overcrowding or funding problems in juvenile correctional institutions (Flowers, 1990; Jordan, 1984).

Approximately 20 percent of youths are in jail for serious or violent offenses (Cottle, 1977; Flowers, 1989; Wisconsin Department of

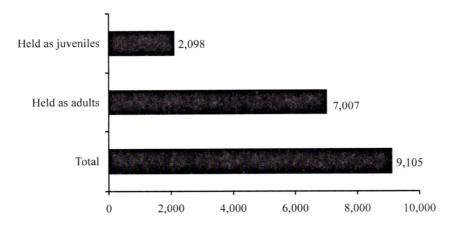

FIGURE 14.1. Juveniles in Jail in the United States, 1997. (*Source:* Derived from Bureau of Justice Statistics, *Correctional Populations in the United States, 1997,* Washington, DC: U.S. Department of Justice, 2000, p. 23.)

Health and Social Services, 1976). Jailed juveniles are most likely to be male, white, older teenagers, and from lower socioeconomic backgrounds (Flowers, 1986).

Juveniles in Prison

Similar to juveniles in jail, juvenile prison inmates constitute only a small portion of the prison population. The *Profile of State Prisoners Under Age 18, 1985-1997,* reported that on December 31, 1997, less than 1 percent of state prisoners were under the age of eighteen (Bureau of Justice Statistics, 2000b). However, the number of juvenile prison inmates younger than eighteen has risen sharply in recent years. As shown in Figure 14.2, between 1985 and 1997, the number of juveniles admitted to state prison in the United States went from 3,400 to 7,400—more than doubling.

Most youths under the age of eighteen sent to prison were convicted of a violent or serious offense. Table 14.1 breaks down the most serious offenses of juveniles admitted to state prison in 1997. Sixty-one percent of the inmates under eighteen were admitted to prison for violent offenses such as murder and nonnegligent manslaughter, sexual assault, robbery, and aggravated assault. Twenty-two percent of admissions were for property crimes such as burglary and motor vehicle theft, and 11 percent were admitted for drug of-

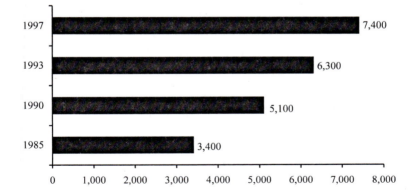

FIGURE 14.2. Trends in Juveniles Admitted to State Prison, 1985-1997. (*Source:* Derived from Bureau of Justice Statistics, *Profile of State Prisoners Under Age 18, 1985-1997,* Special Report, Washington, DC: U.S. Department of Justice, 2000, p. 1.)

TABLE 14.1. Juveniles Under the Age of Eighteen Admitted to State Prison, by Most Serious Offense, 1997a

Most serious offense	Number	Percent
All offenses	7,400	100
Violent offenses	4,510	61
Murder/nonnegligent manslaughter	500	7
Sexual assaultb	300	4
Robbery	2,360	32
Aggravated assault	1,060	14
Property offenses	1,590	22
Burglary	950	13
Larceny-theft	230	3
Motor vehicle theft	160	2
Drug offenses	840	11
Public-order offenses	360	5

Source: Adapted from Bureau of Justice Statistics, *Profile of State Prisoners Under Age 18, 1985-1997,* Special Report (Washington, DC: U.S. Department of Justice, 2000), p. 4.

a All data are based on an estimation, and include only persons under eighteen with a sentence of more than one year.
b Includes forcible rape and other sexual assaults.

fenses. Data show that nearly half the youths under eighteen convicted of violent felonies are incarcerated (Bureau of Justice Statistics, 2000b).

Juvenile prison inmates are predominantly male older teens, and minority, with less than a high school education. The Bureau of Justice Statistics (BJS) reported that in 1997, 97 percent of the youths under eighteen admitted to state prison were male. Nearly 75 percent were seventeen and more than 20 percent were sixteen. Almost 75 percent of juvenile admissions were black or Hispanic, with 25 percent white. Sixty-seven percent of the juveniles admitted to prison had only a ninth- to eleventh-grade education, while more than 25 percent had less than a ninth-grade education (Bureau of Justice Statistics, 2000b).

While few juvenile offenders are confined under the federal prison authority, those being admitted to juvenile corrections are on the rise. According to the federal prisoner data, between 1994 and 1997 the number of persons under eighteen being held in state juvenile correctional facilities under contract to the Federal Bureau of Prisons rose by more than 52 percent. As indicated in Table 14.2, 52 percent of the juvenile federal prisoners admitted in 1997 were adjudicated delinquent for a violent crime, with 31 percent for a property crime. Ninety-five percent of the federal prisoners under eighteen were male, with nearly 90 percent non-Hispanic. Seventy-two percent of juveniles admitted to federal institutions in 1997 were Native American and 18 percent were white.

TABLE 14.2. Persons Under Age Eighteen Admitted to Facilities Under Contract to the Federal Bureau of Prisons, 1997[a]

Characteristic	Percent
Gender	
Male	95
Female	5
Race	
White	18
Black	7
American Indian	72
Asian	3
Hispanic Origin	
Hispanic	11
Non-Hispanic	89
Offense Type	
Violent	52
Property	31
Drug	6
Public-order	11
Number of admissions	189

Source: U.S. Department of Justice, *Juvenile Delinquents in the Federal Criminal Justice System* (Washington, DC: Office of Justice Programs, 1997), p. 9.

[a] Data is for fiscal year ending September 30, 1997.

JUVENILE OFFENDERS IN JUVENILE
CUSTODY FACILITIES

In spite of the crackdown on dangerous juvenile offenders and a shift towards trying, convicting, and incarcerating the most serious and violent youth in the adult criminal justice system, the vast majority of juvenile delinquents continue to be held or confined in juvenile correctional facilities. According to data from the Office of Juvenile Justice and Delinquency Prevention, 105,790 juveniles were being held in public and private juvenile detention, correctional, and shelter facilities on October 29, 1997 (U.S. Department of Justice, 1999).

Table 14.3 reflects the serious offenses for which juveniles were confined to juvenile facilities as of October 29, 1997. More than 33 percent of all institutionalized youths were held for violent offenses—with the highest percentage confined for aggravated assault, robbery, simple assault, and violent sex offenses. Thirty percent of juveniles were in custody facilities for property offenses, including household burglary, theft, and motor vehicle theft. Almost 9 percent of juveniles were held for drug offenses, including drug possession and drug trafficking.

Juveniles in residential placement facilities are predominantly male and older teenagers (see Figures 14.3 and 14.4). In 1997, males constituted 86.5 percent of all juvenile offenders in residential placement, compared to 13.5 percent females. Seventy percent of youths being held were fifteen to seventeen years old, with confinement peaking at age sixteen. More than 26 percent of youths in juvenile correctional facilities in 1997 were sixteen years of age.

Other characteristics of juvenile placement in residential facilities can be seen as follows:

- Juvenile delinquents are more than three times as likely to be held in public facilities as private facilities.
- More than two times as many juveniles in public facilities are committed rather than detained.
- Delinquents being held outnumber status offenders in residential placement facilities by fourteen to one.
- Juvenile person offenders tend to be detained or committed to residential facilities longer than other juvenile offenders.

TABLE 14.3. Juveniles Held in Public or Private Detention, Correctional, and Shelter Facilities in the United States, by Offense, 1997[a]

Offense	Number	Percent
Total[b]	105,790	100.0
Violent offenses	35,357	33.4
Murder/manslaughter	1,927	1.8
Violent sex offense	5,590	5.3
Kidnapping	326	0.3
Robbery	9,451	8.9
Aggravated assault	9,530	9.0
Simple assault	6,630	6.3
Other violent offense	1,903	1.8
Property offenses	31,991	30.2
Household burglary	12,560	11.9
Motor vehicle theft	6,525	6.2
Arson	915	0.9
Property damage	1,758	1.7
Theft	7,294	6.9
Other property offense	2,939	2.8
Drug offenses	9,286	8.8
Drug trafficking	3,045	2.9
Drug possession	5,693	5.4
Other drug offense	548	0.5

Source: Adapted from U.S. Department of Justice, Bureau of Justice Statistics, *Sourcebook of Criminal Justice Statistics 1999* (Washington, DC: Government Printing Office, 2000), p. 495.

[a] Data is as of October 29, 1997.
[b] Total includes public order offenses, other delinquent offenses, status offenses, and probation or parole violation.

MINORITY YOUTHS IN CUSTODY

Racial and ethnic minority juveniles are disproportionately represented in residential placement facilities (Bilchik, 1999; Flowers, 1988). Almost 67 percent of all juveniles in residential placement in

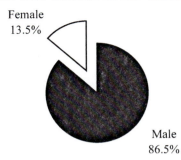

FIGURE 14.3. Juveniles in Residential Placement Facilities, by Sex, 1997[a].
(*Source:* Derived from U.S. Department of Justice, Bureau of Justice Statistics,
Sourcebook of Criminal Justice Statistics 1999, Washington, DC: Government
Printing Office, 2000, p. 495.)
[a]Data as of October 27, 1997.

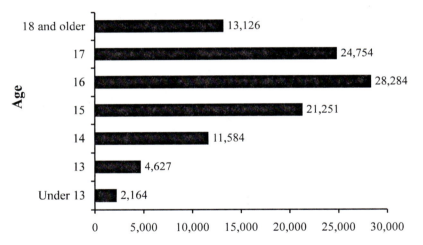

FIGURE 14.4. Juveniles in Residential Placement Facilities by Age, 1997[a].
(*Source:* Derived from U.S. Department of Justice, Bureau of Justice Statistics,
Sourcebook of Criminal Justice Statistics 1999, Washington, DC: Government
Printing Office, 2000, p. 495.)
[a]Data are as of October 29, 1997.

1997 were minorities (U.S. Department of Justice, 1999). This compares to a minority representation of approximately 33 percent of the juvenile population in the United States.

As seen in Table 14.4, minority youths accounted for 62 percent of juveniles held for all delinquent offenses, nearly 58 percent of juve-

TABLE 14.4. Juveniles in Residential Placement Facilities, by Race and Most Serious Offense, 1997 (Percent)[a]

Most serious offense	Total[b]	White	Black	Hispanic	American Indian	Asian
Total juveniles in residential placement	100	37	40	18	2	2
Delinquency	100	36	41	19	1	2
Person	100	31	43	21	1	3
Criminal homicide	100	19	44	30	2	5
Sexual assault	100	51	33	12	2	1
Robbery	100	16	55	24	1	3
Aggravated assault	100	26	41	26	2	4
Simple assault	100	41	38	16	2	2
Other person	100	41	40	15	1	2
Property	100	43	35	17	2	2
Burglary	100	46	32	18	2	2
Theft	100	45	37	15	1	1
Auto theft	100	36	38	20	2	3
Arson	100	52	29	17	1	1
Other property	100	42	38	16	1	2
Drug	100	23	56	19	1	1
Trafficking	100	14	64	21	<1	1
Other drug	100	26	54	18	1	1
Public order	100	38	38	20	2	2
Weapons	100	24	45	27	1	3
Other public order	100	48	33	15	2	2
Violent Crime Index[c]	100	27	45	23	1	3
Property Crime Index[d]	100	43	35	17	2	2

Source: Adapted from U.S. Department of Justice, *Juvenile Offenders and Victims: 1999 National Report* (Washington, DC: Government Printing Office, 1999), p. 195.

[a] As of October 29, 1997.
[b] Detail may not add up due to rounding.
[c] Includes criminal homicide, sexual assault, robbery, and aggravated assault.
[d] Includes burglary, theft, auto theft, and arson.

niles in custody for person offenses, and 77 percent for drug offenses on October 29, 1997. Fifty-six percent of youths in custody for property offenses were minorities.

Black juveniles are particularly overrepresented in serious offender residential-placement figures. Though constituting around 15 percent of the juvenile population, black youths accounted for 43 percent of those confined for violent person offenses and 56 percent held for drug offenses.

Similarly, an overrepresentation of institutionalized Hispanic youths can be seen in the data. While comprising 15 percent of the general juvenile population, Hispanic juveniles made up 18 percent of the total number of juveniles in residential placement facilities in 1997. The disproportion was even higher for person offenses at 21 percent of the total, while representing 30 percent of those held for criminal homicide, 26 percent for aggravated assault, and 24 percent for robbery. Twenty-one percent of juveniles in custody for drug trafficking were Hispanic.

MODES OF ADAPTATION TO THE INSTITUTIONAL SETTING FOR THE JUVENILE OFFENDER

Youths confined to juvenile correctional facilities develop various modes of adaptation to their setting. These are generally dependent upon the juvenile's background, values, and circumstances encountered in the institutional environment. The mode of adaptation most common is to try and make the most out of the time in confinement, including meeting one's needs with the least adverse situations. Other residents take a "playing it cool" adaptation mode, learning to control their emotions while doing whatever is necessary to make the stay as short as possible.

A third mode of adaptation is rebellion, in which hardened juvenile inmates rebel against authority through intimidation, threats, verbal abuse, protest, violence, and inciting others to cause trouble. These youths tend to be leaders of the inmate subculture, exercising a great deal of power over fellow inmates within the correctional institution. A fourth adaptation mode is to withdraw, usually by using drugs or running away from the facility (Flowers, 1990).

Other modes of juvenile adaptation to institutional life that researchers have identified include: innovators, conformists, retreatists, ritualists, con artists, toughs, bushboys, quiet types, and scapegoats (Polsky, 1962; Sieverdes and Bartollas, 1977). For most confined juvenile offenders, survival may hinge on their ability to successfully adapt.

YOUTH OFFENDING IN JUVENILE CORRECTIONAL INSTITUTIONS

Serious and violent institutionalized juvenile offenders can present a problem to correctional administrators in controlling and protecting other youth inmates and staff. Studies have shown that violent and aggressive juvenile inmates are commonly involved in serious behavior that affects residents and staff, including violence, threats, intimidation, and issues with authority (Cohen, Cole, and Bailey, 1976; Flowers, 1989).

Criminologists have explained these patterns of behavior by inmates in secure facilities in terms of deprivation theory and cultural-importation theory (Flowers, 1990). The deprivation perspective regards inmate aggression and violence as a response to the grim conditions, deprivation, and degradation inherent in the institutional setting. In contrast, the cultural importation approach assumes that inmate aggressive and violent behavior is a reflection of values and behavioral patterns possessed prior to entering the institution, which are then used to the inmate's advantage in regard to power, control, respect, and material gain.

In a study of adolescent aggressive behavior in four juvenile correctional institutions with various structures and programming, a history of aggression was found the most significant factor in explaining institutional aggression. In Bartollas, Miller, and Dinitz's (1976) examination of victimization in juvenile corrections, at least 90 percent of the sample studied participated in victimization and exploitation. The researchers found that unlike the traditional socioeconomic and racial structure in American society, black inmates typically occupied the upper rungs of the institutional hierarchy, and were the dominant group with regard to sexually or physically victimizing white inmates. The study further found that:

- Most victimizations related to property appropriation.
- The stronger and more aggressive inmates dominated the weaker and less aggressive inmates.
- Staff members were victimized through "con games," and also exploited the more powerful inmates by using them to maintain order.
- Inmates responded to severe victimization through drug use, attempted suicide, and running away.

AFTERCARE AND THE SERIOUS JUVENILE OFFENDER

Aftercare, or parole, refers to the release of juveniles from correctional facilities and the support and supervisory services and practices accompanying the youths' reintegration into the community. The primary method of juvenile release from juvenile corrections is through the aftercare program (Flowers, 1990).

The increased concern about serious and violent juvenile offending, the high recidivism rate, and less than ideal treatment and rehabilitative practices and results in institutional settings, make it all the more important for innovative and comprehensive strategies in effective intensive aftercare programs (Agee, 1979; Baird and Heinz, 1978; Palmer, 1991). Identifying juveniles at high risk for repeat offending is seen as crucial in successful aftercare. These youths include those with a long history of delinquency and criminality, property offenders, and violent offenders (Coates, 1984; Shannon, 1978; Wolfgang, Figlio, and Sellin, 1972). Other important factors in recidivism include intrafamilial dynamics, substance abuse, school, and peer group pressures (Flowers, 1990; Flowers and Flowers, 2001; Office of Juvenile Justice and Delinquency Prevention, 1994).

Successful aftercare programs balance the needs of the high-risk youth and others susceptible to reoffending with the needs of the community at-large and public safety in the process of reintegration. However, due to overcrowding at secure juvenile residential facilities and the increasing costs of detention, some fear that intensive aftercare strategies may be threatened or reduced by practicalities and bureaucracy, thus releasing dangerous youths back into society to reoffend.

PART IV:
RESPONDING TO JUVENILE DELINQUENCY AND CRIMINALITY

Chapter 15

Prevention and Control of Juvenile Crime

In spite of a decline in juvenile crime, and violent crime in particular, in the United States, a public perception still exists that youth crime and delinquency are out of control. Many believe that this is the result of the easy availability of drugs and guns in our society (Cornell, 1993; Flowers, 1999; Lizotte et al., 1994). Exacerbating the perception of increased juvenile violence and criminality are the recent highly publicized school shootings, juveniles murdering their parents and other family members, and other instances of serious or chronic juvenile offending (Flowers, 2000; Flowers and Flowers, 2001).

Although such highly publicized examples may be isolated instances, serious and violent juvenile delinquent and criminal acts continue to be a major problem in this country. Prevention strategies for reducing the criminality of at-risk youths include legislative efforts for preventing child abuse and neglect, help for youth running away from abusive environments, and attack of juvenile criminality at its roots, as well as differentiating serious from status juvenile offenders (Flowers, 1990, 1994; Office of Justice Programs, 1999; U.S. Department of Health and Human Services, 1999).

In addition, a number of intervention programs and strategies around the country have proven successful in reducing juvenile violence, while helping violent and serious youthful offenders turn their lives around (Esbensen and Osgood, 1997; Kennedy, Piehl, and Braga, 1996; Loeber and Farrington, 1998; Office of Juvenile Justice and Delinquency Prevention, 1998).

FEDERAL RESPONSES TO JUVENILE CRIME AND DELINQUENCY PREVENTION

Since the 1970s, Congress has enacted a number of key laws aimed at preventing and controlling the spread of juvenile crime, as well as addressing the precursors of youth antisocial behavior, including child physical and sexual abuse, and an unstable family environment. These efforts in combination with "get tough" federal and state level juvenile crime legislation have made an impact on the problem of youth violence and serious offending (Flowers, 1990; Office of Justice Programs, 1999; U.S. Department of Justice, 1999). See also Chapter 13 for more discussion on laws and juvenile offenders.

Juvenile Justice and Delinquency Prevention Act

The Juvenile Justice and Delinquency Prevention Act enacted in 1974 and amended in 1980, was intended to identify and deinstitutionalize status offenders, dependent and neglected youth, and to separate juvenile delinquents from adult criminals. The act required: (1) a comprehensive assessment of the effectiveness of the current juvenile justice system, (2) the impetus for development and implementation of innovative alternatives in delinquency prevention and diversion of status offenders from the criminal justice system, and (3) use of juvenile justice system resources to more effectively deal with juvenile delinquents.

In order to receive Formula Grants funding under the provisions of the Act, states were required to submit plans that described their compliance with the requirements set forth (Juvenile Justice and Delinquency Prevention Act, 1974).

Child Abuse Prevention and Treatment Act

The Child Abuse Prevention and Treatment Act was enacted in 1974 and amended in 1978 in response to increasing national concern about child maltreatment and its relationship to juvenile delinquency. The Act provided for:

> (1) the establishment of a National Center on Child Abuse and Neglect, (2) increasing public awareness on child maltreatment, detection, and reporting, (3) assisting states and local communi-

ties in developing more effective mechanisms for delivery of services to families, (4) providing training and technical assistance to state and local communities in dealing with the problems of child abuse and neglect, and (5) supporting research into causal and preventative measures in child victimization. (Child Abuse Prevention and Treatment and Adoption Reform Act, 1978)

To qualify for federal funds, states were required to meet the following criteria: (1) a uniform, comprehensive definition of child abuse and neglect, (2) investigation of child abuse reports, (3) assuring confidentiality of records, and (4) the appointment of guardians ad litem for juveniles involved in abuse or neglect court proceedings.

Protection of Children Against Sexual Exploitation Act

The Protection of Children Against Sexual Exploitation Act was enacted in 1978, following extensive hearings in both houses of Congress on the problem of child sexual abuse and sexual exploitation and its relationship to youth crime and delinquency. The law sought to halt the production and dissemination of child pornography by prohibiting the transportation of minors across state lines for the purpose of sexual exploitation. The Act also extended the federal government's power to prosecute producers and distributors of child pornography. In specific, the law provided:

> Punishment for persons who use, employ, or persuade minors (defined as any persons under 16) to become involved in the production of visual or print materials that depict sexually explicit conduct if the producers know or have reasons to know that the materials will be transported in interstate or foreign commerce or mailed. Punishment is also specifically provided for parents, legal guardians, or other persons having custody or control of minors and who knowingly permit a minor to participate in the production of such material. (Sexual Exploitation Act, 1978)

A number of other federal laws have since passed to further prohibit the sexual misuse and exploitation of children and strengthen penalties against child sexual exploiters (Flowers, 1998, 2001a; Office of Juvenile Justice and Delinquency Prevention, 1999c).

Runaway and Homeless Youth Act

The Runaway and Homeless Youth Act was enacted in 1978 and amended in 1980. It authorized what is now the Secretary of Health and Human Services to provide assistance to local organizations in the operation of temporary runaway shelters. The Act addresses the serious youth problems associated with children running away or being thrown out of the house—such as child abuse, teenage prostitution, juvenile substance abuse, and youth crime and violence—and the need to curb them. The legislation made grant money available for establishing and maintaining shelters for runaways by states, localities, and nonprofit organizations.

To qualify for federal funds for a runaway house, criteria included:

- An accessible location to runaways
- A maximum capacity of twenty children
- A sufficient staff to juvenile ratio
- Aadequate plans for contacting parents or relatives of a juvenile runaway and providing for safe return home
- Maintenance of satisfactory records profiling runaways and their parents

The 1980 amendment to the Act included (1) recognizing that many "runaways" are actually "throwaways," (2) clarification of requirements that shelter services be provided to the families of runaway and homeless youth in addition to the juveniles themselves, and (3) the addition of program authorities for establishing model programs aimed at helping habitual runaways (Runaway and Homeless Youth Act, 1978).

National Center for Missing and Exploited Children

To address the public concern over the tens of thousands of children missing and sexually exploited each year—many of whom become serious and chronic offenders—in 1984, Congress enacted legislation for establishing a permanent National Center for Missing and Exploited Children (Flowers, 2000). The Center hoped to spearhead a national effort to halt the epidemic of missing and exploited youth while addressing the implications associated with the problem.

Furthermore, the Center was designed to act as a central contact point for parents or relatives of missing children and others who may have information on them.

Other key features of the National Center include providing assistance and expertise in legislation, education, advocacy, criminal justice system improvements, and public awareness (Flowers, 1994).

National Center on Child Abuse and Neglect

The National Center on Child Abuse and Neglect (NCCAN) was established in 1974 and reauthorized in 1988 under the Child Abuse, Prevention, Adoption, and Family Services Act. Representing the federal government in regard to child maltreatment matters, the NCCAN administers grants to states, local agencies, and organizations across the country for research, programs, and assistance in identifying, treating, and preventing child abuse and neglect (Child Abuse Prevention, Adoption, and Family Services Act, 1988).

National Child Abuse and Neglect Data System

The National Child Abuse and Neglect Data System (NCANDS) was established in 1988 by the NCCAN. Currently under the Administration of Children, Youth and Families (ACYF), the NCANDS is the primary source of information on abused and neglected children nationwide as known to state child protective services agencies. The Summary Data Component of NCANDS collects data on the nature of reports of child maltreatment, the characteristics of abuse and neglect victims and alleged perpetrators, and the response of local and state child protective services. Such information is made available to policymakers, child welfare professionals, researchers, and concerned citizens for policy, practice, identification, and prevention (U.S. Department of Health and Human Services, 1999).

CHILD PROTECTIVE SERVICES

Child Protective Services (CPS) is the agency primarily responsible for evaluating and preventing possible cases of child maltreatment in every state, and protecting and treating victims of child abuse and neglect (National Center on Child Abuse and Neglect, 1992). Given the strong association between child maltreatment and juvenile delinquency (Flowers, 2000; Fontana, 1964; Helfer and Kempe, 1976), the role of the CPS is critical in identifying at-risk youth for child abuse and neglect and ensuring their safety and well-being. Mandatory child abuse reporting laws exist in every state for reporting suspected child maltreatment.

A secondary goal of the CPS is to try to keep child abusive families together, if possible, for the long-term health and needs of a child in a safe and stable environment. This includes focus on treatment for child abusers. Should this fail, prosecuting such perpetrators in criminal court may become necessary to receive treatment, as a deterrence, and to ensure the welfare of the victim or victims.

DELINQUENCY PREVENTION AND CONTROL STRATEGIES

A number of promising prevention and intervention programs exist around the country in efforts to reduce serious juvenile crime and violence (Hawkins and Catalano, 1992; Olds and Kitzman, 1993; Olweus, 1991; Yoshikawa, 1994). The effectiveness of these programs varies, however all point toward the possibilities for formulating successful strategies in delinquency and youth violence control (Gottfredson, 1987; Klein, Alexander, and Parsons, 1977; McPartland and Nettles, 1991; Murphy, Hutchison, and Bailey, 1983; Office of Juvenile Justice and Delinquency Prevention, 1998).

Experts in juvenile crime and violence believe that the most effective prevention strategies are those that seek a reduction in high-risk factors while enhancing protective factors (Hawkins, Catalano, and Miller, 1992; Institute of Medicine, 1994; Office of Juvenile Justice and Delinquency Prevention, 1998). Current successful intervention programs and strategies in preventing and reducing serious, violent, and chronic juvenile delinquency and criminality include the following:

- Prenatal to age six educational programs
- Classroom management, organization, and instructional strategies

- Curricula focusing on conflict resolution and violence prevention
- Peer counseling and mediation
- Recreation programs after school
- Firearms intervention strategies
- Training of parents
- Marriage and family therapy
- Gang prevention strategies
- Vocational training
- Policing strategies
- Mobilizing of community programs (Office of Juvenile Justice and Delinquency Prevention, 1998)

Youth and Gun Violence

The literature indicates that youth violence is strongly associated with the use of firearms (Howell, 1998; Office of Juvenile Justice and Delinquency Prevention, 1998; Sheley and Wright, 1995). Various intervention models in juvenile criminality have focused on a reduction in gun access and use by juveniles (Ginsberg and Loffredo, 1993; Jung and Jason, 1988; Zimring, 1986). For example, in the Boston Gun Project's Operation Ceasefire—which uses a multijurisdictional approach to law enforcement deterrence strategies in firearms possession—homicides involving males under the age of twenty-five dropped by almost 70 percent after the Ceasefire program was implemented (Kennedy, 1998). Other models have shown similar results in the correlation between a reduction in gun possession by juvenile males and a reduction in youth fatalities (Office of Justice Programs, 1999).

Youth Gangs and Violence

Intervention programs have also targeted youth gang violence. Studies show that members of gangs are much more likely to be involved in violent behavior than youths not affiliated with gangs (Thornberry, 1998; Office of Justice Programs, 1999). Members of gangs are also more violence prone while in them than before they join or leave the gang (Thornberry et al., 1993).

Effective gang-prevention strategies have focused on (1) preventing youths from joining gangs, (2) turning delinquent gangs into harmless youth groups, and (3) mediation and intervention in conflict and confrontation between gangs (Miller, 1962; Office of Juvenile Justice and Delinquency Prevention, 1998; Spergel, 1986; Thompson and Jason, 1988).

One example of a successful strategy in antigang membership was started by the Bureau of Tobacco and Firearms. The Gang Resistance Education and Training (G.R.E.A.T.) program is a school-based curriculum in gang prevention. Early results indicate that students completing the G.R.E.A.T. program had lower levels of gang involvement and delinquent activity (Esbensen and Osgood, 1997).

In examining gang prevention and intervention strategies, Spergel and colleagues found that effective programs involving community mobilization and providing social opportunities, gang suppression, social intervention, and organizational development reduced the rate of youth gang violence (Spergel et al., 1994). However, some studies have found that intervention strategies that seek to shift gang involvement activity to more socially acceptable avenues have generally been unsuccessful (Klein, 1969; Miller, 1962).

Youth and School Violence

The documented relationship between troubled youth and school violence has prompted strong interest in prevention and intervention programs in reducing juvenile school violence (Cernkovich and Giordano, 1992; Felner and Adam, 1988; Gottfredson, 1987; Olweus, 1993; Polk and Schafer, 1972). The recent rash of school shootings has made it all the more important to identify at-risk youth for violent behavior (Flowers, 1994; Flowers and Flowers, 2001).

Some strategies have focused on school bullying, which has been related to various factors of adolescence, including child abuse and juvenile delinquency (Office of Juvenile Justice and Delinquency Prevention, 1998). In the first intervention program to reduce school bullying, begun in Norway in the early 1980s, Olweus (1993) found a reduction in the incidence of bully behavior, victimization, and other juvenile deviance due to the program. Delinquencies that decreased included fighting, theft, and substance abuse. Similarly, a South Carolina anti-bullying program in middle schools indicated that self-reported juvenile delinquent behavior was reduced after a year (Office of Justice Programs, 1999).

Other effective school-related strategies in delinquency prevention and control have been implemented in peer mediation programs, student counseling, and school organizations (Felner, Ginter, and Primavera, 1982; Gottfredson, Karweit, and Gottfredson, 1989; Reyes and Jason, 1991). More such programs are needed in association with other factors present in the lives of at-risk youth for violent and antisocial behavior, including family, child maltreatment, community, and biological and psychological variables.

References

Abrahamsen, D. (1970). *Our Violent Society*. New York: Funk and Wagnalls.

ABT Associates, Inc. (1994). *Conditions of Confinement: Juvenile Detention and Corrections Facilities*. Washington, DC: Office of Juvenile Justice and Delinquency Prevention.

Adams, D. E., H. A. Ishizuka, and K. S. Ishizuka (1977). The Child Abuse Delinquent: An Exploratory/Descriptive Study. Unpublished MSW Thesis. University of South Carolina, Columbia, SC.

Adler, F. (1975). *Sisters in Crime: The Rise of the New Female Criminal*. New York: McGraw-Hill.

Agee, V. L. (1979). *Treatment of the Violent Incorrigible Adolescent*. Lexington, MA: D. C. Heath.

Ageton, S. S. (1983). *Sexual Assault Among Adolescents*. Lexington, MA: D. C. Heath.

Agnew, R. (1985). A Revised Strain Theory of Delinquency. *Social Forces* 64(1): 151-167.

Agnew, R. (1992). Foundation for a General Strain Theory of Crime and Delinquency. *Criminology* 10(1):47-87.

Agnew, R. (1996). Foundation for a General Strain Theory of Crime and Delinquency. In D. G. Rojek and G. F. Jensen (Eds.), *Exploring Delinquency: Causes and Control* (pp. 150-167). Los Angeles: Roxbury.

Aichorn, A. (1935). *Wayward Youth*. New York: Viking Press.

Akers, R. L. (1985). *Deviant Behavior: A Social Learning Approach*, Third Edition. Belmont, CA: Wadsworth.

American Humane Association (1994). *Child Abuse and Neglect Data: AHA Fact Sheet #1*. Englewood, CO: American Humane Association.

American Psychiatric Association (1987). *Diagnostic and Statistical Manual of Mental Disorders* (DSM-III) Third Edition. Washington, DC: American Psychiatric Association.

Amir, M. (1971). *Patterns in Forcible Rape*. Chicago: University of Chicago Press.

Andry, R. G. (1962). Paternal Affection and Delinquency. In M. E. Wolfgang, L. Savitz, and N. Johnston (Eds.), *The Sociology of Crime and Delinquency* (pp. 342-352). New York: John Wiley and Sons.

Arbetter, S. (1995). Family Violence: When We Hurt the Ones We Love. *Health* 22(3):6.

Arias, I., and P. Johnson (1989). Evaluations of Physical Aggression Among Intimate Dyads. *Journal of Interpersonal Violence* 4(3):298-307.

Arias, I., M. Samios, and K. D. O'Leary (1987). Prevalence and Correlates of Physical Aggression During Courtship. *Journal of Interpersonal Violence* 2(1):82-90.

Austin, R. L. (1980). Adolescent Subcultures of Violence. *Sociological Quarterly* 21:545-561.

Averill, J. R. (1982). *Anger and Aggression*. New York: Springer-Verlag.

Avery-Leaf, S. (1997). Efficacy of a Dating Violence Prevention Program or Attitudes Justifying Aggression. *Journal of Adolescent Health* 21(1):11-17.

Bailey, S. (1996). Adolescents Who Murder. *Journal of Adolescence* 19(1):19-39.

Baird, S. C., and R. Heinz (1978). *Risk Assessment in Juvenile Probation and Aftercare*. Madison, WI: Division of Corrections.

Bandura, A., and R. H. Walters (1959). *Adolescent Aggression*. New York: Ronald Press.

Bane, M. J. (1976). Marital Disruption and the Lives of Children. *Journal of Social Issues* 32(1):103-117.

Bartollas, C. (1985). *Juvenile Delinquency*. New York: John Wiley and Sons.

Bartollas, C., S. J. Miller, and S. Dinitz (1976). *Juvenile Victimization: The Institutional Paradox*. New York: Halstead Press.

Bateman, P. (1998). The Context of Date Rape. In B. Levy (Ed.), *Dating Violence: Young Women in Danger* (pp. 94-99). Seattle: Seal Press.

Battin, S. R., K. G. Hill, R. D. Abbott, R. F. Cattalano, and J. D. Hawkins (1998). The Contributions of Gang Membership to Delinquency Beyond Delinquent Friends. *Criminology* 36:93-115.

Becker, H. (1963). *Outsiders, Studies in the Sociology of Deviance*. New York: Macmillan.

Belson, W. (1978). *Television Violence and the Adolescent Boy*. London: Saxon House.

Bender, L., and F. J. Curran (1940). Children and Adolescents Who Kill. *Journal of Criminal Psychopathology* 1(4):297.

Bergman, L. (1992). Dating Violence Among High School Students. *Social Work* 37(1):21-27.

Bernard, M. L., and J. L. Bernard (1983). Violent Intimacy: The Family As a Model for Love Relationships. *Family Relations* 32:283-286.

Bernard, T. J. (1984). Control Criticisms of Strain Theories: An Assessment of Theoretical and Empirical Adequacy. *Journal of Research in Crime and Delinquency* 21:353-372.

Bernard, T. J. (1987). Testing Structural Strain Theories. *Journal of Research in Crime and Delinquency* 24:262-280.

Bilchik, S. (1999). *Minorities in the Juvenile Justice System*. Washington, DC: Office of Juvenile Justice and Delinquency Prevention.

Billingham, R. E., and A. R. Sack (1987). Conflict Resolution Tactics and the Level of Emotional Commitment Among Unmarrieds. *Human Relations* 40:59-74.

Bishop, F. J. (1971). Children at Risk. *Medical Journal of Australia* 1:623-628.

Bjerregaard, B., and A. J. Lizotte (1995). Gun Ownership and Gang Membership. *Journal of Criminal Law and Criminology* 86(1):37-58.

Bjerregaard, B., and C. Smith (1993). Gender Differences in Gang Participation, Delinquency, and Substance Use. *Journal of Quantitative Criminology* 9(4):329-355.

Black, D. J., and A. J. Reiss Jr. (1979). Police Control of Juveniles. *American Sociological Review* 35:63-77.

Blechman, E. (1982). Are Children with One Parent at Psychological Risk? A Methodological Review. *Journal of Marriage and the Family* 44:179-195.

Block, C. R. (1993). Lethal Violence in the Chicago Latino Community. In A. V. Wilson (Ed.), *Homicide: The Victim/Offender Connection* (pp. 267-341). Cincinnati: Anderson.

Block, C. R., A. Christakos, A. Jacob, and R. Przybylski (1996). *Street Gangs and Crime: Patterns and Trends in Chicago*. Research Bulletin. Chicago: Criminal Justice Information Authority.

Block, R., and C. R. Block (1993). *Street Gang Crime in Chicago*. Research in Brief. Washington, DC: National Institute of Justice.

Blum, H. M., M. H. Boyle, and D. R. Offord (1988). Single-Parent Families: Child Psychiatric Disorder and School Performance. *Journal of the American Academy of Child and Adolescent Psychiatry* 27:214-219.

Blumstein, A. (1995). Youth Violence, Guns, and the Illicit-Drug Industry. *Journal of Criminal Law and Criminology* 86(1):10-36.

Blumstein, A. (1996). *Youth Violence, Guns, and Illicit Drug Markets*. Washington, DC: Office of Justice Programs.

Bolton, F. G., J. W. Reich, and S. E. Guiterres (1977). Delinquency Patterns in Maltreated Children and Siblings. *Victimology* 2:349-357.

Bouma, D. H. (1969). *Kids and Cops*. Grand Rapids, MI: William E. Eerdman Publishing Co.

Bowlby, J. (1951). *Maternal Care and Mental Health*. Geneva, Switzerland: World Health Organization.

Boyd, R., and P. J. Richerson (1985). *Culture and the Evolutionary Process*. Chicago: University of Chicago Press.

Brady, C. P., J. H. Bray, and L. Zeeb (1986). Behavior Problems of Clinic Children: Relation to Parental Marital Status, Age, and Sex of Child. *American Journal of Orthopsychiatry* 56:399-412.

Breed v. Jones (1975). 421 U.S. 519, 95 S. Ct. 1779.

Brier, N. (1995). Predicting Antisocial Behavior in Youngsters Displaying Poor Academic Achievement: A Review of Risk Factors. *Developmental and Behavioral Pediatrics* 16:271-276.

Briere, J., and N. A. Malamuth (1983). Predicting Self-Reported Likelihood of Sexually Abusive Behavior: Attitudinal versus Sexual Explanations. *Journal of Research in Personality* 17:315-323.

Brodbelt, S. (1983). College Dating and Violence. *College Student Journal* 17:273-277.

Brodzinsky, D. M. (1987). Looking at Adoption Through Rose-Colored Glasses: A Critique of Marquis and Detweiler's "Does Adoption Mean Different?" An Attributional Analysis. *Journal of Personality and Social Psychology* 52:394-398.

Brown, W. K. (1970). Black Female Gangs in Philadelphia. *International Journal of Offender Therapy and Comparative Criminology* 21(3):221-229.

Brownmiller, S. (1975). *Against Our Will: Men, Women, and Rape.* New York: Simon and Schuster.

Brustin, S. L. (1995). Legal Responses to Teen Dating Violence. *Family Law Quarterly* 29(2):331-337.

Bureau of Justice Statistics (2000a). *Correctional Populations in the United States, 1997.* Washington, DC: Office of Justice Programs.

Bureau of Justice Statistics (2000b). *Profile of State Prisoners Under Age 18, 1985-1997.* Special Report. Washington, DC: U.S. Department of Justice.

Burgess, A. W., C. R. Hartman, and A. McCormack (1987). Abused to Abuser: Antecedents of Socially Deviant Behaviors. *American Journal of Psychiatry* 14(4):1431-1436.

Burgess, R. L., and R. L. Akers (1966). A Differential Association-Reinforcement Theory of Criminal Behavior. *Social Problems* 14:128-147.

Burke, P. J., J. E. Stets, and M. A. Piroz-Good (1989). Gender Identity, Self-Esteem, and Physical and Sexual Abuse in Dating Relationships. In M. A. Piroz-Good and J. E. Stets (Eds.), *Violence in Dating Relationships: Emerging Social Issues* (pp. 172-193). New York: Praeger.

Bursik, R. J. Jr., and H. G. Grasmick (1996). The Use of Contextual Analysis in Models of Criminal Behavior. In J. D. Hawkins (Ed.), *Delinquency and Crime: Current Theories* (pp. 236-267). New York: Cambridge University Press.

Burt, C. (1925). *The Young Delinquent.* London: University of London Press.

Button, A. (1973). Some Antecedents of Felonious and Delinquent Behavior. *Journal of Child Clinical Psychology* 2(3):35-37.

Campbell, A. (1981). *Girl Delinquents.* New York: St. Martin's Press.

Campbell, A. (1991). *The Girls in the Gang,* Second Edition. Cambridge, MA: Basil Blackwell.

Carlson, B. (1987). Dating Violence: A Research Review and Comparison with Spousal Abuse. *Social Casework* 68(1):16-23.

Carpenter, C., B. Blassner, B. D. Johnson, and J. Loughlin (1988). *Kids, Drugs, and Crime.* Lexington, MA: Lexington Books.

Carter, R. M., and M. W. Klein (1976). *Back on the Streets.* Englewood Cliffs, NJ: Prentice-Hall.

Catalano, R. F., and J. D. Hawkins (1996). The Social Development Model: A Theory of Antisocial Behavior. In J. D. Hawkins (Ed.), *Delinquency and Crime: Current Theories* (pp. 149-188). New York: Cambridge University Press.

Cate, R. M., J. M. Henton, J. Koval, F. S. Christopher, and S. Lloyd (1982). Premarital Abuse: A Social Psychological Perspective. *Journal of Family Issues* 3:79-91.

Cavalli-Sforza, L. L., and M. W. Feldman (1981). *Cultural Transmission and Evolution: A Quantitative Approach.* Princeton, NJ: Princeton University Press.

Cernkovich, S. A., and P. C. Giordano (1979). A Comparative Analysis of Male and Female Delinquency. *Sociological Quarterly* 20(1):131-145.

Cernkovich, S. A., and P. C. Giordano (1992). School Bonding, Race, and Delinquency. *Criminology* 30(2):261-291.

Cernkovich, S. A., P. C. Giordano, and M. D. Pugh (1985). Chronic Offenders: The Missing Cases in Self-Reported Delinquency Research. *Journal of Criminal Law and Criminology* 76(3):705-732.

Chaiken, M. R. (2000). *Violent Neighborhoods, Violent Kids.* Washington, DC: Office of Juvenile Justice and Delinquency Prevention.

Chaiken, M. R., and B. D. Johnson (1988). *Characteristics of Different Types of Drug-Involved Offenders.* Washington, DC: Office of Justice Programs.

Chalk, R., and P. A. King (1998). Facing Up to Family Violence. *Issues in Science and Technology* 15(2):39.

Chandler, K. A., C. D. Chapman, M. R. Rand, and B. M. Taylor (1998). *Students' Reports of School Crime: 1989 and 1995.* Washington, DC: Office of Educational Research and Improvement.

Child Abuse Prevention, Adoption, and Family Services Act (1988). P.L. 100-294.

Child Abuse Prevention and Treatment and Adoption Reform Act (1978). P.L. No. 95-266, 92 Stat. 205.

Christiansen, K. O. (1977). Seriousness of Criminality and Concordance Among Danish Twins. In R. Hood (Ed.), *Crime, Criminology and Public Policy* (pp. 281-296). London: Heinemann.

Clinard, M. B. (1964). *Anomie and Deviant Behavior.* New York: Free Press.

Cloninger, R., and I. Gottesman (1987). Genetic and Environmental Factors in Antisocial Behavior Disorders. In S. Mednick, T. Moffitt, and S. Stack (Eds.), *The Causes of Crime: New Biological Approaches* (pp. 92-109). London: Cambridge University Press.

Cloward, R. A., and L. E. Ohlin (1960). *Delinquency and Opportunity.* New York: Free Press.

Coates, R. B. (1984). Appropriate Alternatives for the Violent Juvenile Offender. In R. Mathias, P. DeMuro, and R. Allison (Eds.), *Violent Juvenile Offenders: An Anthology.* San Francisco: National Council on Crime and Delinquency.

Cohen, A. K. (1955). *Delinquent Boys.* New York: Free Press.

Cohen, A. K. (1965). The Sociology of the Deviant Act: Anomie Theory and Beyond. *American Sociological Review* 30:5-14.

Cohen, A. K., G. F. Cole, and R. G. Bailey (1976). *Prison Violence.* Lexington, MA: D. C. Heath.

Cohen, A. K., and J. F. Short Jr. (1958). Research on Delinquent Subculture. *Journal of Social Issues* 14(3):20-37.

Cohen, M. (1998). The Monetary Value of Saving a High-Risk Youth. *Journal of Quantitative Criminology* 14(1):5-33.

Cole, S. (1975). The Growth of Scientific Knowledge: Theories of Deviance As a Case Study. In L. A. Coser (Ed.), *The Idea of Social Structure: Papers in Honor of Robert K. Merton* (pp. 175-220). New York: Harcourt Brace Jovanovich.

Collins, G. (1982). The Violent Child: Some Patterns Emerge. *The New York Times,* September 27, p. A. 3.

Commonwealth Fund, The (1993). First Comprehensive National Health Survey of American Woman Finds Them at Significant Risk. News release. July 14, New York.

Cooley, C. H. (1902). *Human Nature and the Social Order.* New York: Scribners.

Cornell, D. G. (1990). Prior Adjustment of Violent Juvenile Offenders. *Law and Human Behavior* 14:569-577.

Cornell, D. G. (1993). Juvenile Homicide: A Growing National Problem. *Behavioral Sciences and the Law* 11(Autumn):389-396.

Cortes, J. B., and F. M. Gatti (1972). *Delinquency and Crime: A Biopsychosocial Approach.* New York: Seminar Press.

Cottle, T. J. (1977). Children in Jail: Seven Lessons in American Justice. Boston: Beacon Press.

Crason, H. (1943). The Psychopath and the Psychopathic. *Journal of Criminal Psychopathology* 4:522-527.

Cressey, D. R. (1979). Fifty Years of Criminology: From Sociological Theory to Political Control. *Pacific Sociological Review* 22:451-480.

Curry, G. D. (1996). National Youth Gang Surveys: A Review of Methods and Findings. Unpublished Report. Tallahassee, FL: National Youth Gang Center.

Curry, G. D., R. A. Ball, and S. H. Decker (1996). Estimating the National Scope of Gang Crime From Law Enforcement Data. In C. R. Huff (Ed.), *Gangs in America* (pp. 21-36). Newbury Park, CA: Sage.

Curry, G. D., R. A. Ball, and R. J. Fox (1994). *Gang Crime and Law Enforcement Record Keeping.* Washington, DC: Office of Justice Programs.

Curry, G. D., and S. H. Decker (1998). *Confronting Gangs: Crime and Community.* Los Angeles: Roxbury.

Curry, G. D., and I. A. Spergel (1992). Gang Involvement and Delinquency Among Hispanic and African American Males. *Journal of Research in Crime and Delinquency* 29(3):273-291.

Curtis, G. C. (1963). Violence Breeds Violence—Perhaps? *American Journal of Psychiatry* 120:386-387.

Cyriaque, J. (1982). The Chronic Serious Offender: How Illinois Juveniles Match Up. Illinois Department of Corrections. *Illinois* 2:4-5.

Dalgaard, O. S., and E. Kringlen (1976). A Norwegian Twin Study of Criminality. *British Journal of Criminology* 16(3):213-233.

Danield, D., M. Gilula, and F. Ochberg (Eds.) (1970). *Violence and the Struggle for Existence.* Boston: Little, Brown.

Dannefer, D., and R. K. Schmitt (1982). Race and Juvenile Justice Processing in Court and Police Agencies. *American Journal of Sociology* 87(5):1113-1132.

Darwin, C. (1995). *The Origin of Species.* New York: Gramercy.

Davids, L. (1977). Delinquency Prevention Through Father Training: Some Observations and Proposals. In P. C. Friday and V. L. Stewart (Eds.), *Youth, Crime and Juvenile Justice: International Perspectives.* New York: Holt, Rinehart, and Winston.

Deal, J. E., and K. S. Wampler (1986). Dating Violence: The Primacy of Previous Experiences. *Journal of Social and Personal Relationships* 3(4):457-471.

Decker, S. H., and B. Van Winkle (1994). Slinging Dope: The Role of Gangs and Gang Members in Drug Sales. *Justice Quarterly* 11(4):583-604.

Decker, S. H., and B. Van Winkle (1996). *Life in the Gang: Family, Friends, and Violence.* New York: Cambridge University Press.

Denno, D. W. (1985). Sociological and Human Developmental Explanations of Crime: Conflict or Consensus? *Criminology* 23(4):711-741.

Denno, D. W. (1988). Human Biology and Criminal Responsibility: Free Will or Free Ride? *University of Pennsylvania Law Review* 137(2):615-671.

Deykin, E. Y. (1971). Life Functioning in Families of Delinquent Boys: An Assessment Model. *Social Services Review* 46(1):90-91.

DiLalla, L. F., and I. I. Gottesman (1991). Biological and Genetic Contributions to Violence-Widom's Untold Tale. *Psychological Bulletin* 109:125-129.

Dobash, R. E., and R. Dobash (1979). *Violence Against Wives.* New York: Free Press.

Dorfman, A. (1984). The Criminal Mind: Body Chemistry and Nutrition May Lie at the Roots of Crime. *Science Digest* 92(October):44-47.

Dugdale, R. L. (1877). *The Jukes: A Study in Crime, Pauperism, and Heredity.* New York: Putnam.

Durkheim, E. (1933). *The Division of Labor in Society.* New York: Free Press.

Easson, W. M., and R. M. Steinhilber (1961). Murderous Aggression by Children and Adolescents. *Archives of General Psychiatry* 4:1-9.

Eissler, R. S. (1949). Scapegoats of Society. In K R. Eissler (Ed.), *Searchlights on Delinquency.* New York: International University Press.

Elliot, D. S. (1994) Serious Violent Offenders: Onset, Developmental Course, and Termination—The American Society of Criminology 1993 Presidential Address. *Criminology* 32(1):1-21.

Elliot, D. S., and S. S. Ageton (1980). Reconciling Race and Class Differences in Self-Reported and Official Estimates of Delinquency. *American Sociological Review* 45(1):95-110.

Elliot, D., S. S. Ageton, and R. Canter (1979). An Integrated Theoretical Perspective on Delinquent Behavior. *Journal of Research in Crime and Delinquency* 16:3-27.

Elliot, D. S., D. Huizinga, and S. S. Ageton (1985). *Explaining Delinquency and Drug Use.* Beverly Hills: Sage.

Elliot, D. S., D. Huizinga, and S. Menard (1989). *Multiple Problem Youth: Delinquency, Substance Use and Mental Health Problems.* New York: Springer-Verlag.

Elliot, D. S., D. Huizinga, and B. Morse (1986). Self-Reported Violent Offending—A Descriptive Analysis of Juvenile Violent Offenders and Their Offending Careers. *Journal of Interpersonal Violence* 1(4):472-514.

Elliot, D. S., and H. Voss (1974). *Delinquency and Dropout.* Lexington, MA: Heath.

Ellis, L. (1982). Genetics and Criminal Behavior. *Criminology* 20:43-66.

Emerson, R. M. (1969). *Judging Delinquents: Context and Process in Juvenile Court.* Chicago: Aldine-Atherson.

Emery, R. E. (1982). Interpersonal Conflict and the Children of Discord and Divorce. *Psychological Bulletin* 93:310-330.

Erikson, K. (1962). Notes on the Sociology of Deviance. *Social Problems* 9:307-314.

Esbensen, F., and D. Huizinga (1993). Gangs, Drugs, and Delinquency in a Survey of Urban Youth. *Criminology* 31(4):565-587.

Esbensen, F., and D. W. Osgood (1997). *National Education of G.R.E.A.T.* Research in Brief. Washington, DC: National Institute of Justice.

Ewing, C. P. (1990). *Kids Who Kill.* New York: Avon Books.

Ewing, C. P. (1997). *Fatal Families: The Dynamics of Intrafamilial Homicide.* Thousand Oaks, CA: Sage.

Eysench, H. J. (1973). *The Inequality of Man.* San Diego: Edits Publishers.

Farnworth, M. (1984). Family Structure, Family Attributes, and Delinquency in a Sample of Low-Income, Minority Males and Females. *Journal of Youth and Adolescence* 13:349-364.

Farnworth, M., and M. J. Leiber (1989). Strain Theory Revisited: Economic Goals, Educational Means, and Delinquency. *American Sociological Review* 54:263-274.

Farrington, D. P. (1978). The Family Backgrounds of Aggressive Youths. In L. Hersov, M. Berger, and D. Shaffer (Eds.), *Aggression and Antisocial Behavior in Childhood and Adolescence* (pp. 173-193). Oxford: Pergamon.

Farrington, D. P. (1990). Implications of Criminal Career Research for the Prevention of Offending. *Journal of Adolescence* 13(2):93-113.

Farrington, D. P. (1991). Childhood Aggression and Adult Violence: Early Precursors and Later Life Outcomes. In D. J. Peter and K. H. Rubin (Eds.), *The Development and Treatment of Childhood Aggression* (pp. 5-29). Hillsdale, NJ: Erlbaum.

Farrington, D. P. (1996). The Explanation and Prevention of Youthful Offending. In J. D. Hawkins (Ed.), *Delinquency and Crime: Current Theories* (pp. 68-129). New York: Cambridge University Press.

Farrington, D. P., G. Grundy, and D. J. West (1975). The Familial Transmission of Criminality. *Medicine, Science, and the Law* 15:177-186.

Farrington, D. P., R. Loeber, M. Southamer-Loeber, W. B. Van Kammen, and L. Schmidt (1996). Self-Reported Delinquency and a Combined Delinquency Seriousness Scale Based on Boys, Mothers, and Teachers; Concurrent and Predictive Validity for African-Americans and Caucasians. *Criminology* 34(4):493-514.

Federal Bureau of Investigation (2000). *Crime in the United States: Uniform Crime Reports 1999*. Washington, DC: Government Printing Office.

Felner, R. D., and A. M. Adam (1988). The School Transitional Environment Project: An Ecological Intervention and Evaluation. In R. Price, E. Cowen, R. Lorion, and J. Ramos-McKay (Eds.), *Fourteen Ounces of Prevention: A Casebook for Practitioners* (pp. 111-122). Washington, DC: American Psychological Association.

Felner, R. D., M. Ginter, and J. Primavera (1982). Primary Prevention During School Transitions: Social Support and Environmental Structure. *American Journal of Community Psychology* 10:277-290.

Felson, R. B., and S. F. Messner (1996). To Kill or Not to Kill? Lethal Outcomes in Injurious Attacks. *Criminology* 34(4):519-545.

Ferguson, T. (1952). *The Young Delinquent in His Social Setting*. London: Oxford University Press.

Ferracuti, F., and M. Wolfgang (1970). *Violence in Sardina*. Rome: Bulzoni.

Ferster, E. Z., and T. F. Courtless (1969). The Beginning of Juvenile Justice, Police Practices, and the Juvenile Offender. *Vanderbilt Law Review* 22:598-601.

Finkelhor, D., G. Hotaling, and A. Sedlak (1990). *Missing, Abducted, Runaway, and Thrownaway Children in America: First Report*. Washington, DC: Office of Juvenile Justice and Delinquency Prevention.

Finkelhor, D., and R. Ormrod (2000). *Characteristics of Crimes Against Juveniles*. Washington, DC: Office of Juvenile Justice and Delinquency Prevention.

Fishbein, D. H. (1996). Biological Perspectives in Criminology. In D. G. Rojek and G. F. Jensen (Eds.), *Exploring Delinquency: Causes and Control* (pp. 102-108). Los Angeles: Roxbury.

Flowers, R. B. (1986). *Children and Criminality: The Child as Victim and Perpetrator*. Westport, CT: Greenwood.

Flowers, R. B. (1988). *Minorities and Criminality*. Westport, CT: Greenwood.

Flowers, R. B. (1989). *Demographics and Criminality: The Characteristics of Crime in America*. Westport, CT: Greenwood.

Flowers, R. B. (1990). *The Adolescent Criminal: An Examination of Today's Juvenile Offender*. Jefferson, NC: McFarland.

Flowers, R. B. (1994). *The Victimization and Exploitation of Women and Children: A Study of Physical, Mental and Sexual Maltreatment in the United States*. Jefferson, NC: McFarland.

Flowers, R. B. (1995). *Female Crime, Criminals, and Cellmates: An Exploration of Female Criminality and Delinquency*. Jefferson, NC: McFarland.

Flowers, R. B. (1998). *The Prostitution of Women and Girls*. Jefferson, NC: McFarland.

Flowers, R. B. (1999). *Drugs, Alcohol, and Criminality in American Society*. Jefferson, NC: McFarland.

Flowers, R. B. (2000). *Domestic Crimes, Family Violence, and Child Abuse: A Study of Contemporary American Society*. Jefferson, NC: McFarland.

Flowers, R. B. (2001a). *Runaway Kids and Teenage Prostitution: America's Lost, Abandoned, and Sexually Exploited Children*. Westport, CT: Greenwood.

Flowers, R. B. (2001b). *Sex Crimes, Predators, Perpetrators, Prostitutes, and Victims: An Examination of Sexual Criminality and Victimization*. Springfield, IL: Charles C Thomas.

Flowers, R. B., and H. Loraine Flowers (2001). *Murders in the United States: Crimes, Killers, and Victims of the Twentieth Century*. Jefferson, NC: McFarland.

Fontana, V. J. (1964). *The Maltreated Child: The Maltreatment Syndrome in Children*. Springfield, IL: Charles C Thomas.

Frazier, C. E. (1976). *Theoretical Approaches to Deviance: An Evaluation*. Columbus, OH: Charles E. Merrill.

Freedman, J. L. (1986). Television Violence and Aggression: A Rejoiner. *Psychological Bulletin* 100(3):372-378.

Freeman, M.A. (1979). *Violence in the Home*. Farnborough, England: Saxon House.

Freud, S. (1933). *New Introductory Lectures on Psychoanalysis*. New York: W. W. Norton.

Gamache, D. (1998). Domination and Control; The Social Context of Dating Violence. In B. Levy (Ed.), *Dating Violence: Young Women in Danger*. Seattle: Seal Press.

Geismar, L. L., and K. M. Wood (1986). *Family and Delinquency: Resocializing the Young Offender*. New York: Human Sciences Press.

Geller, A., and H. MacLean (1993). Substance Abuse. In H. MacLean (Ed.), *Every Woman's Health: The Complete Guide to Body and Mind* (pp. 381-414), Fifth Edition. Garden City, NY: Guild America Books.

Gelles, R. J. (1972). *The Violent Home: A Study of the Physical Aggression Between Husbands and Wives*. Beverly Hills: Sage.

Gelles, R. J. (1978). Violence Toward Children in the United States. *American Journal of Orthopsychiatry* 48(4):580-592.

Gelles, R. J., and M. A. Straus (1979). Determinants of Violence in the Family: Toward a Theoretical Integration. In W. R. Burr, R. Hill, F. I. Nye, and I. L. Reiss (Eds.), *Contemporary Theories About the Family* (pp. 549-581). New York: Free Press.

Gibbons, T. C. N., and A. Walker (1956). *Cruel Parents*. London: Institute for the Study and Treatment of Delinquency.

Gibson, H. B. (1969). Early Delinquency in Relation to Broken Homes. *Journal of Child Psychology* 10:195-204.

Gil, D. G. (1970). *Violence Against Children: Physical Child Abuse in the United States.* Cambridge, MA: Harvard University Press.

Ginsberg, C., and L. Loffredo (1993). Violence-Related Attitudes and Behaviors of High School Students—New York City, 1992. *Morbidity and Mortality Weekly Report* 42(39):773-777.

Giordano, P. C. (1978). Girls, Guys, and Gangs: The Changing Social Context of Female Delinquency. *Journal of Criminal Law and Criminology* 69(1):126-132.

Girschick, L. (1993). Chicago Department of Public Health. Chicago, IL.

Glueck, S., and E. T. Glueck (1950). *Unraveling Juvenile Delinquency.* Cambridge, MA: Harvard University Press.

Glueck, S., and E. T. Glueck (1956). *Physique and Delinquency.* New York: Harper and Row.

Glueck, S., and E. T. Glueck (1962). *Family Environments and Delinquency.* Boston: Houghton Mifflin.

Glueck, S., and E. T. Glueck (1968). *Delinquents and Non-Delinquents in Perspective.* Cambridge, MA: Harvard University Press.

Goddard, H. H. (1914). *Feeblemindedness, Its Causes and Consequences.* New York: Macmillan.

Goetting, A. (1989). Patterns of Homicide Among Children. *Criminal Justice and Behavior* 16:63-80.

Gold, M., and D. J. Reimer (1975). Changing Patterns of Delinquent Behavior Among Americans 13 Through 16 Years Old: 1967-72. *Crime and Delinquency* 7:483-517.

Goldman, N. (1969). The Differential Selection of Juvenile Offenders for Court Appearance. In W. Chambliss (Ed.), *Crime and the Legal Process* (pp. 264-290). New York: McGraw-Hill.

Goldstein, P. J. (1979). *Prostitution and Drugs.* Lexington, MA: Lexington Books.

Goodchilds, J. B., and G. L. Zellman (1984). Sexual Signaling and Sexual Aggression in Adolescent Relationships. In N. Malamuth and E. Donnerstein (Eds.), *Pornography and Sexual Aggression* (pp. 233-243). Orlando, FL: Academic Press.

Goring, C. (1913). *The English Convict.* Montclair, NJ: Patterson Smith.

Gorman, C. (1996). Liquid X. *Time* 148(9):64.

Gottfredson, D. C., N. L. Karweit, and G. D. Gottfredson (1989). *Reducing Disorderly Behavior in Middle Schools.* Report No. 37. Baltimore: Center for Research on Elementary and Middle Schools, John Hopkins University.

Gottfredson, G. D. (1987). Peer Group Interventions to Reduce the Risk of Delinquent Behavior: A Selective Review and a New Evaluation. *Criminology* 25(3):671-714.

Gottfredson, G. D., and D. C. Gottfredson (1985). *Victimization in Schools.* New York: Plenum.

Gottfredson, M. R., and T. Hirschi (1996). Biological Positivism. In D. G. Rojek and G. F. Jensen (Eds.), *Exploring Delinquency: Causes and Control* (pp. 109-119). Los Angeles: Roxbury.

Gove, W. R., and R. D. Crutchfield (1982). The Family and Juvenile Delinquency. *Sociological Quarterly* 23(Summer):301-319.

Gray H., and V. Foshee (1997). Adolescent Dating Violence: Differences Between One-Sided and Mutually Violent Profiles. *Journal of Interpersonal Violence* 12(1):126-141.

Gray-Ray, P., and M. C. Ray (1990). Juvenile Delinquency in the Black Community. *Youth and Society* 22(1):67-84.

Greenberg, D. F. (1977). Delinquency and the Age Structure of Society. *Contemporary Crises* 1(April):189-224.

Hagan, J. A., R. Gillis, and J. Simpson (1985). The Class Structure of Gender and Delinquency: Toward a Power-Control Theory of Common Delinquent Behavior. *American Journal of Sociology* 90(6):1151-1178.

Hagan, J. A., and R. Peterson (1995). Criminal Inequality in America: Patterns and Consequences. In J. Hagan and R. Peterson (Eds.), *Crime and Inequality* (pp. 14-36). Stanford, CA: Stanford University Press.

Hahn, P. H. (1984). *The Juvenile Offender and the Law*, Third Edition. Cincinnati: W. H. Anderson Co.

Hakeem, M. (1958). A Critique of the Psychiatric Approach. In J. S. Roucek (Ed.), *Juvenile Delinquency* (pp. 89-95). New York: Philosophical Library.

Hamparian, D. (1978). *The Violent Few*. Lexington, MA: Lexington Books.

Hardman, D. G. (1969). Small Town Gangs. *Journal of Criminal Law, Criminology, and Police Science* 60(2):176-177.

Harlan, S., L. L. Rodgers, and B. Slattery (1981). *Male and Female Adolescent Prostitution: Huckleberry House Sexual Minority Youth Services Project*. Washington, DC: Department of Health and Human Services.

Haskell, M. R., and L. Yablonsky (1974a). *Crime and Delinquency*, Second Edition. Chicago: Rand McNally.

Haskell, M. R., and L. Yablonsky (1974b). *Juvenile Delinquency*. Chicago: Rand McNally.

Hawkins, D. F. (1995). Ethnicity, Race, and Crime: A Review of Selected Studies. In D. F. Hawkins (Ed.), *Ethnicity, Race and Crime: Perspectives Across Time and Place* (pp. 11-45). Albany, NY: State University of New York Press.

Hawkins, D. F., J. H. Laub, and J. L. Lauritsen (1998). Race, Ethnicity, and Serious Juvenile Offending. In R. Loeber and D. P. Farrington (Eds.), *Serious and Violent Juvenile Offenders: Risk Factors and Successful Interventions* (pp. 30-46). Thousand Oaks, CA: Sage.

Hawkins, D. F., J. H. Laub, J. L. Lauritsen, and L. Cothern (2000). *Race, Ethnicity and Serious Juvenile Offending*. Washington, DC: Office of Juvenile Justice and Delinquency Prevention.

Hawkins, J. D. (1996). *Delinquency and Crime: Current Theories.* New York: Cambridge University Press.

Hawkins, J. D., and R. F. Catalano (1992). *Communities That Care.* San Francisco: Jossey-Bass.

Hawkins, J. D., R. F. Catalano, and J. Y. Miller (1992). Risk and Protective Factors for Alcohol and Other Drug Problems in Adolescence and Early Adulthood: Implications for Substance Abuse Prevention. *Psychological Bulletin* 112(1):64-105.

Hawkins, J. D., T. Herrenkohl, D. P. Farrington, D. Brewer, R. F. Catalano, and T. W. Harachi (1998). A Review of Predictors of Youth Violence. In D. P. Farrington (Ed.), *Serious and Violent Juvenile Offenders: Risk Factors and Successful Interventions* (pp. 106-146). Thousand Oaks, CA: Sage.

Healy, W., and A. F. Bronner (1936). *New Light on Delinquency and Its Treatment.* New Haven: Yale University Press.

Heide, K. M. (1992). *Why Kids Kill Parents: Child Abuse and Adolescent Homicide.* Columbus: Ohio State Press.

Helfer, R. E. (1975). *The Diagnostic Process and Treatment Programs.* Washington, DC: Office of Child Development.

Helfer, R. E., and C. H. Kempe (1976). *Child Abuse and Neglect: The Family and the Community.* Cambridge, MA: Ballinger.

Henton, J. M., R. M. Cate, J. Koval, S. Lloyd, and F. S. Christopher (1983). Romance and Violence in Dating Relationships. *Journal of Family Issues* 4(3):467-482.

Hersch, P. (1988). Coming of Age on City Streets. *Psychology Today* 22(1):28-30.

Hershorn, M., and A. Rosenbaum (1985). Children of Marital Violence: A Closer Look at the Unintended Victims. *American Journal of Orthopsychiatry* 55(2):260-266.

Hindelang, M. (1978). Race and Involvement in Common Law Personal Crimes. *American Sociological Review* 43(1):93-109.

Hindelang, M. (1981). Variations in Sex-Race-Age-Specific Incidence Rates of Offending. *American Sociological Review* 46(4):461-474.

Hindelang, M., T. Hirschi, and J. G. Weis (1981). *Measuring Delinquency.* Beverly Hills: Sage.

Hippchen, J. (1978). *Ecologic-Biochemical Approaches to Treatment of Delinquents and Criminals.* New York: Van Nostrand Reinhold.

Hirschi, T. (1969). *Causes of Delinquency.* Berkeley: University of California Press.

Hirschi, T. (1975). Labeling Theory and Juvenile Delinquency: An Assessment of the Evidence. In W. R. Gove (Ed.), *The Labeling of Deviance: Evaluating a Perspective* (pp. 181-203). New York: John Wiley.

Hirschi, T., and M. Hindelang (1977). Intelligence and Delinquency: A Revisionist Review. *American Sociological Review* 42(August):571-586.

Holzman, H. R. (1979). Learning Disabilities and Juvenile Delinquency: Biological and Sociological Theories. In C. R. Jeffrey (Ed.), *Biology and Crime*. Beverly Hills: Sage, 1979.

Hooton, E. A. (1939). *Crime and the Man*. Cambridge, MA: Harvard University Press.

Howell, J. C. (1998). *Youth Gangs: An Overview*. Washington, DC: Office of Juvenile Justice and Delinquency Prevention.

Howell, J. C., and J. P. Lynch (2000). *Youth Gangs in Schools*. Washington, DC: Office of Juvenile Justice and Delinquency Prevention.

Howells, K., M. McEwan, B. Jones, and C. Mathews (1983). Social Evaluations of Mental Illness in Relation to Criminal Behavior. *British Journal of Social Psychology* 22:165-166.

Howing, P. T., J. S. Wodarski, P. D. Kurtz, J. M. Gaudin, Jr., and E. N. Herbst (1990). Child Abuse and Delinquency: The Empirical and Theoretical Links. *Social Work* 5:244-249.

Hughes, H. M. (1988). Psychological and Behavioral Correlates of Family Violence in Child Witnesses and Victims. *American Journal of Orthopsychiatry* 58(1):77-90.

Huizinga, D., and D. Elliot (1986). Reassessing the Reliability and Validity of Self-Report Delinquency Measures. *Journal of Quantitative Criminology* 2(4):293-327.

Huizinga, D., R. Loeber, T. P. Thornberry, and L. Cothern (2000). *Co-Occurrence of Delinquency and Other Problem Behaviors*. Washington, DC: Office of Juvenile Justice and Delinquency Prevention.

Hunner, R. J., and Y. E. Walker (Eds.) (1981). *Exploring the Relationship Between Child Abuse and Delinquency* (pp. 117-164). Montclair, NJ: Allanheld, Osmun and Co.

Hutchings, B., and S. A. Mednick (1975). Registered Criminality in the Adoptive and Biological Parents of Registered Male Criminal Adoptees. In R. R. Fiene, D. Rosenthal, and H. Brill (Eds.), *Genetic Research in Psychiatry* (pp. 105-122). Baltimore: John Hopkins University Press.

Hutchings, B., and S. A. Mednick (1977). Criminality in Adoptees and Their Adoptive and Biological Parents: A Pilot Study. In S. Mednick and K. O. Christiansen (Eds.), *Biological Bases of Criminal Behavior* (pp. 127-142). New York: Gardner.

Hutson, H. R., D. Anglin, and M. Eckstein (1996). Drive-by Shootings by Violent Street Gangs in Los Angeles: A Five-Year Review from 1989 to 1993. *Academic Emergency Medicine* 3:300-303.

Hutson, H. R., D. Anglin, D. N. Kyriacou, J. Hart, and K. Spears (1995). The Epidemic of Gang-Related Homicides in Los Angeles County from 1979 through 1994. *Journal of the American Medical Association* 274(13):1031-1036.

Hutson, H. R., D. Anglin, and M. J. Pratts (1994). Adolescents and Children Injured or Killed in Drive-By Shootings in Los Angeles. *New England Journal of Medicine* 330:324-327.

In re Gault (1967). 387 U.S. 1, 87 S. Ct. 1428.

In re Winship (1970). 397 U.S. 358, 90 S. Ct. 1068.

Inciardi, J. A. (1986). *The War on Drugs: Heroin, Cocaine, Crime, and Public Policy.* Palo Alto, CA: Mayfield.

Inciardi, J. A., and A. E. Pottieger (1991). Kids, Crack, and Crime. *Journal of Drug Issues* 21:257-270.

Institute of Medicine (1994). *Reducing Risks for Mental Disorders: Frontiers for Preventive Invention Research.* Washington, DC: National Academy Press.

James. J. (1980). *Entrance into Juvenile Prostitution.* Washington, DC: National Institute of Mental Health.

Jasinski, J. L., and L. M. Williams (Eds.) (1998). *Partner Violence: A Comprehensive Review of 20 Years of Research.* Thousand Oaks, CA: Sage.

Jensen, G. F. (1973). Inner Containment and Delinquency. *Journal of Law and Criminology* 64:464-470.

Jensen, G. F., and D. Brownfield (1983). Parents and Drugs: Specifying the Consequences of Attachment. *Criminology* 21(4):543-554.

Johnson, A. M. (1949). Sanctions for Superego Lacunae of Adolescents. In K. R. Eissler (Ed.), *Searchlights on Delinquency* (pp. 225-245). New York: International University Press.

Johnson, A. M., and E. C. Burke (1955). Parental Permissiveness and Fostering in Child Rearing and Their Relationships to Juvenile Delinquency. *Proceedings of the Staff Meetings of the Mayo Clinic* 30:557-565.

Johnson, B. D. (1973). *Marijuana Users and Drug Subcultures.* New York: John Wiley and Sons.

Johnson, B. D., E. Wish, and D. Huizinga (1986). The Concentration of Delinquent Offending: The Contribution of Serious Drug Involvement to High Rate Delinquency. In B. D. Johnson and E. Wish (Eds.), *Crime Rates Among Drug Abusing Offenders* (pp. 106-143). New York: Interdisciplinary Research Center.

Johnson, J. J. (1992). *Teen Prostitution.* Danbury, CT: Franklin Watts.

Johnson, R. E. (1979). *Juvenile Delinquency and Its Origins.* London: Cambridge University Press.

Johnston, L. D., P. M. O'Malley, and J. G. Bachman (1999). *National Survey Results on Drug Use From the Monitoring the Future Study, 1975-1998. Volume 1: Secondary Students.* Rockville, MD: National Institute on Drug Abuse.

Johnston, L. D., P. M. O'Malley, and J. G. Bachman (2000a). *The Monitoring the Future National Survey Results on Adolescent Drug Use: Overview of Key Findings, 1999.* Rockville, MD: National Institute on Drug Abuse.

Johnston, L. D., P. M. O'Malley, and J. G. Bachman (2000b). *National Survey Results on Drug Use from the Monitoring the Future Study, 1975-1999. Volume 1: Secondary School Students.* Rockville, MD: National Institute on Drug Abuse.

Jordan, M. (1984). More Juveniles Being Tried As Adults. *The Washington Post,* December 30, p. A6.

Jung, R. S., and L. A. Jason (1988). Firearm Violence and the Effects of Gun Control Legislation. *American Journal of Community Psychology* 16(4):515-524.

Justice, B., and R. Justice (1976). *The Abusing Family*. New York: Human Services Press.

Juvenile Justice and Delinquency Prevention Act (1974). P.L. 93-415.

Kanin, E. J. (1957). Male Aggression in Dating-Courtship Relations. *American Journal of Sociology* 63:197-204.

Kanin, E. J., and S. R. Parcell (1977). Sexual Aggression: A Second Look at the Offended Female. *Archives of Sexual Behavior* 6:67-76.

Kann, L., S. A. Kinchen, B. I. Williams, J. G. Ross, R. Lowry, J. A. Grunbaum, and L. J. Kolbe (2000). Youth Risk Behavior Surveillance—United States, 1999. CDC Surveillance Summaries. *Morbidity and Mortality Weekly Report* 49 No. SS-5. Washington, DC: Government Printing Office.

Kantor, G. K., and N. L. Asdigian (1996). When Women Are Under the Influence: Does Drinking or Drug Use by Women Provoke Beatings by Men? In M. Galanter (Ed.), *Recent Developments in Alcoholism* (pp. 315-336). New York: Plenum.

Kantor, G. K., and J. L. Jasinski (Eds.) (1998). Dynamics and Risk Factors in Partner Violence. In J. L. Jasinski, and L. M. Williams (Eds.), *Partner Violence: A Comprehensive Review of 20 Years of Research* (pp. 1-43). Thousand Oaks, CA: Sage.

Kelly, D. H. (1971). School Failure, Academic Self-Evaluation, and School Avoidance and Deviant Behavior. *Youth and Society* 2:489-503.

Kempe, C. H., and R. E. Helfer (1972). *Helping the Battered Child and His Family*. Philadelphia: J. B. Lippincott.

Kennedy, D. M. (1998). Pulling Levers: Getting Deterrence Right. *National Institute of Justice Journal* 7:2-8.

Kennedy, D. M., A. M. Piehl, and A. A. Braga (1996). Youth Violence in Boston: Gun Markets, Serious Youth Offenders, and a Use-Reduction Strategy. *Law and Contemporary Problems* 59:147-196. Special Issue.

Kent v. United States (1966). 383 U.S. 541, 86 S. Ct. 1045.

Keseredy, W. S. (1988). Women Abuse in Dating Relationships: The Relevance of Social Support Theory. *Journal of Family Violence* 3(1):1-14.

King, C. H. (1975). The Ego and the Integration of Violence in Homicidal Youth. *American Journal of Orthopsychiatry* 45:134-145.

Klein, M. W. (1969). Gang Cohesiveness, Delinquency, and a Street-Work Program. *Journal of Research in Crime and Delinquency* 6:135-166.

Klein, M. W. (1995). *The American Street Gang: Its Nature, Prevalence, and Control*. New York: Oxford University Press.

Klein, N. C., J. F. Alexander, and B. V. Parsons (1977). Impact of Family Systems Intervention on Recidivism and Sibling Delinquency: A Model of Primary Prevention and Program Evaluation. *Journal of Consulting and Clinical Psychology* 45:469-474.

Kletschka, H. D. (1966). Violent Behavior Associated with Brain Tumors. *Minnesota Medicine* 49:1835-1855.

Kluegel, J. R., and E. R. Smith (1986). *Beliefs About Inequality*. New York: Aldine Gruyter.

Kolvin, I., F. J. Miller, M. Fleeting, and P. A. Kolvin (1988). Social and Parenting Factors Affecting Criminal-Offense Rates: Findings from the Newcastle Thousand Family Study (1947-1980). *British Journal of Psychiatry* 152:80-90.

Koski, P. R. (1988). Family Violence and Nonfamily Deviance: Taking Stock of the Literature. *Marriage and Family Review* 12:23-46.

Koss, M. P. (1985). The Hidden Rape Victim: Personality, Attitudinal, and Situational Characteristics. *Psychology of Women Quarterly* 9:193-212.

Koss, M. P. (1988). Hidden Rape: Sexual Aggression and Victimization in a National Sample of Students in Higher Education. In A. W. Burgess (Ed.), *Rape and Sexual Assault II* (pp. 3-25). New York: Garland.

Koss, M. P., C. A. Gidycz, and N. Wisniewski (1987). The Scope of Rape: Incidence and Prevalence of Sexual Aggression and Victimization in a National Sample of Higher Education Students. *Journal of Consulting and Clinical Psychology* 55(2):167-170.

Koss, M. P., and K. E. Leonard (1984). Sexually Aggressive Men. In N. A. Malamuth and E. Donnerstein (Eds.), *Pornography and Sexual Aggression* (pp. 173-183). Orlando, FL: Academic Press.

Kozel, N. J., and R. L. DuPont (1977). *Criminal Charges and Drug Use Patterns of Arrestees in the District of Columbia*. Rockville, MD: National Institute on Drug Abuse.

Kratcoski, P. C. (1984). Perspectives in Intrafamily Violence. *Human Relations* 37(8):443-454.

Kratcoski, P. C., and L. D. Kratcoski (1980). *Juvenile Delinquency*, Second Edition. Englewood Cliffs, NJ: Prentice-Hall.

Kratcoski, P. C., and L. D. Kratcoski (1986). *Juvenile Delinquency*, Second Edition. Englewood, NJ: Prentice-Hall.

Kroupa, S. E. (1988). Perceived Parental Acceptance and Female Juvenile Delinquency. *Adolescence* 23(89):171-185.

Kruttschmitt, C., L. Heath, and D. A. Ward (1986). Family Violence, Television Viewing Habits, and Other Adolescent Experiences Related to Violent Criminal Behavior. *Criminology* 24(2):235-267.

Kuehl, S. J. (1998). Legal Remedies for Teen Dating Violence. In B. Levy (Ed.), *Dating Violence: Young Women in Danger* (pp. 209-220). Seattle: Seal Press.

LaFree, G. (1995). Race and Crime Trends in the United States, 1946-1990. In D. F. Hawkins (Ed.), *Ethnicity, Race, and Crime: Perspectives Across Time and Place* (pp. 169-193). Albany, NY: State University of New York Press.

Lane, K. E., and P. A. Gwartney-Gibbs (1985). Violence in the Context of Dating and Sex. *Journal of Family Issues* 6(1):45-49.

Lane, T. W., and G. E. Davis (1987). Child Maltreatment and Juvenile Delinquency: Does a Relationship Exist? In J. D. Burchard and S. N. Burchard (Eds.), *Prevention of Delinquent Behavior* (pp. 122-138). Newbury Park, CA: Sage.

Laner, M. R. (1983). Courtship Abuse and Aggression: Contextual Aspects. *Sociological Spectrum* 3:69-83.

Laner, M. R. (1989). Competition and Combativeness in Courtship: Reports from Men. *Journal of Family Violence* 4(1):47-62.

Laner, M. R., and J. Thompson (1982). Abuse and Aggression in Courting Couples. *Deviant Behavior* 3:229-244.

Lange, J. (1931). *Crime As Destiny*. London: George Allen and Unurn.

Langley, R., and R. C. Levy (1977). *Wife Beating: The Silent Crisis*. New York: E. P. Dutton.

Larson, C. J. (1984). *Crime, Justice, and Society*. Bayside, NY: General-Hall.

Lasseter, D. (1998). *Killer Kids*. New York: Pinnacle.

Laury, G. V. (1970). The Battered Child Syndrome: Parental Motivation, Clinical Aspects. *Bulletin of the New York Academy of Medicine* 46(9):678-685.

LeBlanc, M. (1980). Delinquency as an Epiphenomenon of Adolescence. In R. R. Corrado, M. LeBlanc, and J. Trepanier (Eds.), *Current Issues in Juvenile Justice* (pp. 31-39). Toronto: Butterworth.

Lees, J. P., and L. J. Newson (1954). Family or Sibship Position and Some of Juvenile Delinquency. *British Journal of Delinquency* 5:46-55.

LeFlore, L. (1988). Delinquent Youths and Family. *Adolescence* 23(91):629-642.

Lemert, E. (1967). *Human Deviance, Social Programs, and Social Control*. Englewood Cliffs, NJ: Prentice-Hall.

Leventhal, J. M. (1999). The Challenges of Recognizing Child Abuse: Seeing Is Believing. *Journal of the American Medical Association* 281(7):657.

Levy, B. (Ed.) (1998). *Dating Violence: Young Women in Danger*. Seattle: Seal Press.

Levy, B., and K. Lobel (1998). Lesbian Teens in Abusive Relationships. In B. Levy (Ed.), *Dating Violence: Young Women in Danger* (pp. 203-208). Seattle: Seal Press.

Lewis, D. O., J. H. Pincus, B. Bard, E. Richardson, L. S. Prichep, M. Feldman, and C. Yeager (1988). Neuropsychiatric, Psychoeducational, and Family Characteristics of 14 Juveniles Condemned to Death in the United States. *American Journal of Psychiatry* 145(5):585-589.

Lewis, D. O., S. S. Shanok, and D. A. Balla (1979). Prenatal Difficulties, Head to Face Trauma, and Child Abuse in the Medical Histories of Serious Youthful Offenders. *American Journal of Psychiatry* 136:419-423.

Light, R. J. (1973). Abused and Neglected Children in America: A Study of Alternative Politics. *Harvard Educational Review* 143:574.

Linden, E., and J. C. Hacker (1973). Affective Ties and Delinquency. *Pacific Sociological Review* 16(1):27-46.

Liska, A. E., and M. D. Reed (1985). Ties to Conventional Institutions and Delinquency: Estimating Reciprocal Effects. *American Sociological Review* 50(August):547-560.

Lizotte, A. J., J. M. Tesorio, T. P. Thornberry, and M. D. Krohn (1994). Patterns of Adolescent Firearms Ownership and Use. *Justice Quarterly* 11(1):51-74.

Lloyd, R. (1976). *For Money or Love: Boy Prostitution in America*. New York: Ballantine.

Loeber, R., and D. P. Farrington (1998). *Never Too Early, Never Too Late: Risk Factors and Successful Interventions for Serious and Violent Juvenile Offenders*. Thousand Oaks: Sage.

Loeber, R., and M. Stouthamer-Loeber (1986). Family Factors As Correlates and Predictors of Juvenile Conduct Problems and Delinquency. In M. Tonry and N. Morris (Eds.), *Crime and Justice: An Annual Review of Research* (pp. 219-337). Vol. 7. Chicago: University of Chicago Press.

Loeber, R., and T. Dishion (1983). Early Predictors of Male Delinquency: A Review. *Psychological Bulletin* 94:68-99.

Loeber, R., and T. J. Dishion (1984). Boys Who Fight at Home and School: Conditions Influencing Cross-Setting Consistency. *Journal of Consulting and Clinical Psychology* 52(5):759-768.

Loeber, R., A. W. Weiher, and C. Smith (1991). The Relationship Between Family Interaction and Delinquency and Substance Use. In D. Huizinga, R. Loeber, and T. P. Thornberry (Eds.), *Urban Delinquency and Substance Abuse: Technical Report*. Vol. 1. Washington, DC: Office of Juvenile Justice and Delinquency.

Loehlin, J. C., L. Willerman, and J. M. Horn (1987). Personality Resemblance in Adoptive Families: A 10-Year Follow-Up. *Journal of Personality and Social Psychology* 53(5):961-969.

Lombroso, C. (1918). *Crime, Its Causes and Remedies*. Boston: Little, Brown.

Lombroso, C., and W. Ferrero (1972). *Criminal Man*. Montclair, NJ: Patterson Smith. Originally titled *L'Uormo Delinquents* in its 1876 publication.

Lopez, L. (1989). *Gangs in Denver*. Denver: Denver Public Schools.

Luckenbill, D. F., and D. P. Doyle (1989). Structural Position and Violence: Developing a Cultural Explanation. *Criminology* 27(3):419-436.

Lundberg-Love, P., and R. Geffner (1989). Date Rape: Prevalence, Risk Factors and a Proposed Model. In M. A. Piroz-Good and J. E. Stets (Eds.), *Violence in Dating Relationships: Emerging Social Issues* (pp. 169-184). New York: Praeger.

Lundman, R. J., R. E. Sykes, and J. P. Clark (1980). Police Control of Juveniles: A Replication. In R. J. Lundman (Ed.), *Police Behavior: A Sociological Perspective*. New York: Oxford Press.

Maguin, E., and R. Loeber (1996). Academic Performance and Delinquency. In M. Tonry (Ed.), *Crime and Justice: A Review of Research* (pp. 145-264). Vol. 2. Chicago: University of Chicago Press.

Mahoney, A. R. (1974). The Effect of Labeling upon Youths in the Juvenile Justice System: A Review of the Evidence. *Law and Society Review* 8(4):583-614.

Mahoney, E. R., M. Shively, and M. Traw (1985). Sexual Coercion and Assault: Male Macho and Female Chance. *Sexual Coercion and Assault* 1(1):2-7.

Makepeace, J. M. (1981). Courtship Violence Among College Students. *Family Relations* 30:97-102.

Makepeace, J. M. (1986). Gender Differences in Courtship Violence Victimization. *Family Relations* 36:383-388.

Makepeace, J. M. (1988). The Severity of Courtship Violence Injuries and Individual Precautionary Measures. In G. T. Hotaling, D. Finkelhor, J. T. Kirkpatrick, and M. A. Straus (Eds.), *Family Abuse and Its Consequences: New Directions in Research* (pp. 297-311). Newbury Park, CA: Sage.

Makepeace, J. M. (1989). Dating, Living Together, and Courtship Violence. In M. A. Piroz-Good and J. E. Stets (Eds.), *Violence in Dating Relationships: Emerging Social Issues* (pp. 95-107). New York: Praeger.

Malamuth, W. M. (1981). Rape Proclivity Among Males. *Journal of Social Issues* 37(4):138-157.

Mann, C. R. (1993). *Unequal Justice: The Question of Color*. Bloomington, IN: Indiana University Press.

Marshall, L. L., and P. Rose (1987). Gender, Stress, and Violence in Adult Relationships of a Sample of College Students. *Journal of Social and Personal Relationships* 4:299-316.

Marzuk, P. M. (1996). Violence, Crime, and Mental Illness: How Strong a Link? *Archives of General Psychiatry* 53:481-488.

Matsueda, R. L., and K. Heimer (1987). Race, Family Structure, and Delinquency: A Test of Differential Association and Social Control Theories. *American Sociological Review* 52(6):826-840.

Matthews, W. J. (1984). Violence in College Couples. *College Student Journal* 18:150-158.

Matza, D. (1964). *Delinquency and Drift*. New York: John Wiley and Sons.

Matza, D., and G. M. Sykes (1961). Juvenile Delinquency and Subterranean Values. *American Sociological Review* 26:712-719.

Mawson, R. (1981). Aggression, Attachment, Behavior, and Crimes of Violence. In T. Hirschi and M. Gottfredson (Eds.), *Understanding Crime* (pp. 12-15). Beverly Hills: Sage.

Maxson, C. L. (1995). *Street Gangs and Drug Sales in Two Suburban Cities*. Research in Brief. Washington, DC: National Institute of Justice.

Maxson, C. L., M. A. Gordon, and M. W. Klein (1985). Differences Between Gang and Nongang Homicides. *Criminology* 23(2):209-222.

Maxson, C. L., and M. W. Klein (1990). Street Gang Violence: Twice As Great, or Half As Great? In C. R. Huff (Ed.), *Gangs in America* (pp. 71-100). Newbury Park, CA: Sage.

Maxson, C. L., and M. W. Klein (1996). Defining Gang Homicide: An Updated Look at Member and Motive Approaches. In C. R. Huff (Ed.), *Gangs in America* (pp. 3-20). Second Edition. Thousand Oaks, CA: Sage.

McCabe, K. A., and S. S. Gregory (1998). Elderly Victimization: An Examination Beyond the FBI's Index Crimes. *Research on Aging* 20(3):363.

McCord, J. (1979). Some Child-Rearing Antecedents of Criminal Behavior in Adult Men. *Journal of Personality and Social Psychology* 37:1477-1486.

McCord, J. (1982). A Longitudinal View of the Relationship Between Paternal Absence and Crime. In J. Gunn and D. P. Farrington (Eds.), *Abnormal Offenders, Delinquency, and the Criminal Justice System* (pp. 113-128). New York: John Wiley and Sons.

McCord, J., W. McCord, and A. Howard (1963). Family Interaction as Antecedent to the Direction of Male Aggressiveness. *Journal of Abnormal Social Psychology* 66(6):239-242.

McCord, W. (1958). The Biological Bases of Juvenile Delinquency. In J. S. Roucek (Ed.), *Juvenile Delinquency*. Freeport, NY: Philosophical Library.

McCord, W., and J. McCord (1964). *The Psychopath*. Princeton, NJ: Van Nostrand.

McCord, W., J. McCord, and I. K. Zola (1959). *Origins of Crime*. New York: Columbia University Press.

McEachern, A. W., and R. Bauzer (1967). Factors Related to Disposition in Juvenile-Police Contacts. In M. W. Klein (Ed.), *Juvenile Gangs in Context* (pp. 44-160). Englewood Cliffs, NJ: Prentice-Hall.

McFarlane, J. (1989). Battering in Pregnancy: The Tip of the Iceberg. *Women and Health* 15(3):69-84.

McKeiver v. Pennsylvania (1971). 403 U.S. 528, 91 S. Ct. 1976.

McKinney, K. (1986a). Measures of Verbal, Physical, and Sexual Dating Violence by Gender. *Free Inquiry into Creative Sociology* 14(1):55-60.

McKinney, K. (1986b). Perceptions of Courtship Violence: Gender, Difference, and Involvement. *Free Inquiry into Creative Sociology* 14(1):61-66.

McMichael, P. (1979). The Hen or the Egg? Which Comes First—Antisocial Emotional Disorders or Reading Disability? *British Journal of Educational Psychology* 49:226-238.

McPartland, J. M., and S. M. Nettles (1991). Using Community Adults as Advocates or Mentors for At-Risk Middle School Students: A Two-Year Evaluation of Project RAISE. *American Journal of Education* 99(4):568-586.

Mednick, S. A., W. F. Gabrielli Jr., and B. Hutchings (1984). Genetic Influences in Criminal Convictions: Evidence from an Adoption Cohort. *Science* 224:891-894.

Mednick, S. A., W. F. Gabrielli Jr., and B. Hutchings (1987). Genetic Factors in the Etiology of Criminal Behavior. In S. A. Mednick, T. E. Moffitt, and S. A. Stack (Eds.), *The Causes of Crime: New Biological Approaches* (pp. 74-91). London: Cambridge University Press.

Mednick, S. A., T. F. Moffitt, and S. A. Stack (1987*). The Causes of Crime: New Biological Approaches*. New York: Cambridge University Press.

Meehan, P. J., and P. W. O'Carroll (1992). Gangs, Drugs, and Homicide in Los Angeles. *American Journal of the Disabled Child* 146:683-687.

Mercy, J., and M. L. Rosenberg (1998). Preventing Firearm Violence in and Around Schools. In D. S. Elliot, B. A. Hamburg, and K. R. Williams (Eds.), *Violence in American Schools* (pp. 159-187). New York: Cambridge University Press.

Merton, R. (1938). Social Structure and Anomie. *American Sociological Review* 3:672-682.

Merton, R. K. (1957). *Social Theory and Social Structure*. Glencoe, IL: Free Press.

Milavsky, J. R., R. Kessler, H. Stipp, and W. S. Rubens (1996). Television and Aggression: Results of a Panel Study. In D. G. Rojek and G. F. Jensen (Eds.), *Exploring Delinquency: Causes and Control* (pp. 246-255). Los Angeles: Roxbury.

Miller, B. (1988). Date Rape: Time for a New Look at Prevention. *Journal of College Student Development* 29:553-555.

Miller, B., and J. Marshall (1987). Coercive Sex on the University Campus. *Journal of College Student Personnel* 28(1):38-47.

Miller, W. B. (1958). Lower Class Culture As a Generating Milieu of Gang Delinquency. *Journal of Social Issues* 14(3):5-19.

Miller, W. B. (1962). The Impact of a "Total Community" Delinquency Control Project. *Social Problems* 10:168-191.

Miller, W. B. (1966). Violent Crimes in City Gangs. *Annals of the American Academy of Political and Social Science* 364:96-112.

Miller, W. B. (1970). White Gangs. In J. F. Short, Jr. (Ed.), *Modern Criminals* (pp. 57-64). Chicago: Aldine.

Miller, W. B. (1974). American Youth Gangs: Past and Present. In A. Blumberg (Ed.), *Current Perspectives on Criminal Behavior* (pp. 291-320). New York: Knopf.

Miller, W. B. (1975). *Violence by Youth Gangs As a Crime Problem in Major American Cities*. Washington, DC: Law Enforcement Administration.

Miller, W. B. (1980). Gangs, Groups, and Serious Youth Crime. In D. Schichor and D. H. Kelly (Eds.), *Critical Issues in Juvenile Delinquency*. Lexington, MA: Lexington Books.

Miller, W. B. (1992). *Crime by Youth Gangs and Groups in the United States*. Washington, DC: Office of Juvenile Justice and Delinquency Prevention.

Minty, B. (1988). Public Care or Distorted Family Relationships: The Antecedents of Violent Crime. *Howard Journal* 27(3):172-187.

Molidor, C., and R. M. Tolman (1998). Gender and Contextual Factors in Adolescent Dating Relationships. *Violence Against Women* 4:180-194.

Mones, P. (1991). *When a Child Kills: Abused Children Who Kill Their Parents*. New York: Pocket Books.

Moore, J. W. (1978). *Homeboys: Gangs, Drugs, and Prison in the Barrios of Los Angeles*. Philadelphia: Temple University Press.

Moore, J. W. (1988). Introduction: Gangs and the Underclass: A Comparative Perspective. In J. Hagedorn (Ed.), *People and Folks* (pp. 3-17). Chicago: Lake View.

Moore, J. W. (1990). Gangs, Drugs, and Violence. In M. De La Rosa, E. Y. Lambert, and B. Gropper (Eds.), *Drugs and Violence: Causes, Correlates, and Consequences* (pp. 160-176). Rockville, MD: National Institute on Drug Abuse.

Morales, A. (1998). Seeking a Cure for Child Abuse. *USA Today*, 127(September), pp. 34-35.

Morris, N., and G. Hawkins (1970). *The Honest Politician's Guide to Crime Control*. Chicago: University of Chicago Press.

Mouzakitis, C. M. (1981). An Inquiry into the Problem of Child Abuse and Juvenile Delinquency. In R. J. Hunner and Y. E. Walker (Eds.), *Exploring the Relationship Between Child Abuse and Delinquency* (pp. 175-219). Montclair, NJ: Allanheld, Osmun and Co.

Muehlenhard, C. L., and M. A. Linton (1987). Date Rape and Sexual Aggression in Dating Situations: Incidence and Risk Factors. *Journal of Counseling Psychology* 34:186-196.

Mueller, C. W. (1983). Environmental Stressors and Aggressive Behavior. In R. G. Geen and E. I. Donnerstein (Eds.), *Theoretical and Empirical Reviews*. Vol. 2. New York: Academic Press.

Murphy, H. A., J. M. Hutchison, and J. S. Bailey (1983). Behavioral School Psychology Goes Outdoors: The Effect of Organized Games on Playground Aggression. *Journal of Applied Behavior Analysis* 16:29-35.

Murray, C. A. (1976). *The Link Between Learning Disabilities and Juvenile Delinquency*. Washington, DC: Government Printing Office.

Myerhoff, H. L., and B. G. Myerhoff (1964). Field Observations of Middle Class "Gangs." *Social Forces* 42:328-336.

National Center for Education Statistics (1998). *Violence and Discipline Problems in U. S. Public Schools: 1996-97*. Washington, DC: U. S. Department of Education.

National Center for Juvenile Justice (1999). *Juvenile Court Statistics 1996*. Washington, DC: Office of Juvenile Justice and Delinquency Prevention.

National Center on Child Abuse and Neglect (1992). *Child Abuse and Neglect: A Shared Community Concern*. Washington, DC: National Center on Child Abuse and Neglect.

National Drug Intelligence Center (1996). *National Street Gang Survey Report*. Johnstown, PA: National Drug Intelligence Center.

National Governors' Association (1999). *NGA Policy Positions February 1999*. Washington, DC: National Governors' Association.

National Youth Gang Center (1999). *1996 National Youth Gang Survey*. Washington, DC: Office of Juvenile Justice and Delinquency Prevention.

Newson, J., E. Newson, and M. Adams (1993). The Social Origins of Delinquency. *Criminal Behavior and Mental Health* 3:19-29.

Newton, G. D., and F. E. Zimring (1969). *Firearms and Violence in American Life: A Staff Report to the National Commission on the Causes and Prevention of Violence*. Washington, DC: Government Printing Office.

Nye, F. I. (1958). *Family Relations and Delinquent Behavior.* New York: John Wiley and Sons.

Odem, M. E., and J. Clay-Warner (Eds.) (1998). *Confronting Rape and Sexual Assault.* Wilmington, DE: Scholarly Resources, Inc.

Office of Justice Programs (1999). *Report to Congress on Juvenile Violence Research.* Washington, DC: Office of Juvenile Justice and Delinquency Prevention.

Office of Juvenile Justice and Delinquency Prevention (1994). *Intensive Aftercare for High-Risk Juveniles: A Community Care Model.* Washington, DC: U.S. Department of Justice.

Office of Juvenile Justice and Delinquency Prevention (1998). *Guide for Implementing the Comprehensive Strategy for Serious, Violent, and Chronic Juvenile Offenders.* Washington, DC: Office of Justice Programs.

Office of Juvenile Justice and Delinquency Prevention (1999a). *Juvenile Justice: A Century of Change.* Washington, DC: Office of Justice Programs.

Office of Juvenile Justice and Delinquency Prevention (1999b). *Juvenile Offenders in Residential Placement, 1997.* Washington, DC: U.S. Department of Justice.

Office of Juvenile Justice and Delinquency Prevention (1999c). *Prostitution of Children and Child-Sex Tourism: An Analysis of Domestic and International Responses.* Arlington, VA: National Center for Missing and Exploited Children.

Office of National Drug Control Policy (1996). *Fact Sheet: Drug Summary.* Rockville, MD: ONDCP Drugs and Crime Clearinghouse.

Office of National Drug Control Policy (1997). *Juveniles and Drugs: Facts and Figures.* Rockville, MD: ONDCP Drugs and Crime Clearinghouse.

O'Keefe, N., K. Brockopp, and E. Chew (1986). Teen Dating Violence. *Social Work* 31:465-468.

Olds, D. I., and H. Kitzman (1993). Review of Research on Home Visiting for Pregnant Women and Parents of Young Children. *The Future of Children* 3(3):53-92.

Olweus, D. (1980). Familial and Temperamental Determinants of Aggressive Behavior in Adolescents: A Causal Analysis. *Developmental Psychology* 14:644-660.

Olweus, D. (1991). Bully/Victim Problems Among Schoolchildren: Basic Facts and Effects of a School-Based Intervention Program. In D. J. Pepler and K. H. Rubin (Eds.), *The Development and Treatment of Childhood Aggression* (pp. 80-84). Hillsdale, NJ: Erlbaum.

Olweus, D. (1993). *Bullying at School: What We Know and What We Can Do.* Cambridge, MA: Blackwell.

Osmond, M., and P. Martin (1975). Sex and Sexism: A Comparison of Male and Female Sex-Role Attitudes. *Journal of Marriage and the Family* 37:744-758.

Ounsted, C., R. Oppenheimer, and J. Lindsay (1975). The Psychopathology and Psychotherapy of the Families: Aspects Bounding Failure. In A. Franklin (Ed.), *Concerning Child Abuse.* London: Churchill Livingston.

Palmer, T. B. (1991). Interventions with Juvenile Offenders: Recent and Long-Term Changes. In T. L. Armstrong (Ed.), *Intensive Interventions with High-Risk Youths: Promising Approaches in Juvenile Probation and Parole* (pp. 85-120). Monsey, NY: Criminal Justice Press.

Park, R. E., and E. W. Burgess (1925). *The City*. Chicago: University of Chicago Press.

Parrot, A., and L. Bechhofer (Eds.) (1991). *Acquaintance Rape: The Hidden Crime*. New York: John Wiley and Sons.

Patterson, E. P. (1996). Poverty, Income Inequality, and Community Crime Rates. In D. G. Rojek and G. F. Jensen (Eds.), *Exploring Delinquency: Causes and Control* (pp. 142-149). Los Angeles: Roxbury.

Patterson, G. R. (1986). Performance Models for Antisocial Boys. *American Psychologist* 41(4):432-444.

Peters, K. D., K. Kochanek, and S. Murphy (1998). Community and Dating Violence Among Adolescents: Perpetration and Victimization. *Journal of Adolescent Health* 21:291-302.

Peterson, K. S. (1983). The Nightmare of a Battered Parent. *USA Today*, March 18, p. A6.

Piliavin, I., and S. Briar (1964). Police Encounters with Juveniles. *American Journal of Sociology* 70:206-214.

Plant, M. A. (Ed.) (1990). *AIDS, Drugs, and Prostitution*. London: Routledge.

Plass, M. S., and J. C. Gessner (1983). Violence in Courtship Relations: A Southern Example. *Free Inquiry in Creative Sociology* 11(2):198-202.

Platt, A. (1968). *The Child-Savers: The Invention of Delinquency*. Chicago: University of Chicago Press.

Polansky, N. A., C. DeSaix, and S. A. Sharlin (1972). *Child Neglect: Understanding and Reaching the Parents*. New York: Child Welfare League of America.

Polk, K., and W. E. Schafer (1972). *Schools and Delinquency*. Englewood Cliffs, NJ: Prentice-Hall.

Pollock, V., S. A. Mednick, and W. F. Gabrielli Jr. (1983). Crime Causation: Biological Theories. In S. H. Kadish (Ed.), *Encyclopedia of Crime and Justice*. Vol. l. New York: Free Press.

Polsky, H. (1962). *Cottage Six*. New York: Russell Sage Foundation.

Poole, E. D., and R. M. Regoli (1983). Violence in Juvenile Institutions. *Criminology* 21(2):214.

Pope, C., and W. Feyerherm (1993). *Minorities and the Juvenile Justice System*. Washington, DC: Office of Juvenile Justice and Delinquency Prevention.

Portune, R. (1971). *Changing Adolescent Attitudes Toward Police*. Cincinnati: W. H. Anderson Co.

Powell, C. (1998). Dealing with Dating Violence in Schools. In B. Levy (Ed.), *Dating Violence: Young Women in Danger* (pp. 279-283). Seattle: Seal Press.

President's Commission on Mental Health (1978). *Report to the President*. Vol. l. Washington, DC: Government Printing Office.

PRIDE Surveys (2000). *1988-99 National Summary, Grades 6 Through 8*. Bowling Green, KY: PRIDE Surveys.

Puig, A. (1984). Predomestic Strife: A Growing College Counseling Concern. *Journal of College Student Personnel* 25:268-269.

Quay, H. C. (1983). Crime Causation: Psychological Theories. In S. H. Kadish (Ed.), *Encyclopedia of Crime and Justice* (pp. 340-345). Vol. 1. New York: Free Press.

Rapaport, K., and B. R. Burkhart (1984). Personality and Attitudinal Characteristics of Sexually Coercive College Males. *Journal of Abnormal Psychology* 93:216-221.

Rausch, S. (1983). Court Processing versus Diversion of Status Offenders: A Test of Deterrence and Labeling Theories. *Journal of Research in Crime and Delinquency* 20:39-54.

Reckless, W. C. (1970). Self-Concept As an Insulator Against Delinquency. In J. E. Teele (Ed.), *Juvenile Delinquency: A Reader*. Itasca, IL: Peacock.

Reiss, A. J. Jr. (1961). Social Correlates of Psychological Types of Delinquency. *American Sociological Review* 17:710-718.

Reyes, O., and L. A. Jason (1991). An Evaluation of a High School Dropout Prevention Program. *Journal of Community Psychology* 19(2):221-230.

Rhoades, P. W., and S. L. Parker (1981). *The Connection Between Youth Problems and Violence in the Home*. Portland, OR: Oregon Coalition Against Domestic and Sexual Violence.

Rhodes, A. L., and A. J. Reiss Jr. (1969). Apathy, Truancy and Delinquency As an Adaptation to School Failure. *Social Forces* 48:12-22.

Rich, A. (1980). Compulsory Heterosexuality and Lesbian Existence. *Signs* 5(4):631-660.

Richards, R. J. (2000). *Charles Darwin*. San Diego: Greenhaven Press.

Riggs, D. S., K. D. O'Leary, and F. C. Breslin (1990). Multiple Correlates of Physical Aggression in Dating Couples. *Journal of Interpersonal Violence* 5(1):61-73.

Riley, D., and M. Shaw (1985). *Paternal Supervision and Juvenile Delinquency*. London: Her Majesty's Stationery Office.

Riley, K. J. (1997). *Crack, Powder Cocaine, and Heroin: Drug Purchase and Use Patterns in Six U.S. Cities*. Washington, DC: Office of Justice Programs.

Robins, L. N. (1966). *Deviant Children Grown Up*. Baltimore: Williams and Wilkins.

Robinson, E. A., and N. S. Jacobson (1987). Social Learning Theory and Family Psychopathology: A Kantian Model in Behaviorism. In T. Jacob (Ed.), *Family Interaction and Psychopathology: Theories, Methods, and Findings* (pp. 117-162). New York: Plenum.

Rodriguez, O. (1988). Hispanics and Homicides in New York City. In J. F. Kraus, S. B. Sorenson, and P. D. Juarez (Eds.), *Proceedings of Research Conference on Violence and Homicide in Hispanic Communities* (pp. 67-84). Los Angeles: University of California.

Rojek, D. G., and G. F. Jensen (Eds.) (1996). *Exploring Delinquency: Causes and Control*. Los Angeles: Roxbury.

Roscoe, B., and J. E. Callahan (1985). Adolescents' Self-Report of Violence in Families and Dating Relations. *Adolescence* 20:545-553.

Roscoe, B., and T. Kelsey (1986). Dating Violence Among High School Students. *Psychology* 23(1):53-59.

Rosen, L., and K. Neilson (1978). The Broken Home and Delinquency. In L. D. Savitz and N. Johnston (Eds.), *Crime in Society* (pp. 406-415). New York: John Wiley and Sons.

Rosen, L., and K. Neilson (1982). Broken Homes and Delinquency. In L. Savitz and N. Johnston (Eds.), *Contemporary Criminology* (pp. 406-415). New York: John Wiley and Sons.

Rosenthal, R. (1986). Media Violence, Antisocial Behavior, and the Social Consequences of Small Effects. *Journal of Social Issues* 42(2):141-154.

Rothman, D. J. (1990). *The Discovery of the Asylum: Social Order and Disorder in the New Republic*. Boston: Little, Brown, and Co.

Rouse, L., R. Breen, and M. Howell (1988). Abuse in Intimate Relationships: A Comparison of Married and Dating College Students. *Journal of Interpersonal Violence* 3(4):415-419.

Rowe, D. C. (1996). An Adaptive Strategy Theory of Crime and Delinquency. In J. D. Hawkins (Ed.), *Delinquency and Crime: Current Theories* (pp. 268-314). New York: Cambridge University Press.

Rowe, D. C., and D. W. Osgood (1984). Heredity and Sociological Theories of Delinquency: A Reconsideration. *American Sociological Review* 49:526-540.

Runaway and Homeless Youth Act (1978). 42 U.S.C. §5701-5702 (Supp. II).

Russell, D. E. (1990). *Rape in Marriage*. Indianapolis: Indiana University Press.

Rutter, M. (1977). The Family Influences. In M. Rutter and L. Hersov (Eds.), *Child Psychiatry: Modern Approaches*. Oxford: Blackwell.

Samenow, S. E. (1984). *Inside the Criminal Mind*. New York: Time Books.

Sampson, R. J., and J. Lauritsen (1997). Racial and Ethnic Disparities in Crime and Criminal Justice in the United States. In M. Tonry (Ed.), *Crime and Justice: An Annual Review of Research* (pp. 311-374). Vol. 22. Chicago: University of Chicago Press.

Sampson, R. J., and W. J. Wilson (1995). Toward a Theory of Race, Crime, and Urban Inequality. In J. Hagan and R. Peterson (Eds.), *Crime and Inequality* (pp. 37-54). Stanford, CA: Stanford University Press.

Sanday, P. R. (1990). *Fraternity Gang Rape: Sex, Brotherhood, and Privilege on Campus*. New York: New York University Press.

Sandberg, A. A., G. F. Koepf, T. Ishiara, and T. S. Hanschka (1961). An XYY Human Male. *Lancet* 262:488-489.

Sanders, W. B. (1981). *Juvenile Delinquency: Causes, Patterns, and Reactions*. New York: Holt, Rinehart and Winston.

Sante, L. (1991). *Low Life: Lures and Snares of Old New York.* New York: Vintage Books.

Sargeant, D. (1971). Children Who Kill—A Family Conspiracy? In J. Howell (Ed.), *Theory and Practice of Family Psychiatry.* New York: Brunner-Mazel.

Sarri, R. (1983). The Use of Detention and Alternatives in the United States Since the Gault Decision. In R. C. Corrado, M. LeBlanc, and J. Trepanier (Eds.), *Current Issues in Juvenile Justice.* Toronto: Butterworth.

Schall v. Martin (1984). 467 U.S. 253, 104 S. Ct. 2403.

Scheff, T. J. (1966). *Being Mentally Ill.* Chicago: Aldine.

Schmitt, B. D., and C. H. Kempe (1975). Neglect and Abuse in Children. In V. C. Vaugh and R. McKay (Eds.), *Nelson Textbook of Pediatrics* (pp. 107-111) Tenth Edition. Philadelphia: W. B. Saunders.

Schoenfeld, C. G. (1975). A Psychoanalytic Theory of Juvenile Delinquency. In E. E. Peoples (Ed.), *Readings in Correctional Casework and Counseling* (pp. 23-26). Pacific Palisades, CA: Goodyear.

Schuessler, K. F., and D. R. Cressey (1950). Personality Characteristics of Criminals. *American Journal of Sociology* 55:476-484.

Schulsinger, F. (1972). Psychopathy: Heredity and Environment. *International Journal of Mental Health* 1:190-206.

Schulsinger, F. (1980). Biological Psychopathology. *Annual Review of Psychology* 31:583-606.

Schur, E. (1972). *Labeling Deviant Behavior.* New York: Harper and Row.

Sellin, T. (1938). *Culture, Conflict, and Crime.* New York: Research Council.

Sellin, T. (1961). The Significance of Records and Crime. *The Law Quarterly Review* 67:489-504.

Seng, M. J. (1989). Child Sexual Abuse and Adolescent Prostitution: A Comparative Analysis. *Adolescence* 24:665-671.

Sexual Exploitation Act (1978). U.S.C. §2251, 2253-2254.

Shannon, L. W. (1978). A Longitudinal Study of Delinquency and Crime. In C. Wellford (Ed.), *Quantitative Studies in Criminology.* Beverly Hills: Sage.

Shaw, C. R. (1929). *Delinquency Areas.* Chicago: University of Chicago Press.

Shaw, C. R., and H. D. McKay (1932). Are Broken Homes a Causative Factor in Juvenile Delinquency? *Social Forces* 10:514-524.

Shaw, C. R., and H. D. McKay (1969). *Juvenile Delinquency and Urban Areas.* Chicago: University of Chicago Press.

Sheldon, W. H. (1942). *Varieties of Temperament.* New York: Harper and Row.

Sheley, J. F. (1985). *America's "Crime Problem": An Introduction to Criminology.* Belmont, CA: Wadsworth.

Sheley, J. F., and J. D. Wright (1993). *Gun Acquisition and Possession in Selected Juvenile Samples.* Research in Brief. Washington, DC: Office of Justice Programs.

Sheley, J. F., and J. D. Wright (1995). *In the Line of Fire.* Hawthorne, NY: Aldine de Gruyter.

Shore, M. F. (1971). Psychological Theories on the Causes of Antisocial Behavior. *Crime and Delinquency* 17(4):456-458.

Short, J. F. (1957). Differential Association and Delinquency. *Social Problems.* 4:233-239.

Short, J. F. Jr. (1964). Gang Delinquency and Anomie. In M. B. Clinard (Ed.), *Anomie and Deviant Behavior* (pp. 98-127). New York: Free Press.

Siegel, L. J., and J. J. Senna (1991). *Juvenile Delinquency,* Fourth Edition. St. Paul, MN: West Publishing.

Sieverdes, C. M., and C. Bartollas (1977). Modes of Adaptation and Game Behavior at Two Juvenile Institutions. In P. C. Friday and V. L. Stewart (Eds.), *Youth Crime and Juvenile Justice: International Perspectives* (pp. 27-35). New York: Holt, Rinehart and Winston.

Sigelman, C. K., C. J. Berry, and K. A. Wiles (1984). Violence in College Students' Dating Relationships. *Journal of Applied Social Psychology* 14(6):530-548.

Silbert, M. H. (1982). Delancey Street Study: Prostitution and Sexual Assault. Summary of Results. San Francisco: Delancey Street Foundation.

Silver, L. B., C. C. Dublin, and R. S. Lourie (1969). Does Violence Breed Violence? Contributions from a Study of the Child Abuse Syndrome. *American Journal of Psychiatry* 126:404-407.

Silverstein, H. (1994). *Date Abuse (Issues in Focus).* Hillside, NJ: Enslow Publishers.

Simmons, H. E. (1970). *Protective Services for Children,* Second Edition. Sacramento: Citadel Press.

Simons, R. L., J. F. Robertson, and W. R. Downs (1989). The Nature of the Association Between Parental Rejection and Delinquent Behavior. *Journal of Youth and Adolescence* 18(3):297-310.

Simonton, D. K. (1985). Intelligence and Personal Influence in Groups: Four Nonlinear Models. *Psychological Review* 92:532-547.

Slocum, W., and C. L. Stone (1963). Family Culture Patterns and Delinquent-Type Behavior. *Marriage and Family Living* 25:202-208.

Smith, D. A., C. A. Visher, and L. A. Davidson (1984). Equity and Discretionary Justice: The Influence of Race on Police Arrest Decisions. *Journal of Criminal Law and Criminology* 75: 234-249.

Snyder, H. N. (1997). *Serious, Violent, and Chronic Juvenile Offenders: An Assessment of the Extent of and Trends in Officially Recognized Serious Criminal Behavior in a Delinquent Population.* Pittsburgh: National Center for Juvenile Justice.

Snyder, H. N. (1999). *Juvenile Arrests 1998.* Bulletin. Washington, DC: Office of Juvenile Justice and Delinquency Prevention.

Snyder, H. N., and M. Sickmund (1996). Juvenile Offenders and Victims: A National Report. In D. G. Rojek and G. F. Jensen (Eds.), *Exploring Delinquency: Causes and Control* (pp. 57-61). Los Angeles: Roxbury.

Snyder, J., and G. Patterson (1987). Family Interaction and Delinquent Behavior. In H. C. Quay (Ed.), *Handbook of Juvenile Delinquency* (pp. 220-225). New York: Wiley-Interscience.

Snyder, S. (1991). Movies and Juvenile Delinquency: An Overview. *Adolescence* 26(101):121-132.

Solomon, T. (1973). History and Demography of Child Abuse. *Pediatrics* 51(4): 773-776.

Sorrells, J. M. (1977). *Kids Who Kill.* Crime and Delinquency 23(2):312-320.

Sousa, C. A. (1999). Teen Dating Violence. The Hidden Epidemic. *Family and Conciliation Courts Review* 37(3):356-375.

Spence, J. T., R. L. Helmreich, and J. Stapp (1975). Ratings of Self and Peers on Sex Role Attributes and Their Relation to Self-Esteem and Conceptions of Masculinity and Femininity. *Journal of Personality and Social Psychology* 32:29-39.

Spergel, I. A. (1986). The Violent Gang Problem in Chicago: A Local Community Approach. *Social Service Review* 60:94-131.

Spergel, I. A. (1990). Youth Gangs: Continuity and Change. In M. Tonry and N. Morris (Eds.), *Crime and Justice: A Review of Research* (pp. 171-275). Vol. 12. Chicago: University of Chicago.

Spergel, I. A. (1995). *The Youth Gang Problem: A Community Approach.* New York: Oxford University Press.

Spergel, I. A., and L. Bobrowski (1989). *Proceedings of the Law Enforcement Youth Gang Definitional Conference Draft.* Washington, DC: Office of Justice Programs.

Spergel, I. A., R. Chance, K. Ehrensaft, T. Regulus, C. Kane, R. Laseter, A. Alexander, and S. Oh (1994). *Gang Suppression and Intervention: Community Models: Research Summary.* Washington, DC: Office of Juvenile Justice and Delinquency Prevention.

Sroufe, L. A. (1986). Bowlby's Contribution to Psychoanalytic Theory and Developmental Psychology. *Journal of Child Psychology and Psychiatry* 27:841-849.

Steele, B. F. (1976). Violence Within the Family. In R. E. Helfer and C. H. Kempe (Eds.), *Child Abuse and Neglect: The Family and the Community* (pp. 12-14). Cambridge, MA: Ballinger.

Steele, B. F., and C. Pollock (1968). A Psychiatric Study of Parents Who Abuse Infants and Small Children. In R. E. Helfer and C. H. Kempe (Eds.), *The Battered Child* (pp. 89-133). Chicago: University of Chicago Press.

Steinmetz, S. K. (1977). *The Cycle of Violence: Assertive, Aggressive, and Abusive Family Interaction.* New York: Praeger.

Stinchcombe, A. L. (1964). *Rebellion in a High School.* Chicago: Quadrangle Books.

Stouthamer-Loeber, M., R. Loeber, D. Huizinga, and P. Porter (1997). The Onset of Persistent Serious Offending. Unpublished report. Washington, DC: Office of Justice Programs.

Strasberg, P. A. (1978). *Violent Delinquents: A Report to the Ford Foundation from the Vera Institute of Justice.* New York: Monarch.

Straus, M. A. (1973). A General Systems Theory Approach to a Theory of Violence Between Family Members. *Social Science Information* 12(3):105-125.

Straus, M. A. (1979). Measuring Intrafamily Conflict and Violence: The Conflict Tactics Scale. *Journal of Marriage and the Family* 41:75-88.

Straus, M. A. (1992). Children As Witnesses to Marital Violence; A Risk Factor for Lifelong Problems Among a Nationally Representative Sample of American Men and Women. Paper presented at the Twenty-Third Ross Roundtable on Critical Approaches to Common Pediatric Problems, Columbus, Ohio.

Straus, M. A., and R. J. Gelles (1990). *Physical Violence in American Families: Risk Factors and Adaptations to Violence in 8,145 Families*. New Brunswick, NJ: Transaction.

Straus, M. A., R. J. Gelles, and S. K. Steinmetz (1980). *Behind Closed Doors: Violence in the American Family*. Garden City, NY: Doubleday/Anchor.

Sugarman, D. B., and G. T. Hotaling (1998). Dating Violence: A Review of Contextual and Risk Factors. In B. Levy (Ed.), *Dating Violence: Young Women in Danger* (pp. 100-118). Seattle: Seal Press.

Sutherland, E. H. (1939). *Principles of Criminology*. Philadelphia: J. B. Lippincott.

Sutherland, E. H., and D. R. Cressey (1978). *Criminology*, Tenth Edition. Philadelphia: J. B. Lippincott.

Szasz, T. S., and G. J. Alexander (1968). Mental Illness As an Excuse for Civil Wrongs. *Journal of Nervous and Mental Disease* 147(4):113-123.

Task Force on Juvenile Justice and Delinquency Prevention (1977). *Juvenile Justice and Delinquency Prevention*. Washington, DC: Government Printing Office.

Tatem-Kelley, B., D. Huizinga, T. P. Thornberry, and R. Loeber (1997). *Epidemiology of Serious Violence*. Washington, DC: Office of Juvenile Justice and Delinquency Prevention.

Taylor, S. P., and S. T. Chermack (1993). Alcohol, Drugs, and Human Physical Aggression. *Journal of Studies on Alcohol* 11:78-88.

Teeters, N. K., and J. D. Reinemann (1950). *The Challenge of Delinquency*. New York: Prentice-Hall.

Thompson, D. W., and L. A. Jason (1988). Street Gangs and Preventive Interventions. *Criminal Justice and Behavior* 15(3):323-333.

Thompson, W. E. (1986). Courtship Violence: Toward a Conceptual Understanding. *Youth and Society* 18(2):162-176.

Thornberry, T. P. (1987). Toward an Interactional Theory of Delinquency. *Criminology* 25(4):863-891.

Thornberry, T. P. (1998). Membership in Youth Gangs and Involvement in Serious and Violent Offending. In R. Loeber and D. P. Farrington (Ed.), *Serious and Violent Offenders: Risk Factors and Successful Interventions* (pp. 147-166). Thousand Oaks, CA: Sage.

Thornberry, T. P., M. D. Krohn, A. J. Lizotte, and D. Chard-Wierschem (1993). The Role of Juvenile Gangs in Facilitating Delinquent Behavior. *Journal of Research in Crime and Delinquency* 30(1):55-87.

Thornberry, T. P., M. Moore, and R. L. Christenson (1985). The Effect of Dropping Out of High School on Subsequent Criminal Behavior. *Criminology* 23(1):3-18.

Thrasher, F. M. (1927). *The Gang*. Chicago: University of Chicago Press.

Tittle, C. R. (1975). Labeling and Crime: An Empirical Evaluation. In W. R. Gove (Ed.), *The Labeling of Deviance: Evaluating a Perspective* (pp. 157-179). New York: John Wiley and Sons.

Tittle, C. R., M. J. Burke, and E. F. Jackson (1986). Modeling Sutherland's Theory of Differential Association: Toward an Empirical Clarification. *Social Forces* 65:404-432.

Toby, J. (1957). The Differential Impact of Family Disorganization. *American Sociological Review* 22:505-512.

Tonry, M. (1995). *Malign Neglect: Race, Crime, and Punishment in America*. New York: Oxford University Press.

Tontodonato, P., and B. K. Crew (1988). The Role of Alcohol and Dating Violence: Some Preliminary Findings. Paper presented at the American Society of Criminology meetings. Chicago, IL.

Tooley, K. (1975). The Small Assassins. *Journal of the American Academy of Child Psychiatry* 14:306.

Torbet, P., and L. Szymanski (1998). *State Legislative Responses to Violent Juvenile Crime: 1996-97 Update*. Washington, DC: Office of Juvenile Justice and Delinquency Prevention.

U.S. Department of Health and Human Services (1997). Fact Sheet. *Substance Abuse—A National Challenge: Prevention, Treatment and Research at HHS*. Washington, DC: Government Printing Office.

U.S. Department of Health and Human Services (1998). Children's Bureau. *Child Maltreatment 1996: Reports From the States to the National Child Abuse and Neglect Data System*. Washington, DC: Government Printing Office.

U.S. Department of Health and Human Services (1999). *Child Maltreatment 1997: Reports From the States to the National Child Abuse and Neglect Data System*. Washington, DC: Government Printing Office.

U.S. Department of Health and Human Services (2000). Centers for Disease Control and Prevention. *Fact Sheet: Youth Risk Behavior Trends* (Online). <http://www.cdc.gov/nccdphp/dash/yrbs/trend.htm>

U.S. Department of Justice (1980). *Juvenile Justice Before and After the Onset of Delinquency*. Washington, DC: Office of Juvenile Justice and Delinquency Prevention.

U.S. Department of Justice (1994). Bureau of Justice Statistics Special Report. *Family Violence*. Washington, DC: Government Printing Office.

U.S. Department of Justice (1997a) Bureau of Justice Statistics. *Sex Offenses and Offenders: An Analysis of Data on Rape and Sexual Assault*. Washington, DC: Office of Justice Programs.

U.S. Department of Justice (1997b). Bureau of Justice Statistics Special Report. *Violence-Related Injuries Treated in Hospital Emergency Departments*. Washington, DC: Government Printing Office.

U.S. Department of Justice (1997c). *Juvenile Delinquents in the Federal Criminal Justice System.* Washington, DC: Office of Justice Programs.

U.S. Department of Justice (1998). Bureau of Justice Statistics Factbook. *Violence by Intimates.* Washington, DC: Government Printing Office.

U.S. Department of Justice (1999). *Juvenile Offenders and Victims: 1999 National Report.* Washington, DC: Office of Justice Programs.

U.S. Department of Justice (2000a). Bureau of Justice Statistics. *Sourcebook on Criminal Justice Statistics 1999.* Washington, DC: Government Printing Office.

U.S. Department of Justice (2000b). *Criminal Victimization in the United States, 1995: A National Crime Victimization Survey Report.* Washington, DC: Office of Justice Programs.

U.S. Department of Justice (2000c). National Institute of Justice. *1999 Annual Report on Drug Use Among Adult and Juvenile Arrestees.* Washington, DC: Office of Justice Programs.

U.S. Departments of Education and Justice (2000). *Indicators of School Crime and Safety 2000.* Washington, DC: Offices of Educational Research and Improvement and Justice Programs.

Utting, D., J. Bright, and C. Henricson (1993). *Crime and the Family.* London: Family Policy Studies Centre.

Valdez, R., B. Nourjah, and P. Nourjah (1988). Homicide in Southern California, 1966-1985: An Examination Based on Vital Statistics Data. In J. F. Kraus, S. B. Sorenson, and P. D. Juarez (Eds.), *Quieter Riots: Race and Poverty in the United States* (pp. 85-100). New York: Pantheon.

Volenik, A. (1978). Right to Treatment: Case Developments in Juvenile Law. *Justice System Journal* 3:303-304.

Volkonsky, A. (1995). Legalizing the "Profession" Would Sanction the Abuse. *Insight on the News* 11:21.

Wadsworth, M. J. (1979). *Roots of Delinquency: Infancy, Adolescence, and Crime.* London: Martin Robertson.

Waldo, G., and S. Dinitz (1967). Personality Attributes of the Criminal: An Analysis of Research Studies, 1950-1965. *Journal of Research in Crime and Delinquency* 4:185-202.

Waldorf, D. (1993). Don't Be Your Own Best Customer—Drug Use of San Francisco Gang Drug Sellers. *Crime, Law, and Social Change* 19:1-15.

Walker, L. E. (1979). *The Battered Woman.* New York: Harper and Row.

Walker, L. E. (1984). *The Battered Woman Syndrome.* New York: Springer.

Wang, Z. (1995). Gang Affiliation Among Asian-American High School Students: A Path Analysis of a Social Developmental Model. *Journal of Gang Research* 2(3):1-13.

Warren, C. A. (1978). Parent Batterers: Adolescent Violence and the Family. Paper presented at the Pacific Sociological Association, April, Anaheim, CA.

Warshaw, R. (1988). *I Never Called It Rape: The Ms. Report on Recognizing, Fighting and Surviving Date and Acquaintance Rape.* New York: Harper and Row.

Waterman, C. K., L. J. Dawson, and M. J. Bologna (1989). Sexual Coercion in Gay Male and Lesbian Relationships: Predictors and Implications for Support Services. *Journal of Sex Research* 26(1):118-124.

Weeks, H. A., and M. G. Smith (1939). Juvenile Delinquency and Broken Homes in Spokane, Washington. *Social Forces* 18:48-49.

Weinberg, S. K. (1958). Sociological Processes and Factors in Juvenile Delinquency. In J. S. Roucek (Ed.), *Juvenile Delinquency* (pp. 113-132). New York: Philosophical Library.

Weinberg, S. K. (1966). *Incest Behavior.* New York: Citadel Press.

Weisberg, D. K. (1985). *Children of the Night: A Study of Adolescent Prostitution.* Lexington, MA: Lexington Books.

Welfare and Institution Code (2002). Sect. 602. Amended Ch. 1748. Stats.

Wells, L. E., and J. H. Rankin (1986). The Broken Homes Model of Delinquency: Analytic Issues. *Journal of Research in Crime and Delinquency* 23(1):68-93.

Welsh, R. S. (1976). Severe Parental Punishment and Delinquency: A Developmental Theory. *Journal of Clinical Child Psychology* 5(1):17-21.

Werthman, C., and I. Piliavin (1967). Gang Members and the Police. In D. J. Bordual (Ed.), *The Police.* New York: John Wiley and Sons.

West, D. J., and D. P. Farrington (1973). *Who Becomes Delinquent?* London: Heinemann.

Widom, C. S. (1989). Does Violence Beget Violence? A Critical Examination of the Literature. *Psychological Bulletin* 106(1):3-28.

Wiebush, R. G. (1993). Juvenile Intensive Supervision: The Impact on Felony Offenders Diverted From Institutional Placement. *Crime and Delinquency* 39(1): 68-89.

Wiehe, V. (1997). *Sibling Abuse: Hidden Physical, Emotional, and Sexual Trauma.* Newbury Park, CA: Sage.

Wilkinson, K. (1980). The Broken Home and Delinquent Behavior: An Alternative Interpretation of Contradictory Findings. In T. Hirschi and M. Gottfredson (Eds.), *Understanding Crime: Current Theory and Research* (pp. 21-42). Beverly Hills: Sage.

Wilson, A. (Ed.) (1993). *Homicide: The Victim/Offender Connection.* Cincinnati: Anderson.

Wilson, J. Q. (1968). Dilemmas of Police Administration. *Public Administration Review* 28:14-18.

Wilson, J. Q., and R. Herrnstein (1985). *Crime and Human Nature.* New York: Simon and Schuster.

Wilson, R. (1978). Juvenile Inmates: The Long-Term Trend Is Down. *Corrections* 4:3-11.

Winfree, L. T. Jr., and C. T. Griffiths (1977). Adolescents' Attitudes Toward the Police: A Survey of High School Students. In Theodore Ferdinand (Ed.), *Juvenile Delinquency: Little Brother Grows Up* (pp. 77-99). Beverly Hills: Sage.

Wisconsin Department of Health and Social Services (1976). *Juvenile Detention in Wisconsin, 1976. Final Report*. Madison, WI: Wisconsin Department of Heath and Social Services.

Witkin, H., S. Mednick, F. Schulsinger, E. Bakkestrom, K. Christiansen, D. Goodenough, K. Hirschorn, C. Lundsteen, D. Owen, J. Philip, D. Rubin, and M. Stocking (1977). Criminality, Aggression, and Intelligence Among XYY and XXY Men. In S. Mednick, and K. O. Christiansen (Eds.), *Biosocial Bases of Criminal Behavior* (pp. 165-187). New York: Gardner.

Wolak, J., and D. Finkelhor (1998). Children Exposed to Partner Violence. In J. L. Jasinski and L. M. Williams (Eds.), *Partner Violence: A Comprehensive Review of 20 Years of Research* (pp. 73-111). Thousand Oaks, CA: Sage.

Wolfe, S. (1998). As America Ages: Look for Signs of Abuse. *RN* 61(8):48.

Wolfgang, M. E. (1963). Uniform Crime Reports: A Critical Appraisal. *University of Pennsylvania Law Review* 3:408-438.

Wolfgang, M. E., and F. Ferracuti (1967). *The Subculture of Violence: Toward and Integrated Theory in Criminology*. London: Tavistock.

Wolfgang, M. E., R. M. Figlio, and T. Sellin (1972). *Delinquency in a Birth Cohort*. Chicago: University of Chicago Press.

Woolard, J. L., S. L. Gross, E. P. Mulvey, and N. D. Repucci (1992). Legal Issues Affecting Mentally Disordered Youth in the Juvenile Justice System. In J. J. Coczza (Ed.), *Responding to the Mental Health Needs of Youth in the Juvenile Justice System* (pp. 91-106). Seattle: National Coalition for the Mentally Ill in the Criminal Justice System.

Wright, K. N., and K. E. Wright (1996). Family Life, Delinquency, and Crime: A Policymaker's Guide. In D. G. Rojek and G. F. Jensen (Eds.), *Exploring Delinquency: Causes and Control* (pp. 192-209). Los Angeles: Roxbury.

Yablonsky, L. (1962). *The Violent Gang*. Baltimore: Penguin.

Yochelson, S., and S. E. Samenow (1976). *The Criminal Personality*. Vol. 1. New York: Jason Arsonson.

Yoshihama, M., A. L. Parekh, and D. Boyington (1998). Dating Violence in Asian/Pacific Communities. In B. Levy (Ed.), *Dating Violence: Young Women in Danger* (pp. 184-195). Seattle: Seal Press.

Yoshikawa, H. (1994). Prevention as Cumulative Protection: Effects of Early Family Support and Education on Chronic Delinquency and Its Risks. *Psychological Bulletin* 115:28-54.

Zalba, S. (1966). The Abused Child: A Survey of the Problem. *Social Work* 11(4):3-16.

Zillman, D. (1979). *Hostility and Aggression*. Hillsdale, NJ: Lawrence Erlbaum.

Zimring, F. E. (1986). Gun Control. *Bulletin of the New York Academy of Medicine* 62:615-621.

Zimring, F. E. (1996). Kids, Guns, and Homicide: Policy Notes on an Age-Specific Epidemic. *Law and Contemporary Problems* 59:25-38.

Index

Page numbers followed by the letter "f" indicate figures; those followed by the letter "t" indicate tables.

Order a copy of this book with this form or online at:
http://www.haworthpressinc.com/store/product.asp?sku=4620

KIDS WHO COMMIT ADULT CRIMES
Serious Criminality by Juvenile Offenders

_____ in hardbound at $49.95 (ISBN: 0-7890-1129-8)
_____ in softbound at $24.95 (ISBN: 0-7890-1130-1)

COST OF BOOKS_____

OUTSIDE USA/CANADA/
MEXICO: ADD 20%____

POSTAGE & HANDLING_____
*(US: $4.00 for first book & $1.50
for each additional book)
Outside US: $5.00 for first book
& $2.00 for each additional book)*

SUBTOTAL_____

in Canada: add 7% GST____

STATE TAX____
*(NY, OH & MIN residents, please
add appropriate local sales tax)*

FINAL TOTAL____
*(If paying in Canadian funds,
convert using the current
exchange rate, UNESCO
coupons welcome.)*

Prices in US dollars and subject to change without notice.

❏ **BILL ME LATER:** ($5 service charge will be added)
(Bill-me option is good on US/Canada/Mexico orders only;
not good to jobbers, wholesalers, or subscription agencies.)

❏ Check here if billing address is different from
shipping address and attach purchase order and
billing address information.

Signature_____

❏ **PAYMENT ENCLOSED:** $_____

❏ **PLEASE CHARGE TO MY CREDIT CARD.**

❏ Visa ❏ MasterCard ❏ AmEx ❏ Discover
❏ Diner's Club ❏ Eurocard ❏ JCB

Account # _____

Exp. Date_____

Signature_____

NAME_____
INSTITUTION_____
ADDRESS_____
CITY_____
STATE/ZIP_____
COUNTRY_____ COUNTY (NY residents only)_____
TEL_____ FAX_____
E-MAIL_____

May we use your e-mail address for confirmations and other types of information? ❏ Yes ❏ No
We appreciate receiving your e-mail address and fax number. Haworth would like to e-mail or fax special
discount offers to you, as a preferred customer. **We will never share, rent, or exchange your e-mail address
or fax number.** We regard such actions as an invasion of your privacy.

Order From Your Local Bookstore or Directly From
The Haworth Press, Inc.
10 Alice Street, Binghamton, New York 13904-1580 • USA
TELEPHONE: 1-800-HAWORTH (1-800-429-6784) / Outside US/Canada: (607) 722-5857
FAX: 1-800-895-0582 / Outside US/Canada: (607) 722-6362
E-mail: getinfo@haworthpressinc.com
PLEASE PHOTOCOPY THIS FORM FOR YOUR PERSONAL USE.
www.HaworthPress.com

BOF02